General

2023 Test Guide

Study and prepare for your aviation mechanic FAA Knowledge Exam

AVIATION SUPPLIES & ACADEMICS, INC.
NEWCASTLE, WASHINGTON

The FAA Knowledge Exam Questions can change throughout the year. Stay current with test changes; sign up for ASA's free email update service at **asa2fly.com/testupdate**

General Mechanic Test Guide
2023 Edition

Aviation Supplies & Academics, Inc.
7005 132nd Place SE
Newcastle, Washington 98059
asa@asa2fly.com | 425.235.1500 | asa2fly.com

Visit **asa2fly.com/AMG** for additional information and resources related to this book.

Cover photo: iStock.com/Ziviani

ASA-AMG-23
ISBN 978-1-64425-235-2

Additional format available:
eBook PDF ISBN 978-1-64425-236-9

Also sold as *General Mechanic Test Guide Plus*, which includes this book plus Prepware software.
ASA-TPP-AMG-23, ISBN 978-1-64425-252-9

Printed in the United States of America
2023 2022 5 4 3 2 1

Aviation Supplies & Academics, Inc. (ASA) is an industry leader in the development and sale of aviation supplies and publications for pilots, flight instructors, aviation maintenance technicians, aircraft dispatchers, air traffic controllers, flight attendants, and drone operators. We manufacture and publish more than 1,000 products and have been providing trusted and reliable training materials to the aviation industry for over 80 years. Visit **asa2fly.com** to learn more.

Contents

Updates and Practice Tests

Free Test Updates for the One-Year Life Cycle of Test Guide Books

The FAA modifies tests as needed throughout the year. ASA keeps abreast of changes to the tests and posts free Test Updates on the ASA website. Before taking your test, be certain you have the most current information by visiting the ASA Test Updates webpage: **asa2fly.com/testupdate**. Additionally, sign up for free email notifications, which are sent when new Test Updates are available.

We Invite Your Feedback

After you take your FAA exam, let us know how you did. Were you prepared? Did ASA's products meet your needs and exceed your expectations? We want to continue to improve these products to ensure applicants are prepared and become safe aviators. Send your feedback to: **cfi@asa2fly.com**.

Introduction

Welcome to the Aviation Supplies & Academics, Inc., (ASA) Test Guide Series, based on the original Fast-Track series written by Dale Crane. This series has been helping aviation mechanics prepare for FAA Knowledge Exams with great success for more than 60 years. We are confident that with the proper use of this book you will score very well on your FAA Knowledge Exam. Additionally, the ASA Test Guides include typical oral test questions and practical projects to help you prepare for the final step in the Aviation Mechanic certification process.

Begin your studies with an instructor-led or home-study ground school course, which will involve reading a comprehensive textbook for aviation maintenance technicians (AMTs). Once complete, visit the Reader Resources for this Test Guide (**asa2fly.com/AMG**) and become familiar with the FAA guidance material available for this certification exam. Then use this Test Guide to prepare for your exam: Read the question, select your choice for the correct answer, and then read the explanation. Use the references that accompany the correct answer at the bottom of each page to identify additional resources for further study. Upon completion of your studies, take practice tests at **prepware.com** (see inside the front cover for your activation code).

Prior to taking an FAA Airman Knowledge Test, all applicants must establish an FAA Tracking Number (FTN) by creating a profile in the Integrated Airman Certification and Rating Application (IACRA) system at **iacra.faa.gov**. Then visit **faa.psiexams.com** to register for your exam and take FAA-created practice tests to become familiar with the computer testing platform.

The FAA exams are "closed tests" which means the exact database of questions is not available to the public. The question and answer choices in this book are based on our extensive history and experience with the FAA testing process as well as the FAA's publicly available information. You might see similarly worded questions on your official FAA exam and answer stems may be rearranged from the A, B, C order you see in this book. Therefore, be sure to fully understand the intent of each question and corresponding answer while studying, rather than memorizing the letter associated with the correct response. Studying and understanding the information in this book and the associated references will give you the tools to answer question variations with confidence.

If your study leads you to question an answer choice, we recommend you seek the assistance of a local instructor. We welcome your questions, recommendations or concerns—send them to:

Aviation Supplies & Academics, Inc.
7005 132nd Place SE
Newcastle, WA 98059-3153
Email: cfi@asa2fly.com
Voice: 425-235-1500
Fax: 425-235-0128
Website: asa2fly.com

The FAA appreciates testing experience feedback. Contact them at:

Federal Aviation Administration
AFS-630, Airman Testing Standards Branch
PO Box 25082
Oklahoma City, OK 73125
Email: afs630comments@faa.gov

Instructions

The general qualifications for an Aviation Mechanic certificate require you to have a combination of experience, knowledge, and skill. If you are pursuing an Aviation Mechanic certificate with Airframe and Powerplant ratings, you should review the appropriate sections of 14 CFR Part 65 for detailed information pertaining to eligibility requirements. Further information may be obtained from **faa.gov/mechanics**.

The table below lists the number of questions, allotted testing time, and required passing score for each aviation mechanic knowledge exam, as well as the Test Code you'll use to register for your test.

Test Code	Test Name	Number of Questions	Min. Age	Allotted Time (hrs)	Passing Score
AMG	Aviation Mechanic—General	60	N/A	2.0	70
AMA	Aviation Mechanic—Airframe	100	N/A	2.0	70
AMP	Aviation Mechanic—Powerplant	100	N/A	2.0	70

Description of the Knowledge Test

All test questions are objective multiple-choice and can be answered by the selection of a single response. Each test question is independent of other questions; therefore, a correct response to one does not depend upon, or influence, the correct response to another. Considerable effort is expended to write each question in a clear, precise manner. Make sure you read the instructions given with the test, as well as the statements in each test item. When taking a test, keep the following points in mind:

1. Answer each question in accordance with the latest regulations and guidance publications.
2. Read each question carefully before looking at the possible answers. You should clearly understand the problem before attempting to solve it.
3. After formulating an answer, determine which choice corresponds with that answer. The answer chosen should completely resolve the problem.
4. From the answers given, it may appear that there is more than one possible answer; however, there is only one answer that is correct and complete. The other answers are either incomplete, erroneous, or represent common misconceptions.
5. If a certain question is difficult for you, mark it for review and proceed to the next question. After you answer the less difficult questions, return to those you marked for review and answer them. The review marking procedure will be explained to you prior to starting the test. Although the computer should alert you to unanswered questions, make sure every question has an answer recorded. This procedure will enable you to use the available time to maximum advantage.
6. When solving a calculation problem, select the answer closest to your solution. The problem has been checked several times by various individuals; therefore, if you have solved it correctly, your answer will be closer to the correct answer than any of the other choices.

Your test will be graded immediately upon completion and your score will display on the computer screen.

Knowledge Test Eligibility Requirements

Before taking the certification knowledge and practical tests, you must meet the eligibility requirements for authorization. Applicants may present one or more of the following acceptable forms of authorization:

- Original FAA Form 8610-2, Airman Certificate and/or Rating Application. The proctor will verify that applicable blocks are marked (in upper left corner of form). Those not applicable will have a line drawn through them (identifying Airframe and/or Powerplant).
- Certificate of graduation or completion from an FAA-certificated Aviation Maintenance Technician School (AMTS).
- Military Certificate of Eligibility.

Learn more about the FAA's test authorization requirement by reviewing 14 CFR Parts 65 and 141 and the FAA Airman Knowledge Testing Authorization Requirements matrix posted in the reader resources at **asa2fly.com/AMG**.

Taking the Knowledge Test

The FAA testing provider authorizes hundreds of test center locations that offer a full range of airman knowledge tests. For information on authorized testing centers and to register for the knowledge test, visit **faa.psiexams.com**.

When you contact a knowledge testing center, be prepared to select a test date and make a payment. You may register for test(s) several weeks in advance online or with a telephone call, and you may cancel in accordance with the testing center's cancellation policy. Regardless of your registration method, you will need an FAA Tracking Number (FTN). This FTN will follow you throughout your aviation career. You will obtain your FTN by creating a profile in the Integrated Airman Certificate and Rating Application (IACRA) system at **iacra.faa.gov**. This FTN will be printed on your Airman Knowledge Test Report (AKTR).

For more information, contact:
PSI Services LLC
844-704-1487 or examschedule@psionline.com
faa.psiexams.com

On the day of the Airman Knowledge Test the applicant must provide the following information to be collected in order to complete the registration process at the testing center prior to the test proctor administering the Airman Knowledge Test: Name, FAA Tracking Number (FTN), physical address, date of birth, email address, photo identification, phone number, test authorization (credentials of the individual such as an instructor endorsement), and previous number of test attempts. The **faa.psiexams.com** website, your instructor, or local FAA office can assist you with what documentation to take to the testing facility. Testing center personnel will not begin the test until your identification is verified. Acceptable forms of authorization are:

- FAA Form 8610-2.
- A graduation certificate or certificate of completion from an affiliated testing center.
- A failed, passing, or expired AKTR.

Upon completion of your test, you will receive your AKTR which will state your score. Visit **faa.psiexams.com** to request a duplicate or replacement Airman Test Report due to loss or destruction. The AKTR must be presented to the examiner prior to taking the Oral and Practical Exam. During the oral portion of the test, the examiner is required to evaluate the noted areas of deficiency.

Retesting Procedure

Retests do not require a 30-day waiting period if the applicant presents a signed statement from an airman holding the certificate and rating sought by the applicant. This statement must certify that the airman has given the applicant additional instruction in each of the subjects failed, and that the airman considers the applicant ready for retesting. A 30-day waiting period is required for retesting if the applicant presents a failed airman knowledge test report, but no authorized instructor endorsement.

Applicants taking retests ***after failure*** are required to submit the applicable test report indicating failure to the testing center prior to retesting. The original failed test report shall be retained by the proctor and attached to the applicable sign-in/out log. The latest test taken will reflect the official score.

Applicants retesting ***in an attempt to achieve a higher passing score*** may retake the same test for a better grade after 30 days. The latest test taken will reflect the official score. Applicants are required to submit the ***original*** applicable test report indicating previous passing score to the testing center prior to testing. Testing center personnel must collect and destroy this report prior to issuing the new test report.

Use of Test Aids and Materials

Airman knowledge tests require applicants to analyze the relationship between variables needed to solve aviation problems, in addition to testing for accuracy of a mathematical calculation. The intent is that all applicants are tested on concepts rather than rote calculation ability. It is permissible to use certain calculating devices when taking airman knowledge tests, provided they are used within the following guidelines. The term "calculating devices" is interchangeable with such items as calculators, computers, or any similar devices designed for aviation-related activities.

1. Guidelines for use of test aids and materials. The applicant may use test aids and materials within the guidelines listed below, if actual test questions or answers are not revealed.
    a. Applicants may use test aids, such as a calculating device that is directly related to the test. In addition, applicants may use any test materials provided with the test.
    b. The test proctor may provide a calculating device to applicants and deny them use of their personal calculating device if the applicant's device does not have a screen that indicates all memory has been erased. The test proctor must be able to determine the calculating device's erasure capability. The use of calculating devices incorporating permanent or continuous type memory circuits without erasure capability is prohibited.
    c. The use of magnetic cards, magnetic tapes, modules, computer chips, or any other device upon which prewritten programs or information related to the test can be stored and retrieved is prohibited. Printouts of data will be surrendered at the completion of the test if the calculating device used incorporates this design feature.
    d. The use of any booklet or manual containing instructions related to the use of the applicant's calculating device is not permitted.
    e. Dictionaries are not allowed in the testing area.
    f. The test proctor makes the final determination relating to test materials and personal possessions that the applicant may take into the testing area.
2. Guidelines for applicant's with learning or reading disabilities. An applicant with a learning or reading disability may request approval from the local Flight Standards Office to take an airman knowledge test using one of the following options listed in preferential order:

    (1) The applicant may request up to 1½ times the standard time allotted to complete the knowledge test.

    (2) The applicant may use a self-contained electronic device which pronounces and displays typed-in words (e.g., the Franklin Speaking Wordmaster®) to facilitate the testing process. The applicant must provide his or her own device, with approval of the device to be determined by the administrator. Note: The device should consist of an electronic thesaurus that audibly pronounces typed-in words and presents them on a display screen. The device should also have a built-in headphone jack for private listening in order to avoid disturbing others during testing.

Cheating or Other Unauthorized Conduct

Computer testing centers are required to follow strict security procedures to avoid test compromise. These procedures are established by the FAA and are covered in FAA Order 8080.6, Conduct of Airman Knowledge Tests. The FAA has directed testing centers to terminate a test at any time a test proctor suspects a cheating incident has occurred. An FAA investigation will then be conducted. If the investigation determines that cheating or other unauthorized conduct has occurred, then any airman certificate or rating that you hold may be revoked, and you will be prohibited for 1 year from applying for or taking any test for a certificate or rating under 14 CFR Part 65.

Validity of Airman Test Reports

Airman Knowledge Test Reports are valid for the 24-calendar month period preceding the month you complete the practical test. If the Airman Test Report expires before completion of the practical test, you must retake the knowledge test.

Learning Statement Codes

The expression *learning statement* refers to measurable statements about the knowledge a student should be able to demonstrate following a certain segment of training.

Your AKTR will list the Learning Statement Codes (LSCs) for questions you have answered incorrectly. Match the codes given on your test report to the ones listed below. Your instructor can provide instruction on each of the areas of deficiency listed on your AKTR to help you prepare for your Oral and Practical Exam. The AKTR must be presented to the examiner conducting your Oral and Practical Exam. During the oral portion of the test, the examiner will evaluate the noted areas of deficiency.

Learning Statement Codes are prefixed with a letter-identifier (for example, AMG031). For the purposes of reference within this ASA Test Guide, the letter prefix is omitted; therefore throughout this book, LSCs are referred to by their number-identifiers only, in parentheses.

LSC	**Subject area**
AMG001	Ability to draw/sketch repairs/alterations
AMG002	Calculate center of gravity
AMG003	Calculate weight and balance
AMG004	Determine correct data
AMG005	Determine regulatory requirement
AMG006	Interpret drag ratio from charts
AMG007	Recall aerodynamic fundamentals
AMG008	Recall air density
AMG009	Recall aircraft cleaning—materials/techniques
AMG010	Recall aircraft component markings
AMG011	Recall aircraft control cables—install/inspect/repair/service
AMG012	Recall aircraft corrosion—principles/control/prevention
AMG013	Recall aircraft drawings—detail/assembly
AMG014	Recall aircraft drawings/blueprints—lines/symbols/sketching
AMG015	Recall aircraft electrical system—install/inspect/repair/service
AMG016	Recall aircraft engines—performance charts
AMG017	Recall aircraft hardware—bolts/nuts/fasteners/fittings/valves
AMG018	Recall aircraft instruments—tachometer indications/dual tachometers
AMG019	Recall aircraft metals—inspect/test/repair/identify/heat treat
AMG020	Recall aircraft metals—types/tools/fasteners
AMG021	Recall aircraft publications—aircraft listings
AMG022	Recall aircraft records—required/destroyed
AMG023	Recall aircraft repair—major
AMG024	Recall airframe—inspections
AMG025	Recall airworthiness certificates—validity/requirements
AMG026	Recall ATA codes
AMG027	Recall basic physics—matter/energy/gas
AMG028	Recall data—approved
AMG029	Recall dissymmetry
AMG030	Recall effects of frost/snow on airfoils
AMG031	Recall electrical system—components/operating principles/characteristics/symbols
AMG032	Recall environmental factors affecting maintenance performance

LSC	Subject area
AMG033	Recall external loading
AMG034	Recall flight characteristics—autorotation/compressibility
AMG035	Recall flight operations—air taxi
AMG036	Recall fluid lines—install/inspect/repair/service
AMG037	Recall fluid lines—material/coding
AMG038	Recall forces acting on aircraft—angle of incidence
AMG039	Recall forces acting on aircraft—yaw/adverse yaw
AMG040	Recall fuel—types/characteristics/contamination/fueling/defueling/dumping
AMG041	Recall fundamental inspection principles—airframe/engine
AMG042	Recall fundamental material properties
AMG043	Recall generator system—components/operating principles/characteristics
AMG044	Recall geometry
AMG045	Recall ground operations—start/move/service/secure aircraft
AMG046	Recall helicopter engine control system
AMG047	Recall helicopter flight controls
AMG048	Recall information on an Airworthiness Directive
AMG049	Recall instrument panel mounting
AMG050	Recall maintenance error management
AMG051	Recall maintenance publications—service/parts/repair
AMG052	Recall maintenance resource management
AMG053	Recall mathematics—percentages/decimals/fractions/ratio/general
AMG054	Recall penalties—falsification/cheating
AMG055	Recall physics—work forces
AMG056	Recall pitch control—collective/cyclic
AMG057	Recall precision measuring tools—meters/gauges/scales/calipers
AMG058	Recall reciprocating engine—components/operating principles/characteristics
AMG059	Recall regulations—aircraft inspection/records/expiration
AMG060	Recall regulations—aircraft operator certificate
AMG061	Recall regulations—aircraft registration/marks
AMG062	Recall regulations—Airworthiness Directives
AMG063	Recall regulations—airworthiness requirements/responsibilities
AMG064	Recall regulations—certificate of maintenance review requirements
AMG065	Recall regulations—Certificate of Release
AMG066	Recall regulations—certification of aircraft and components
AMG067	Recall regulations—change of address
AMG068	Recall regulations—check periods
AMG069	Recall regulations—determine mass and balance
AMG070	Recall regulations—display/inspection of licenses and certificates
AMG071	Recall regulations—emergency equipment
AMG072	Recall regulations—flight/operating manual marking/placard
AMG073	Recall regulations—housing and facility requirements
AMG074	Recall regulations—instrument/equipment requirements
AMG075	Recall regulations—maintenance control/procedure manual

LSC	Subject area
AMG076	Recall regulations—maintenance reports/records/entries
AMG077	Recall regulations—maintenance requirements
AMG078	Recall regulations—minimum equipment list
AMG079	Recall regulations—minor/major repairs
AMG080	Recall regulations—persons authorized for return to service
AMG081	Recall regulations—persons authorized to perform maintenance
AMG082	Recall regulations—privileges/limitations of maintenance certificates/licenses
AMG083	Recall regulations—privileges of approved maintenance organizations
AMG084	Recall regulations—reapplication after revocation/suspension
AMG085	Recall regulations—reporting failures/malfunctions/defects
AMG086	Recall regulations—return to service
AMG087	Recall regulations—special airworthiness certificates/requirements
AMG088	Recall regulations—special flight permit
AMG089	Recall regulations—weighing an aircraft
AMG090	Recall repair fundamentals—turnbuckles
AMG091	Recall rotor system—components/operating principles/characteristics
AMG092	Recall rotorcraft vibration—characteristics/sources
AMG093	Recall starter/ignition system—components/operating principles/characteristics
AMG094	Recall starter system—starting procedures
AMG095	Recall turbine engines—components/operational characteristics/associated instruments
AMG096	Recall turbine engines—install/inspect/repair/service/hazards
AMG097	Recall type certificate data sheet (TCDS)/supplemental type certificate (STC)
AMG098	Recall welding types/techniques/equipment
AMG099	Recall work/power/force/motion
AMG100	Recall mathematics—extract roots/radical/scientific notation
AMG101	Recall positive/negative algebraic operations—addition/subtraction/multiplication/division
AMG102	Recall aircraft electrical circuit diagrams—read/interpret/troubleshoot
AMG103	Define maintenance resource management
AMG104	Recall human reliability—in maintenance errors
AMG105	Recall environmental factors leading to maintenance errors
AMG106	Recall fatigue in maintenance errors causes/interventions
AMG107	Recall error management
AMG108	Recall maintenance resource management
AMG109	Recall error management in shift turnover
AMG110	Recall error capture/duplicate inspection
AMG111	Recall ergonomic interventions to maintenance errors
AMG112	Recall interventions to prevent cross-connection maintenance errors
AMG113	Recall interventions to prevent shift/task turnover errors
AMG114	Recall environmental factors affecting maintenance performance
AMG115	Recall environmental factors affecting maintenance performance—lighting/temperature/noise/air quality
AMG116	Recall error intervention—interruptions/access

Knowledge Exam References

The FAA references the following documents to write the FAA Knowledge Exam questions. You should be familiar with all of these as part of your classroom studies, which you should complete before starting test preparation:

FAA-H-8083-30	*Aviation Maintenance Technician Handbook—General* (FAA)
FAA-H-8083-31, Vol. 1 & 2	*Aviation Maintenance Technician Handbook—Airframe* (FAA)
FAA-H-8083-32, Vol. 1 & 2	*Aviation Maintenance Technician Handbook—Powerplant* (FAA)
FAA-H-8083-3	*Airplane Flying Handbook* (FAA)
FAA-G-8082-11	*Inspection Authorization Test Guide* (FAA)

14 CFR Parts 1, 3, 21, 23, 39, 43, 45, 47, 65, 91, 147

Advisory Circulars (AC) 21-12, 23-21, 23.1309-1, 43.9-1, 43.13-1

Additional resources helpful for AMT studies:

AMT-G	*Aviation Mechanic Series: General* (ASA)
AMT-STRUC	*Aviation Mechanic Series: Airframe Structures* (ASA)
AMT-SYS	*Aviation Mechanic Series: Airframe Systems* (ASA)
AMT-P	*Aviation Mechanic Series: Powerplant* (ASA)
DAT	*Dictionary of Aeronautical Terms* (ASA)
AIM	*Aeronautical Information Manual* (FAA)

Acronyms

For reference, acronyms appearing in this book are defined below.

AC	Advisory Circular
AC	Air Corp (fitting, specification standard)
AC	alternating current
AD	Airworthiness Directive
AD	ashless dispersant (oil)
amp	ampere
AN	Army-Navy (specification standard)
ATA	Air Transport Association (specification standard)
BHP	brake horsepower
BMEP	brake mean effective pressure
CG	center of gravity
CO	carbon monoxide
CO_2	carbon dioxide
DC	direct current
EGT	exhaust gas temperature
EMF	electromotive force
FCF	fuel crossfeed
hp	horsepower
IA	inspection authorization
ITT	interstage turbine temperature
KV	kilovolt (1,000 volts)
L/D	lift over drag (ratio)
LEMAC	leading edge of mean aerodynamic chord
LTS	left tank switch
MEDA	Maintenance Error Decision Aid
MEK	methyl ethyl ketone
METO	maximum except for takeoff (power)
MS	military specification (standard)
NAS	National Aerospace Standard (specification)
OAT	outside air temperature
OD	outside diameter
PCO	pressure crossfeed valve open
PHDAN	physically dangerous materials
psi	pounds per square inch
RPM	rotations per minute
RTS	right tank switch
SAE	SAE International, previously the Society of Automotive Engineers
SHEL	software, hardware, environment, liveware (human factors model)
STC	Supplemental Type Certificate
TCC	thrust control computer
TCDS	Type Certificate Data Sheet
TCO	thermal cutoff
TEL	tetraethyl lead
TEMAC	trailing edge of mean aerodynamic chord
TIT	turbine inlet temperature
TSO	Technical Standard Order
V	volt
W	watt

General Test Questions, Explanations, Answers, and References

Answers are printed at the bottom of the page, with other coded items as explained below:

This is the question number.

The brackets enclose the letter answer selected by ASA's researchers. (For those questions for which none of the answer choices provide an accurate response, we have noted [X] as the Answer.)

8001 [C] (031) AMT-G Ch 4

The parentheses enclose the appropriate Learning Statement Code (LSC)—refer to Pages ix–xi. FAA Learning Statement Codes have letter-identifying prefixes, but for reference purposes in this book the letter prefix ("AMG") is omitted and only the number-identifying portion of the code is shown in parentheses.

The reference following the Learning Statement Code is the source from which the answer was derived. The meanings of these abbreviations are found on Page xii. The number following the abbreviations is the specific chapter within that source to study for more information about the derived answer.

Basic Electricity

8001. The working voltage of a capacitor in an AC circuit should be

A—equal to the highest applied voltage.
B—at least 20 percent greater than the highest applied voltage.
C—at least 50 percent greater than the highest applied voltage.

The working voltage of a capacitor is the highest voltage that can be steadily applied to it without the danger of the dielectric breaking down.

The working voltage depends upon the material used as the dielectric and on its thickness.

A capacitor used in an AC circuit should have a working voltage at least 50 percent greater than the highest voltage that will be applied to it.

8002. The term that describes the combined resistive forces in an AC circuit is

A—resistance.
B—reactance.
C—impedance.

Impedence (Z) is the vector sum of the resistance and the total reactance in a circuit. It is expressed in ohms, and found using the formula:

$$Z = \sqrt{R^2 + X^2}$$

There are three types of resistive forces in an AC circuit: inductive reactance, which causes the current to lag the voltage; capacitive reactance, which causes the current to lead the voltage; and resistance, which allows the current and voltage to remain in phase.

Inductive and capacitive reactance are 180° out of phase and cancel each other.

8002-1. What is the opposition to the flow of AC produced by an electromagnetic field (EMF) with generated back voltage called?

A—Inductive reactance.
B—Capacitive reactance.
C—Mutual inductance.

Alternating current is in a constant state of change; EMF causes continuously inducted voltage opposition to the current in the circuit. This opposition is called inductive reactance (X_L), and is measured in ohms just as resistance is measured. Inductance is the property of a circuit to oppose any change in current and is measured in henries. Inductive reactance is a measure of how much the countering EMF in the circuit will oppose current variations.

8002-2. Electrostatic fields are also known as

A—dielectric fields.
B—electrostatic fields.
C—static fields.

A field of force exists around a charged body. This is an electrostatic field (sometimes called a dielectric field) and it is represented by lines that extend in all directions from the charged body which terminate where there is an equal and opposite charge.

8003. The basis for transformer operation in the use of alternating current is mutual

A—inductance.
B—capacitance.
C—reactance.

A transformer operates on the basis of mutual inductance. The changing current in the primary windings produces a changing magnetic field whose flux cuts across the turns of the secondary winding and induces a voltage into it.

8004. The opposition offered by a coil to the flow of alternating current (ignoring resistance) is called

A—impedance.
B—reluctance.
C—inductive reactance.

When alternating current flows in a coil of wire, the changing lines of flux cutting across the turns of wire in the coil induce a voltage in it. The polarity of this voltage (the counter EMF) is opposite to the polarity of the voltage that caused it.

The counter EMF decreases the total voltage across the coil, and this decreases the current flowing through it.

This opposition to the flow of alternating current is called inductive reactance (X_L) and is measured in ohms. It opposes the flow of current, but it does not cause heat nor use any power.

8004-1. What factors strengthen a coil inductor?

A—Limiting and separating the coils.
B—Adding and separating the coils.
C—Adding coils close together.

As more loops are added close together, the strength of the magnetic field increases. Many loops close together will result in a strong electromagnet.

Answers *Note: All Learning Statement Codes (in parentheses) are preceded by "AMG." See explanation on Page 1.*

8001 [C] (031) AMT-G Ch 4	8002 [C] (031) AMT-G Ch 4	8002-1 [A] (102) FAA-H-8083-30	8002-2 [A] (031) FAA-H-8083-30
8003 [A] (015) AMT-G Ch 4	8004 [C] (031) AMT-G Ch 4	8004-1 [C] (031) FAA-H-8083-30	

8005. An increase in which of the following factors will cause an increase in the inductive reactance of a circuit?

A—Inductance and frequency.
B—Resistance and voltage.
C—Resistance and capacitive reactance.

The inductive reactance (X_L) in an AC circuit is increased when either the frequency of the alternating current or the inductance of the circuit is increased.

Resistance, voltage, or capacitive reactance have no effect on the inductive reactance of a circuit.

The formula for inductive reactance is:

$$X_L = 2\pi fL$$

8006. (Refer to Figure 1.) When different rated capacitors are connected in series in a circuit, the total capacitance is

A—less than the capacitance of the lowest rated capacitor.
B—greater than the capacitance of the highest rated capacitor.
C—equal to the sum of all the capacitances.

$$C_T = \frac{1}{1/C_1 + 1/C_2 + 1/C_3...}$$

Figure 1. Equation

When capacitors of different values are connected in series, the total capacitance is less than that of the lowest rated capacitor.

8006-1. Capacitors are sometimes used in DC circuits to

A—counteract inductive reactance at specific locations.
B—smooth out slight pulsations in current/voltage.
C—assist in stepping voltage and current up and/or down.

Capacitors store electrical charges and are sometimes used in DC circuits to smooth out slight pulsations in current or voltage. Capacitors accept electrons when there is an excess and release them back into the circuit when the values decrease.

8007. In an AC circuit, the effective voltage is

A—equal to the maximum instantaneous voltage.
B—greater than the maximum instantaneous voltage.
C—less than the maximum instantaneous voltage.

The effective voltage of sine wave alternating current is 0.707 time its peak voltage.

The effective voltage, also called the root mean square (rms) voltage, is the voltage measured by most of the AC voltmeters. Peak voltage is measured with a special peak voltmeter or an oscilloscope.

8008. The amount of electricity a capacitor can store is directly proportional to the

A—distance between the plates and inversely proportional to the plate area.
B—plate area and is not affected by the distance between the plates.
C—plate area and inversely proportional to the distance between the plates.

Three factors affect the amount of electricity a capacitor can store:

1. *The area of the plates. The larger the plate area, the greater the capacity.*
2. *The thickness of the dielectric (the distance between the plates). The closer the plates are together, the stronger the electrical field will be and the greater the capacity.*
3. *The material from which the dielectric is made (its dielectric constant). The higher the dielectric constant, the greater the capacity.*

8009. (Refer to Figure 2.) What is the total capacitance of a certain circuit containing three capacitors with capacitances of .02 microfarad, .05 microfarad, and .10 microfarad, respectively?

A—.170 µF.
B—0.125 pF.
C—.0125 µF.

$$C_T = \frac{1}{1/C_1 + 1/C_2 + 1/C_3}$$

Figure 2. Equation

Answers

8005 [A] (031) AMT-G Ch 4	8006 [A] (031) AMT-G Ch 4	8006-1 [B] (031) AMT-G Ch 4	8007 [C] (031) AMT-G Ch 4
8008 [C] (031) AMT-G Ch 4	8009 [C] (031) AMT-G Ch 4		

When a 0.02-microfarad, a 0.05-microfarad, and a 0.10-microfarad capacitor are connected in series, the total capacitance is 0.0125 microfarad.

$$C_T = \frac{1}{\frac{1}{C_1}+\frac{1}{C_2}+\frac{1}{C_3}}$$

$$= \frac{1}{\frac{1}{.02}+\frac{1}{.05}+\frac{1}{.1}}$$

$$= 0.0125\ \mu F$$

8009-1. What is the total capacitance of a circuit containing three capacitors in parallel with capacitances of .02 microfarad, .05 microfarad, and .10 microfarad, respectively?

A—.170 µF.
B—0.125 µF.
C—.0125 µF.

Use the formula $C_T = C_1 + C_2 + C_3$. When capacitors are connected together in parallel, the plate area of all the capacitors add together and the total capacitance is the sum of the individual capacitances.

$.02 + .05 + .10 = .170\ \mu F$

8009-2. Convert farads to microfarads by

A—multiplying farads by 10 to the power of 6
B—multiplying picofarads by 10 to the power of 6
C—multiplying microfarads by 10 to the power of 6

One farad is equal to 10^6 microfarads. Example: 2 farads is equal to 2×10^6 (2,000,000) microfarads.

8009-3. Convert farads to picofarads by:

A—multiplying farads by 10 to the power of 12
B—multiplying microfarads by 10 to the power of -12
C—multiplying picofarads by 10 to the power of 12

One farad is equal to 10^{12} picofarads. Example: 2 farads is equal to 2×10^{12} (2,000,000,000) picofarads.

8010. Unless otherwise specified, any values given for current or voltage in an AC circuit are assumed to be

A—instantaneous values.
B—effective values.
C—maximum values.

Almost all measuring instruments used for electrical system servicing measure the effective rms values of alternating current.

Unless peak values, peak-to-peak values, or average values are specifically called out, effective rms values are assumed.

8011. When different rated capacitors are connected in parallel in a circuit, the total capacitance is

(Note: $C_T = C_1 + C_2 + C_3 \ldots$)

A—less than the capacitance of the lowest rated capacitor.
B—equal to the capacitance of the highest rated capacitor.
C—equal to the sum of all the capacitances.

When capacitors are connected in parallel, the effective area of the plates combine, and the total capacitance is the sum of the individual capacitances.

8012. When inductors are connected in series in a circuit, the total inductance (where the magnetic fields of each inductor do not affect the others) is

(Note: $L_T = L_1 + L_2 + L_3 \ldots$)

A—less than the inductance of the lowest rated inductor.
B—equal to the inductance of the highest rated inductor.
C—equal to the sum of the individual inductances.

When several inductors are connected together in such a way that there is no inductive coupling, the total inductance is the sum of the individual inductances.

8013. (Refer to Figure 3.) When more than two inductors of different inductances are connected in parallel in a circuit, the total inductance is

A—less than the inductance of the lowest rated inductor.
B—equal to the inductance of the highest rated inductor.
C—equal to the sum of the individual inductances.

$$L_T = \frac{1}{1/L_1 + 1/L_2 + 1/L_3 \ldots}$$

Figure 3. Equation

When two or more inductors having different inductances are connected in parallel, the total inductance is less than the inductance of the lowest rated inductor.

Answers

8009-1 [A] (031) AMT-G Ch 4	8009-2 [A] (102) AMT-G Ch 4	8009-3 [A] (102) AMT-G Ch 4	8010 [B] (031) AMT-G Ch 4
8011 [C] (031) AMT-G Ch 4	8012 [C] (015) AMT-G Ch 4	8013 [A] (031) AMT-G Ch 4	

8014. What is the total capacitance of a certain circuit containing three capacitors with capacitances of .25 microfarad, .03 microfarad, and .12 microfarad, respectively?

(Note: $C_T = C_1 + C_2 + C_3$)

A—.4 μF.
B—.04 pF.
C—.04 μF.

When three capacitors are connected in parallel, their total capacitance is the sum of the individual capacitances.

$$\begin{aligned} C_T &= C_1 + C_2 + C_3 \\ &= 0.25 + 0.03 = 0.12 \\ &= 0.4\ \mu F \end{aligned}$$

8015. Which requires the most electrical power during operation?

(Note: 1 horsepower = 746 watts)

A—A 12-volt motor requiring 8 amperes.
B—Four 30-watt lamps in a 12-volt parallel circuit.
C—Two lights requiring 3 amperes each in a 24-volt parallel system.

The 12-volt motor requires 96 watts of power.

The four 30-watt lamps require 120 watts of power.

The two 24-volt, 3-amp lights require 144 watts of power.

8016. How much power must a 24-volt generator furnish to a system which contains the following loads?

Unit	**Rating**
One motor (75 percent efficient)	1/5 hp
Three position lights	20 watts each
One heating element	5 amp
One anticollision light	3 amp

(Note: 1 horsepower = 746 watts)

A—402 watts.
B—385 watts.
C—450 watts.

The motor is 1/5 hp, therefore 746 watts (1 hp) ÷ 5 = 149 watts. This is the output of the engine. It takes more energy to produce 149 watts; find this with the efficiency rating: 149/X = 75/100; X = 199. Therefore, the 1/5 hp motor that is 75 percent efficient requires 199 watts.

The three position lights require a total of 60 watts.

The heating element requires 120 watts.

The anticollision light requires 72 watts.

The total power the generator must produce is 451 watts.

8017. A 12-volt electric motor has 1,000 watts input and 1 horsepower output. Maintaining the same efficiency, how much input power will a 24-volt, 1-horsepower electric motor require?

(Note: 1 horsepower = 746 watts)

A—1,000 watts.
B—2,000 watts.
C—500 watts.

The power produced by an electric motor is the product of its voltage and its current.

A 12-volt motor will require 83.3 amps of current for its 1,000 watts of input power to produce 746 watts (1 horsepower) of output power.

A 24-volt motor operating at the same efficiency will also require 1,000 watts of input power for its 746 watts of output power, but it will need only 41.7 amps of current.

8018. How many amperes will a 28-volt generator be required to supply to a circuit containing five lamps in parallel, three of which have a resistance of 6 ohms each and two of which have a resistance of 5 ohms each?

A—1.11 amperes.
B—1 ampere.
C—25.23 amperes.

A current of 4.67 amps flows through each of the three six-ohm lamps. And a current of 5.6 amps flows through each of the 5-ohm lamps.

Since all of these lamps are in parallel, the total current is the sum of the currents flowing through each lamp. The total current is 25.21 amps.

8019. A 24-volt, 1-horsepower DC electric motor that is 80 percent efficient requires 932.5 watts. How much power will a 12-volt, 1-horsepower DC electric motor that is 75 percent efficient require?

(Note: 1 horsepower = 746 watts)

A—932.5 watts.
B—1,305.5 watts.
C—994.6 watts.

When we know the horsepower output and the efficiency of an electric motor, the voltage does not enter into the computation. To find the number of watts required, divide the wattage for the total horsepower by the decimal equivalent of the efficiency.

746 ÷ 0.75 = 994.6 watts

Answers
8014 [A] (031) AMT-G Ch 4
8015 [C] (015) AMT-G Ch 4
8016 [C] (031) AMT-G Ch 4
8017 [A] (031) AMT-G Ch 4
8018 [C] (031) AMT-G Ch 4
8019 [C] (031) AMT-G Ch 4

8020. The potential difference between two conductors which are insulated from each other is measured in

A—volts.
B—amperes.
C—coulombs.

The potential difference between two conductors is a measure of the electrical pressure difference between the conductors.

Electrical pressure is measured in volts.

8020-1. Which effect does not apply to the movement of electrons flowing in a conductor?

A—Magnetic energy.
B—Thermal energy.
C—Static energy.

Current flowing through a conductor produces a magnetic field and also dissipates thermal energy.

8021. A 24-volt source is required to furnish 48 watts to a parallel circuit consisting of four resistors of equal value. What is the voltage drop across each resistor?

A—12 volts.
B—6 volts.
C—24 volts.

Since the resistors are all in parallel across the 24-volt power source, each resistor has the entire 24 volts dropped across it.

8022. When calculating power in a reactive or inductive AC circuit, the true power is

A—more than the apparent power.
B—less than the apparent power in a reactive circuit and more than the apparent power in an inductive circuit.
C—less than the apparent power.

True power in an AC circuit is the product of the circuit voltage and only that part of the current in phase with the voltage.

Apparent power is the circuit voltage multiplied by all of the current.

True power is always less than the apparent power in a reactive circuit which is any AC circuit containing either inductance or capacitance.

8023. (Refer to Figure 4.) How much power is being furnished to the circuit?

A—575 watts.
B—2,875 watts.
C—2,645 watts.

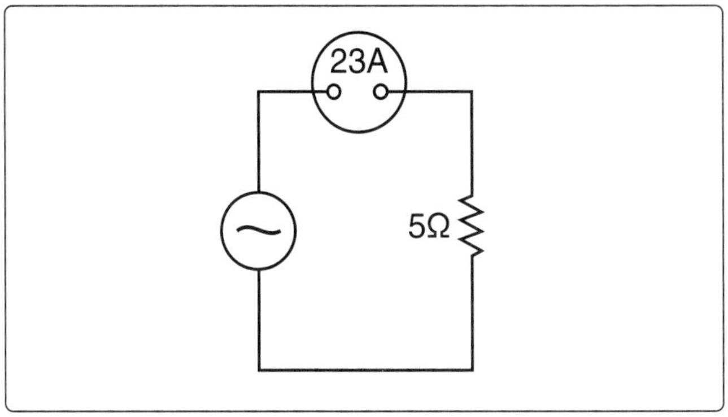

Figure 4. Circuit Diagram

This is a resistive circuit. The power is the product of the square of the current times the resistance.

$P = I^2 \times R = 23^2 \times 5 = 2{,}645$ *watts*

8024. (Refer to Figure 5.) What is the impedance of an AC-series circuit consisting of an inductor with a reactance of 10 ohms, a capacitor with a reactance of 4 ohms, and a resistor with a resistance of 8 ohms?

A—22 ohms.
B—5.29 ohms.
C—10 ohms.

$$Z = \sqrt{R^2+(X_L-X_C)^2}$$

Z = Impedance
R = Resistance
X_L = Inductive reactance
X_C = Capacitive reactance

Figure 5. Formula

The total reactance in this circuit is the difference between the inductive reactance and the capacitive reactance.

Total reactance is 10 – 4 = 6 ohms.

The impedance is the square root of the resistance squared plus the reactance squared. This is the square root of 64 plus 36, or the square root of 100.

The circuit impedance is 10 ohms.

Answers
8020 [A] (031) AMT-G Ch 4
8020-1 [C] (031) AMT-G Ch 4
8021 [C] (015) AMT-G Ch 4
8022 [C] (031) AMT-G Ch 4
8023 [C] (031) AMT-G Ch 4
8024 [C] (031) AMT-G Ch 4

8025. (Refer to Figure 6.) If resistor R_5 is disconnected at the junction of R_4 and R_3 as shown, what will the ohmmeter read?

A—2.76 ohms.
B—3 ohms.
C—12 ohms.

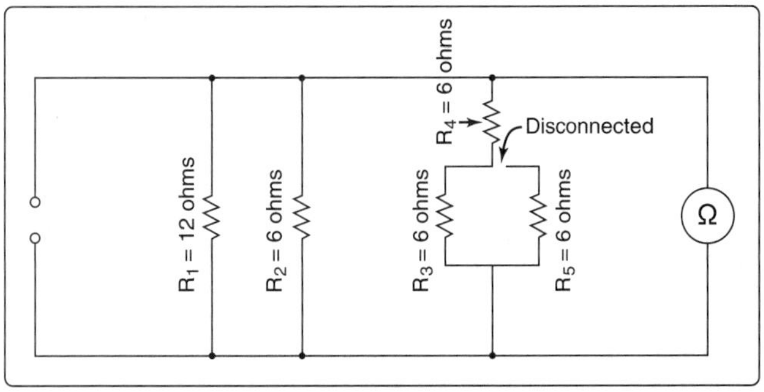

Figure 6. Circuit diagram

With resistor R_5 disconnected, the ohmmeter reads the parallel resistance of R_1 and R_2 in parallel with R_4 and R_3, which are in series. The total resistance is found by the formula:

$$R_P = \frac{1}{\frac{1}{R_1}+\frac{1}{R_2}+\frac{1}{R_3+R_4}}$$

$$= \frac{1}{\frac{1}{12}+\frac{1}{6}+\frac{1}{6+6}}$$

$$= 3\Omega$$

8026. (Refer to Figure 7.) If resistor R_3 is disconnected at terminal D, what will the ohmmeter read?

A—Infinite resistance.
B—10 ohms.
C—20 ohms.

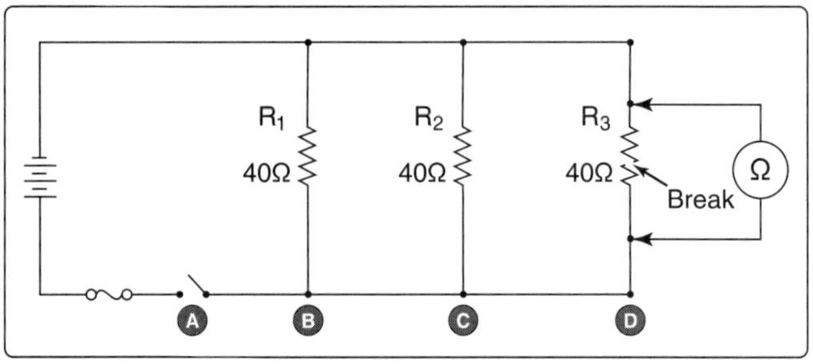

Figure 7. Circuit diagram

When resistor R_3 is disconnected at terminal D, it is isolated from the rest of the circuit, and the ohmmeter will read only the resistance of R_3.

Because R_3 is open (it has a break in it), its resistance is infinite.

8027. (Refer to Figure 8.) With an ohmmeter connected into the circuit as shown, what will the ohmmeter read?

A—20 ohms.
B—Infinite resistance.
C—10 ohms.

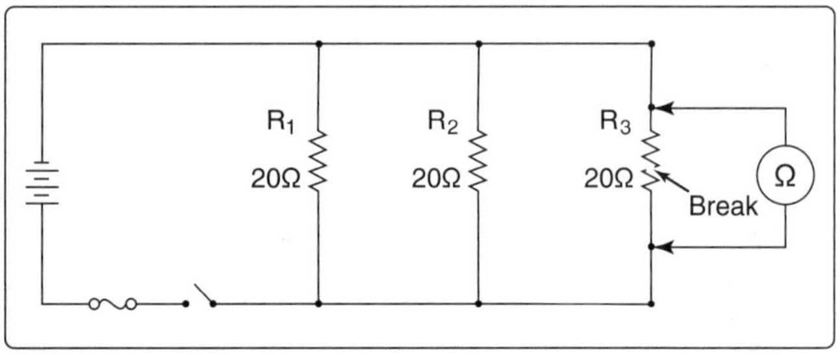

Figure 8. Circuit Diagram

The ohmmeter will read the resistance of R_1 and R_2 in parallel; this is 10 ohms.

The open circuit (break) in resistor R_3 gives it an infinite resistance, and it does not affect the reading of the ohmmeter.

Answers
8025 [B] (015) AMT-G Ch 4 8026 [A] (031) AMT-G Ch 4 8027 [C] (015) AMT-G Ch 4

8028. (Refer to Figure 9.) How many instruments (voltmeters and ammeters) are installed correctly?

A—Three.
B—One.
C—Two.

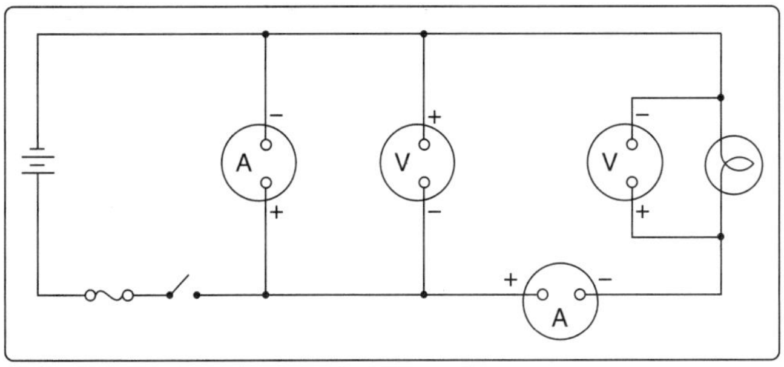

Figure 9. Circuit diagram

The first ammeter is installed across the voltage. This is wrong; the ammeter will burn out.

The first voltmeter will measure the source voltage (the voltage of the battery), but its polarity is wrong. It will read backward.

The voltmeter across the light bulb is installed correctly.

The ammeter in series with the light bulb and the battery is correct. It will read the current flowing through the light bulb.

8029. The correct way to connect a test voltmeter in a circuit is

A—in series with a unit.
B—between the source voltage and the load.
C—in parallel with a unit.

A voltmeter must always be connected in a circuit in parallel with the unit whose voltage is to be measured.

8029-1. What will a voltmeter read if properly connected across a closed switch in a circuit with electrical power on?

A—Voltage drop in the component(s) the switch is connected to.
B—System voltage.
C—Zero voltage.

When a voltmeter is connected across a closed switch in perfect condition or a good fuse, it will read zero voltage. A voltage drop of up to 0.2 volts is acceptable with maximum circuit current flow through the switch.

8029-2. What does the letter Q symbolize when measuring electrical charge?

A—Farad.
B—Electron.
C—Coulomb.

The general formula for capacitance in terms of charge and voltage is C = Q/E, where:

C = Capacitance measured in farads

E = Applied voltage measured in volts

Q = Charge measured in coulombs

8030. Which term means .001 ampere?

A—Microampere.
B—Kiloampere.
C—Milliampere.

The metric prefix "milli-" means one thousandth.

0.001 ampere is one milliampere.

8031. A cabin entry light of 10 watts and a dome light of 20 watts are connected in parallel to a 30-volt source. If the voltage across the 10-watt light is measured, it will be

A—equal to the voltage across the 20-watt light.
B—half the voltage across the 20-watt light.
C—one-third of the input voltage.

When lights are connected in parallel across a voltage source, the voltage across each of the lights will be the same as the voltage of the source.

8032. A 14-ohm resistor is to be installed in a series circuit carrying .05 ampere. How much power will the resistor be required to dissipate?

A—At least .70 milliwatt.
B—At least 35 milliwatts.
C—Less than .035 watt.

Power dissipated in a resistor is found by multiplying its resistance by the square of the current.

$P = I^2 \times R = 0.05^2 \times 14 = 0.035$ *watts*

0.035 watts is 35 milliwatts.

8033. .002 kV equals

A—20 volts.
B—2.0 volts.
C—.2 volt.

One kilovolt (kV) is 1,000 volts. Two thousandths (.002) of a kilovolt is equal to 2.0 volts.

Answers

8028 [C] (015) AMT-G Ch 4
8029-2 [C] (031) AMT-G, Ch 4
8033 [B] (015) AMT-G Ch 4
8029 [C] (015) AMT-G Ch 4
8030 [C] (031) AMT-G Ch 4
8029-1 [C] (015) AMT-G Ch 4, AC43.13 Ch 11
8031 [A] (031) AMT-G Ch 4
8032 [B] (031) AMT-G Ch 4

8034. (Refer to Figure 10.) What is the measured voltage of the series-parallel circuit between terminals A and B?

A—1.5 volts.
B—3.0 volts.
C—4.5 volts.

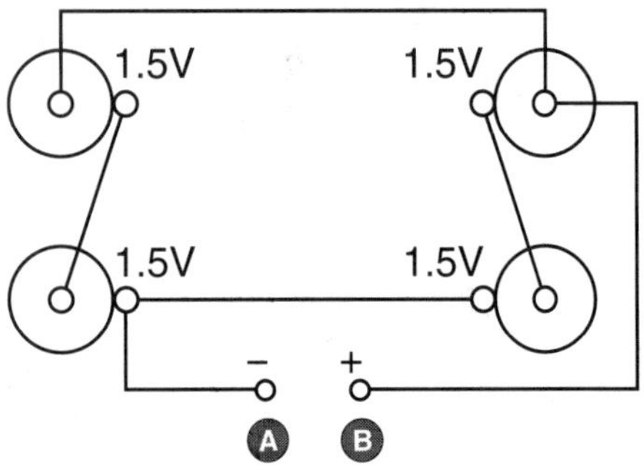

Figure 10. Battery circuit

The two batteries on the left side are connected in series and the two batteries on the right side are connected in series. The two pairs of batteries are connected in parallel.

The series connections between terminals A and B give this circuit a voltage of 3.0 volts.

8035. (Refer to Figure 64.) A 24-volt source is required to furnish 48 watts to a parallel circuit consisting of two resistors of equal value. What is the value of each resistor?

A—24 ohms.
B—12 ohms.
C—6 ohms.

$$R_t = E^2/P$$

Figure 64. Resistance total

To solve this problem, first find the total resistance of the circuit.

$$R_T = E^2 \div P$$
$$= 24^2 \div 48$$
$$= 12\Omega$$

There are two resistors of equal value in parallel that provide this resistance, therefore each resistor must have a resistance of twice this value, or 24 ohms.

8036. Which requires the most electrical power?

(Note: 1 horsepower = 746 watts)

A—A 1/5-horsepower, 24-volt motor which is 75 percent efficient.
B—Four 30-watt lamps arranged in a 12-volt parallel circuit.
C—A 24-volt anticollision light circuit consisting of two light assemblies which require 3 amperes each during operation.

The 1/5-horsepower motor operating at 75 percent efficiency uses 198.93 watts of power.

The four 30-watt lamps use 120 watts of power.

The anticollision light circuit uses 144 watts of power.

8037. What unit is used to express electrical power?

A—Volt.
B—Watt.
C—Ampere.

A watt is a measure of electrical power.

A volt is a measure of electrical pressure.

An ampere is a measure of electrical current flow.

8037-1. What is the basic unit of electrical quantity?

A—Electromotive force.
B—Ampere.
C—Coulomb.

The coulomb is the basic unit of electrical quantity. One coulomb is equal to 6.28×10^{18} *electrons.*

8038. What is the operating resistance of a 30-watt light bulb designed for a 28-volt system?

A—1.07 ohms.
B—26 ohms.
C—0.93 ohm.

A 30-watt light bulb operating in a 28-volt electrical system has a hot resistance (operating resistance) of 26.13 ohms.

$$R = \frac{E^2}{P}$$
$$= \frac{28^2}{30}$$
$$= 26.13\Omega$$

Answers

8034 [B] (031) AMT-G Ch 4	8035 [A] (031) AMT-G Ch 4	8036 [A] (031) AMT-G Ch 4	8037 [B] (031) AMT-G Ch 4
8037-1 [C] (031) AMT-G Ch 4	8038 [B] (015) AMT-G Ch 4		

8039. When referencing resistance in a parallel DC circuit, which of the following statements is true?

A—The current is equal in all portions of the circuit.
B—The total current is equal to the sum of the currents through the individual branches of the circuit.
C—The current in amperes can be found by dividing the source voltage in volts by the sum of the resistors in ohms.

According to Kirchhoff's current law, the current flowing in a parallel circuit is equal to the sum of the currents flowing through each of the individual branches of the circuit.

8039-1. Which of the following is commonly used as a rectifier in electrical circuits?

A—Diodes and anodes.
B—Diodes and cathodes.
C—Diodes.

Diodes are two element electronic components that act as electron check valves. They allow electrons to pass freely in one direction but block their flow in the opposite direction. They are used as rectifiers in electrical circuits.

8040. Diodes are used in electrical power supply circuits primarily as

A—switches.
B—rectifiers.
C—relays.

A diode (either a semiconductor diode or an electron-tube diode) is an electron check valve.

A diode allows electrons to pass in one direction, but blocks their flow in the reverse direction. This is the action of a rectifier.

8041. Transfer of electric energy from one circuit to another without the aid of electrical connections

A—is called induction.
B—is called capacitance.
C—can cause excessive arcing and heat, and as a result is practical for use only with low voltages/amperages.

The continually changing current in an AC circuit causes a changing magnetic field to cut across conductors in an adjacent circuit. When the changing field cuts across a conductor, it induces a voltage in it.

Induction allows electrical energy to be transferred from one circuit to another without the aid of electrical connections.

8042. If three resistors of 3 ohms, 5 ohms, and 22 ohms are connected in series in a 28-volt circuit, how much current will flow through the 3-ohm resistor?

A—9.3 amperes.
B—1.05 amperes.
C—0.93 ampere.

In a series circuit, the total resistance is the sum of the individual resistances. In this circuit, the total resistance is 30 ohms.

All of the current flows through each resistor. Therefore, the current through each resistor is 0.93 amp.

$$I = \frac{E}{R} = \frac{28}{3+5+22} = \frac{28}{30} = 0.933 \text{ amp}$$

8043. A circuit has an applied voltage of 30 volts and a load consisting of a 10-ohm resistor in series with a 20-ohm resistor. What is the voltage drop across the 10-ohm resistor?

A—10 volts.
B—20 volts.
C—30 volts.

In a series circuit, the voltage drop across each resistor is determined by its resistance.

In this circuit, the total resistance is 30 ohms and the total voltage is 30 volts.

One amp of current flows through each resistor and this gives a 10-volt drop across the 10-ohm resistor.

$$E = I \times R = 1 \times 10 = 10 \text{ volts}$$

Answers

8039 [B] (015) AMT-G Ch 4	8039-1 [C] (031) AMT-G Ch 4	8040 [B] (031) AMT-G Ch 4	8041 [A] (031) AMT-G Ch 4
8042 [C] (031) AMT-G Ch 4	8043 [A] (031) AMT-G Ch 4		

8044. (Refer to Figure 11.) Find the total current flowing in the wire between points C and D.

A—6.0 amperes.
B—2.4 amperes.
C—3.0 amperes.

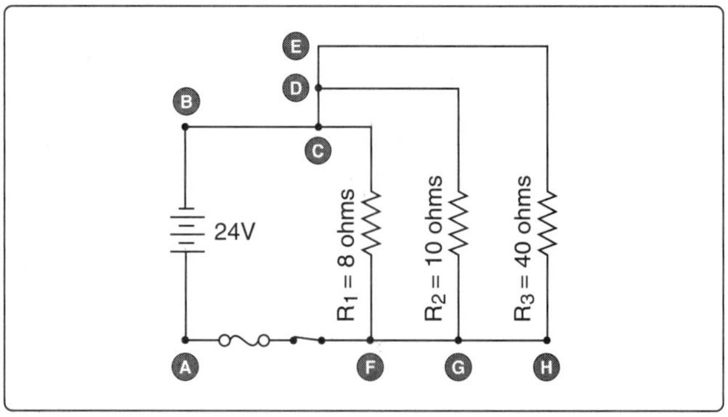

Figure 11. Circuit diagram

The total resistance between points D–E and G–H is 8 ohms. This is the resistance of resistors R_2 and R_3 in parallel.

$$R^{2-3} = \frac{10 \times 40}{10 + 40} = \frac{400}{50} = 8\Omega$$

There is a voltage of 24 volts across these two parallel resistors, so the current through the line between C and D is three amps.

$$I = \frac{E}{R} = \frac{24}{8} = 3 \text{ amps}$$

8045. (Refer to Figure 11.) Find the voltage across the 8-ohm resistor.

A—8 volts.
B—20.4 volts.
C—24 volts.

The 8-ohm resistor, R_1, is across the full 24 volts of the battery.

8045-1. In a parallel circuit with four 6-ohm resistors across a 24-volt battery, what is the total voltage across resistor-three (VR3) in the circuit?

A—6 volts.
B—18 volts.
C—24 volts.

In a parallel circuit the source or battery voltage is applied to each of the individual resistors.

8045-2. If each cell, connected in series, equals 2 volts, how would a 12-cell lead acid battery be rated?

A—24 volts.
B—12 volts.
C—6 volts.

The voltage of a battery is determined by the number of cells connected in series to form the battery. Although the voltage of one lead-acid cell just removed from a charger is approximately 2.2 volts, a lead-acid cell is normally rated at approximately 2 volts. A battery rated at 12 volts consists of 6 lead-acid cells connected in series, and a battery rated at 24 volts is composed of 12 cells.

8046. (Refer to Figure 12.) Find the total resistance of the circuit.

A—16 ohms.
B—2.6 ohms.
C—21.2 ohms.

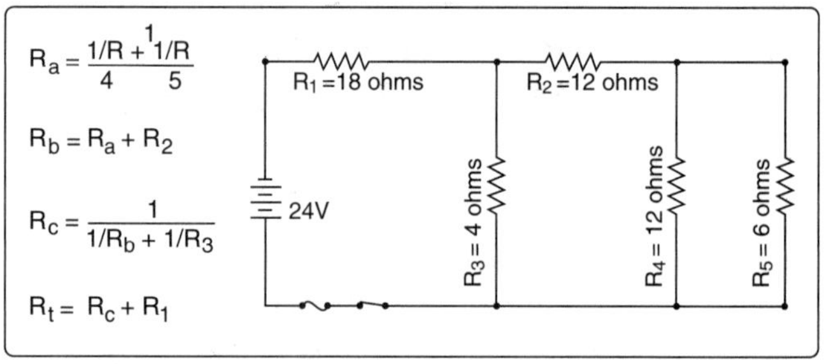

Figure 12. Circuit diagram

This problem can be solved in four steps:

1. *Combine resistors R_4 and R_5 in parallel.*

$$R^{4-5} = \frac{R_4 \times R_5}{R_4 + R_5} = \frac{12 \times 6}{12 + 6} = \frac{72}{18} = 4\Omega$$

Answers

8044 [C] (031) AMT-G Ch 4	8045 [C] (031) AMT-G Ch 4	8045-1 [C] (102) AMT-G Ch 4	8045-2 [A] (031) AMT-G Ch 4
8046 [C] (015) AMT-G Ch 4			

2. *Combine resistor R_2 with R_{4-5} in series.*

$$R_{2-4-5} = R_2 + R_{4-5} = 12 + 4 = 16\Omega$$

3. *Combine resistors R_{2-4-5} with R_3 in parallel.*

$$R^{2-3-4-5} = \frac{R_{2-4-5} \times R_3}{R_{2-4-5} + R_3} = \frac{16 \times 4}{16 + 4} = \frac{64}{20} = 3.2\Omega$$

4. *Combine resistors $R_{2-3-4-5}$ with R_1 in series.*

$$R_T = R_{2-3-4-5} + R_1 = 3.2 + 18 = 21.2\Omega$$

8047. Which is correct in reference to electrical resistance?

A—Two electrical devices will have the same combined resistance if they are connected in series as they will have if connected in parallel.
B—If one of three bulbs in a parallel lighting circuit is removed, the total resistance of the circuit will become greater.
C—An electrical device that has a high resistance will use more power than one with a low resistance with the same applied voltage.

In a parallel electrical circuit, each bulb provides a path for current to flow. The more paths there are, the less the circuit resistance will be. When one bulb is removed, the circuit resistance increases.

8048. What happens to the current in a voltage step-up transformer with a ratio of 1 to 4?

A—The current is stepped down by a 1 to 4 ratio.
B—The current is stepped up by a 1 to 4 ratio.
C—The current does not change.

The power (voltage times current) in the secondary of a transformer is equal to the power in the primary. When the voltage in the secondary is four times that in the primary, the current in the secondary is one fourth of that in the primary.

8049. (Refer to Figure 13.) Determine the total current flow in the circuit.

A—0.2 ampere.
B—1.4 amperes.
C—0.8 ampere.

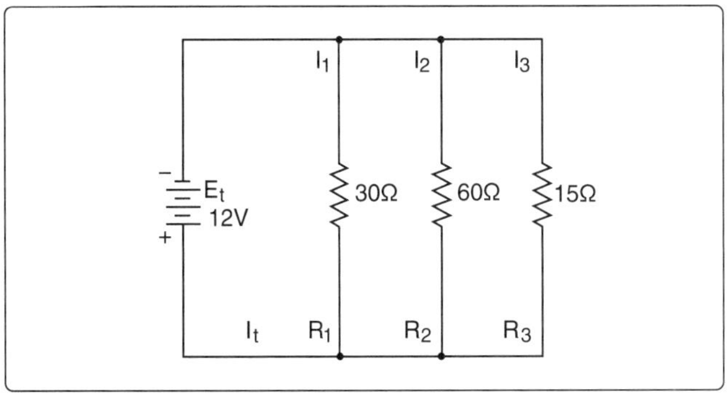

Figure 13. Circuit diagram

The total resistance of this circuit is 8.57 ohms.

$$R_P = \frac{1}{\frac{1}{R_1} + \frac{1}{R_2} + \frac{1}{R_3}} = \frac{1}{\frac{1}{30} + \frac{1}{60} + \frac{1}{15}} = 8.57\Omega$$

The total current flowing in this circuit is 1.4 amps.

$$I = \frac{E}{R} = \frac{12}{8.57} = 1.4 \text{ amps}$$

8049-1. In a parallel circuit with three 6-ohm resistors across a 12-volt battery, what is the total current (I_t) value in the circuit?

A—2 amps.
B—6 amps.
C—12 amps.

The total resistance of this circuit is 2 ohms. The total current flowing in this circuit is 6 amps.

Answers
8047 [B] (015) AMT-G Ch 4 | 8048 [A] (031) AMT-G Ch 4 | 8049 [B] (015) AMT-G Ch 4 | 8049-1 [B] (102) AMT-G Ch 4

8050. (Refer to Figure 14.) The total resistance of the circuit is

A—25 ohms.
B—35 ohms.
C—17 ohms.

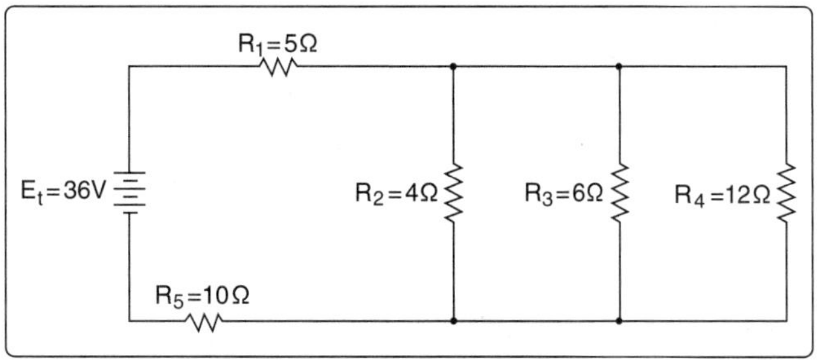

Figure 14. Circuit diagram

The total resistance can be found in two steps:

1. *Combine resistances R_2, R_3, and R_4 in parallel.*

$$R_{2\text{-}3\text{-}4} = \frac{1}{\frac{1}{R_2}+\frac{1}{R_3}+\frac{1}{R_4}} = \frac{1}{\frac{1}{4}+\frac{1}{6}+\frac{1}{12}} = 2\Omega$$

2. *Combine resistances R_1, R_{2-3-4}, and R_5 in series.*

$$R_T = R_1 + R_{2-3-4} + R_5 = 5 + 2 + 10 = 17\Omega$$

8051. Which of these will cause the resistance of a conductor to decrease?

A—Decrease the length or the cross-sectional area.
B—Decrease the length or increase the cross-sectional area.
C—Increase the length or decrease the cross-sectional area.

The resistance of a conductor varies directly as its length, inversely as its cross-sectional area, and directly with the resistivity of its material.

Either decreasing the length or increasing the cross-sectional area of a conductor will cause its resistance to decrease.

8052. Through which material will magnetic lines of force pass the most readily?

A—Copper.
B—Iron.
C—Aluminum.

The permeability of a material is a measure of the ease with which lines of magnetic force can pass through it. Iron has the highest permeability of all the metals listed in this question.

8053. (Refer to Figure 64.) A 48-volt source is required to furnish 192 watts to a parallel circuit consisting of three resistors of equal value. What is the value of each resistor?

A—36 ohms.
B—4 ohms.
C—12 ohms.

$$R_t = E^2/P$$

Figure 64. Resistance total

The total resistance needed to dissipate 192 watts of electrical power from a 48-volt source is 12 ohms.

$$R_T = E^2 \div P = 48^2 \div 192 = 12\Omega$$

Since three resistors in parallel give 12 ohms, each resistor must have a resistance three times this value.

8054. Which is correct concerning a parallel circuit?

A—Total resistance will be smaller than the smallest resistor.
B—Total resistance will decrease when one of the resistances is removed.
C—Total voltage drop is the same as the total resistance.

In a parallel circuit each resistor forms a path for the current to follow and the total resistance is always smaller than that of the smallest resistor.

Answers
8050 [C] (015) AMT-G Ch 4 8051 [B] (031) AMT-G Ch 4 8052 [B] (042) AMT-G Ch 4 8053 [A] (015) AMT-G Ch 4
8054 [A] (031) AMT-G Ch 4

8055. The voltage drop in a circuit of known resistance is dependent on

A—the voltage of the circuit.
B—only the resistance of the conductor and does not change with a change in either voltage or amperage.
C—the amperage of the circuit.

The voltage drop across a circuit is determined by two things: the resistance of the circuit and the amount of current flowing through it (the amperage).

In this question, the resistance of the circuit is fixed; therefore, the voltage drop is determined by the amperage in the circuit.

8056. A thermal switch, or thermal protector, as used in an electric motor, is designed to

A—close the integral fan circuit to allow cooling of the motor.
B—open the circuit in order to allow cooling of the motor.
C—reroute the circuit to ground.

A thermal switch is another name for a built-in thermal circuit breaker. This is a circuit protection device that opens the circuit when the windings of the motor get too hot.

If the motor overheats for any reason, the thermal switch will open the power circuit to the motor and allow the motor to cool.

8057. (Refer to Figure 15.) With the landing gear retracted, the red indicator light will not come on if an open occurs in wire

A—19.
B—7.
C—17.

With the landing gear retracted, the red indicator light will not come on if there is an open in wire 19.

Wire 19 supplies power from the bus to the red indicator light, through the up-limit switch and through wire 8.

Wire 7 supplies power to the red indicator light for the press-to-test circuit.

Wire 17 supplies power to the green indicator light for its press-to-test circuit.

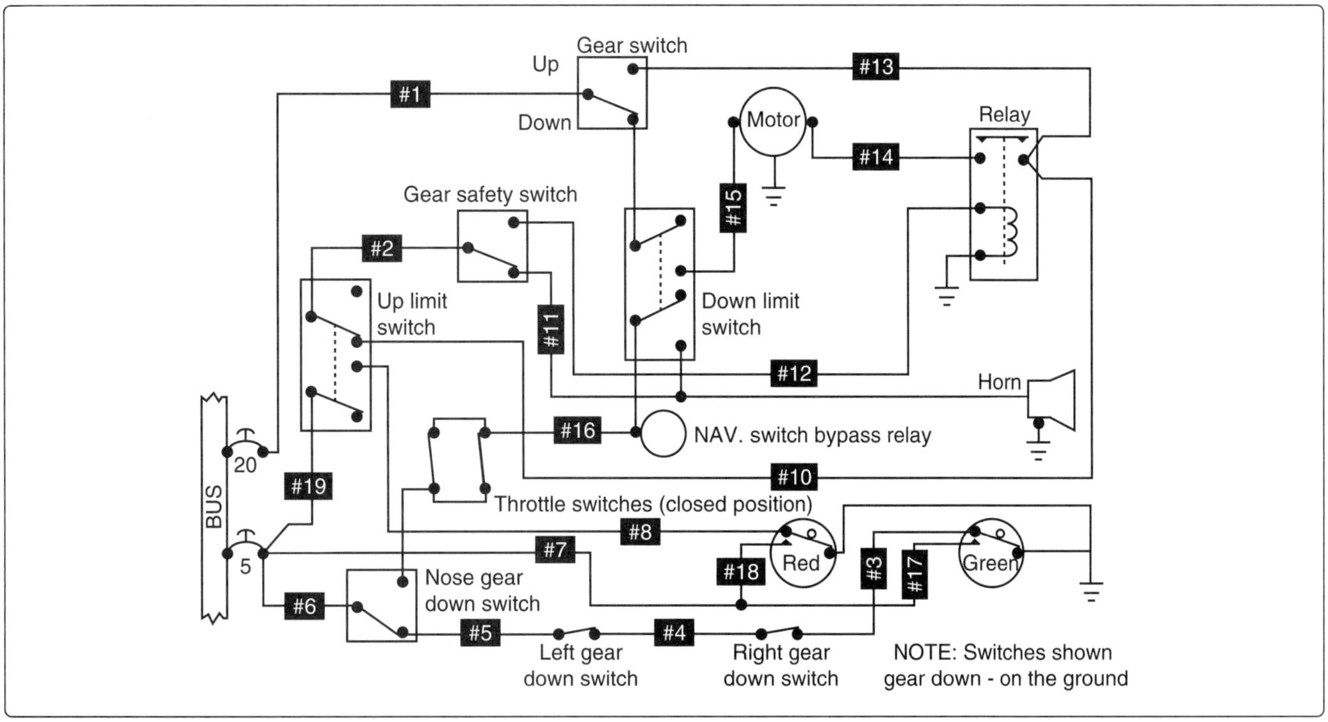

Figure 15. Landing gear circuit

Answers
8055 [C] (015) AC 43.13-1
8056 [B] (031) AMT-G Ch 4
8057 [A] (015) AMT-G Ch 4

8058. (Refer to Figure 15.) Wire 7 is used to

A—close the PUSH-TO-TEST circuit.
B—open the UP indicator light circuit when the landing gear is retracted.
C—close the UP indicator light circuit when the landing gear is retracted.

Wire 7 supplies power to both the red and green indicator lights from the 5-amp circuit breaker.

When either of the press-to-test lamps is pushed, the circuit is completed to ground, allowing the lamp to light up as long as it remains pressed.

Press-to-test lamps are used to allow the pilot to ascertain that the bulb in the lamp is good.

8059. (Refer to Figure 15.) When the landing gear is down, the green light will not come on if an open occurs in wire

A—7.
B—6.
C—17.

The green light will not come on when the landing gear is down if there is an open in wire 6. (Note: The switches in Figure 15 are shown in the position for the gear down and the airplane on the ground.)

Wire 7 supplies power to both the red and green indicator lights from the 5-amp circuit breaker for the push-to-test circuit.

Wire 17 supplies power to the green indicator light for its push-to-test circuit.

8060. (Refer to Figure 16.) What will be the effect if the PCO relay fails to operate when the left-hand tank is selected?

A—The fuel pressure crossfeed valve will not open.
B—The fuel tank crossfeed valve open light will illuminate.
C—The fuel pressure crossfeed valve open light will not illuminate.

PCO relay provides 24-volt DC power from the bus through a 5-amp circuit breaker to the fuel pressure crossfeed valve open caution warning light in the cockpit.

If PCO relay fails to operate, contacts 13 will not complete the circuit and the light will not illuminate, but the rest of the system will operate normally.

8061. (Refer to Figure 16.) The TCO relay will operate if 24-volts DC is applied to the bus and the fuel tank selector is in the

A—right-hand tank position.
B—crossfeed position.
C—left-hand tank position.

The fuel-selector switch must be in the crossfeed position for the relay TCO to close contacts 14.

When the tank selector is put in the crossfeed position, contacts 17 of the FCF relay close, and current flows from the 24-volt DC bus, through a 5-amp circuit breaker, into the "open" coils of the fuel tank crossfeed valve motor.

When the motor opens this valve, contacts 19 close and current flows to theTCO relay closing contacts 14.

8062. (Refer to Figure 16.) With power to the bus and the fuel selector switched to the right-hand tank, how many relays in the system are operating?

A—Three.
B—Two.
C—Four.

When the fuel selector switch is in the right-hand tank position and power is supplied from the bus, three relays (RTS, PCO, and TCC) will actuate.

Current flowing through the fuel-selector switch energizes the coil for relay RTS. This closes contacts 8 and opens contacts 7.

Current from the bus flows through closed contacts 5 of relay LTS, through contacts 8 of relay RTS that has just closed, and through the "open" winding of the fuel pressure crossfeed valve motor.

As soon as this motor fully opens the valve, contacts 12 close and energize the PCO relay to close contacts 13 in the circuit for the fuel pressure crossfeed valve open light.

Current flows from the bus through the right-hand 5-amp circuit breaker and through the normally closed contacts 18 of the FCF relay, through contacts 20 in the fuel tank crossfeed valve to the coil of relay TCC which opens its contacts 16.

8063. (Refer to Figure 16.) When electrical power is applied to the bus, which relays are energized?

A—PCC and TCC.
B—TCC and TCO.
C—PCO and PCC.

Answers

8058 [A] (015) AMT-G Ch 4	8059 [B] (015) AMT-G Ch 4	8060 [C] (015) AMT-G Ch 4	8061 [B] (015) AMT-G Ch 4
8062 [A] (015) AMT-G Ch 4	8063 [A] (015) AMT-G Ch 4		

As soon as electrical power is supplied to the 24-volt bus, two relays, PCC and TCC, are energized.

Current flows from the bus through the left-hand, 5-amp circuit breaker and through contacts 5, 7, and 9 of the relays controlled by the fuel selector switch. It flows from contacts 9, through contacts 11 in the fuel pressure crossfeed valve, to the coil of the PCC relay.

At the same time, current flows through the right-hand 5-amp circuit breaker, through contacts 18 and then through contacts 20 in the fuel tank crossfeed valve to the coil of the TCC relay.

8064. (Refer to Figure 16.) Energize the circuit with the fuel tank selector switch selected to the left-hand position. Using the schematic, identify the switches that will change position.

A—5, 9, 10, 11, 12, 13, and 15.
B—3, 5, 6, 7, 11, and 13.
C—5, 6, 11, 12, 13, 15, and 16.

When power is supplied to the bus with the fuel selector switch in the left-hand position, seven switches change their position (5, 6, 11, 12, 13, 15, and 16).

Current flows from the bus through the left-hand, 5-amp circuit breaker, through the left-hand tank position of the fuel selector switch, into the coil of the LTS relay. This changes the position of switches 5 and 6.

Since current can no longer flow through switch 5, the coil of the PCC relay is de-energized and this changes the position of switch 15.

Current can now flow through switch 6 into the "open" motor coil of the fuel-pressure crossfeed valve. When this valve is open, switches 11 and 12 change their position.

Current now flows through switch 12 to the coil of the PCO relay. This closes switch 13.

At the same time all of this is happening, current is flowing from the right-hand, 5-amp circuit breaker, through switches 18 and 20, to the coil of the TCC relay. When the TCC relay is energized, it changes the position of switch 16.

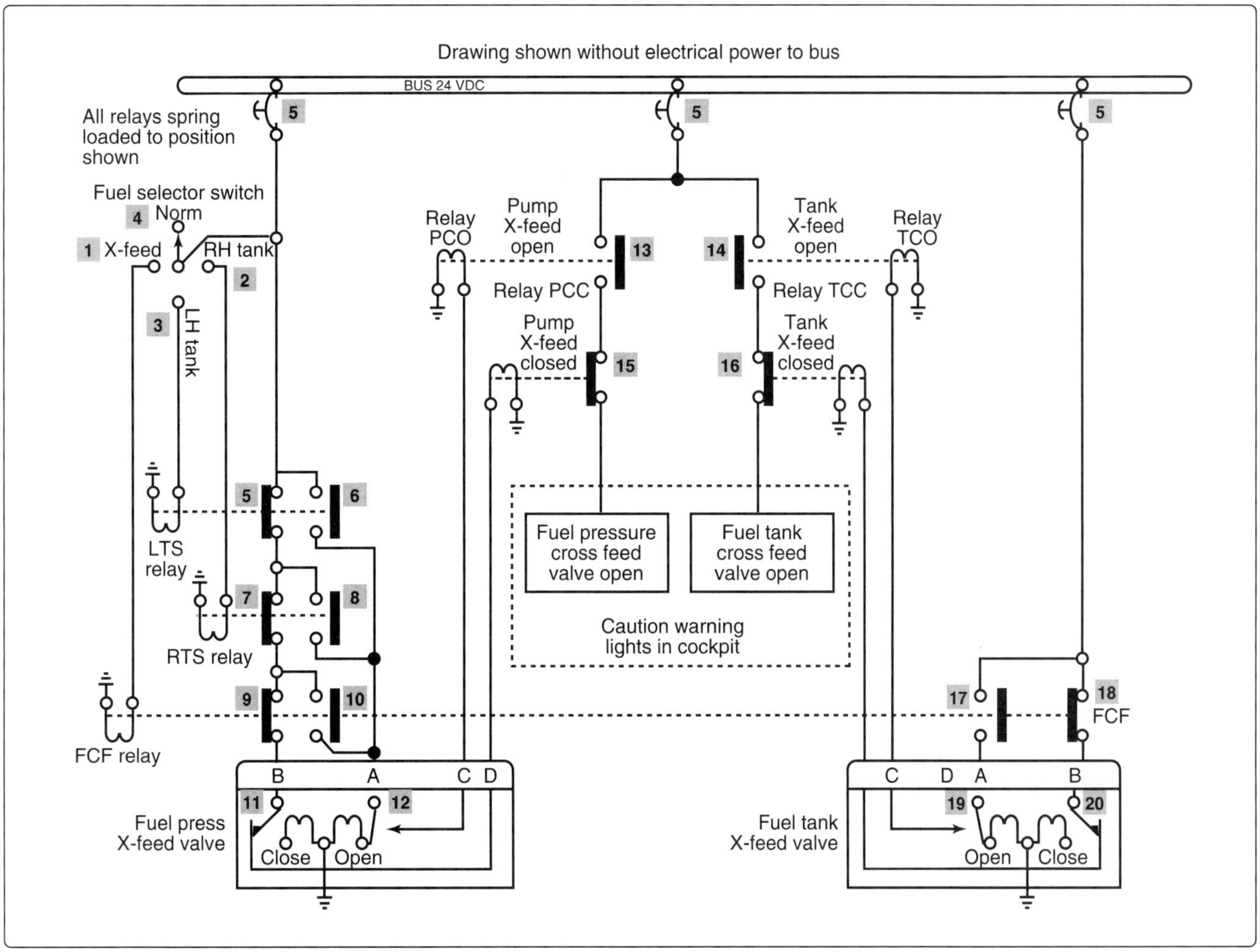

Figure 16. Fuel system circuit

Answers
8064 [C] (015) AMT-G Ch 4

8065. (Refer to Figure 17.) Which of the components is a potentiometer?

A—5.
B—3.
C—11.

The component identified as 3 is a potentiometer.
The component identified as 5 is a variable capacitor.
The component identified as 11 is an inductor (choke).

8066. (Refer to Figure 17.) The electrical symbol represented at number 5 is a variable

A—inductor.
B—resistor.
C—capacitor.

A variable capacitor is shown by symbol 5.
An inductor is shown by symbol 11.
A variable resistor (potentiometer) is shown by symbol 3.

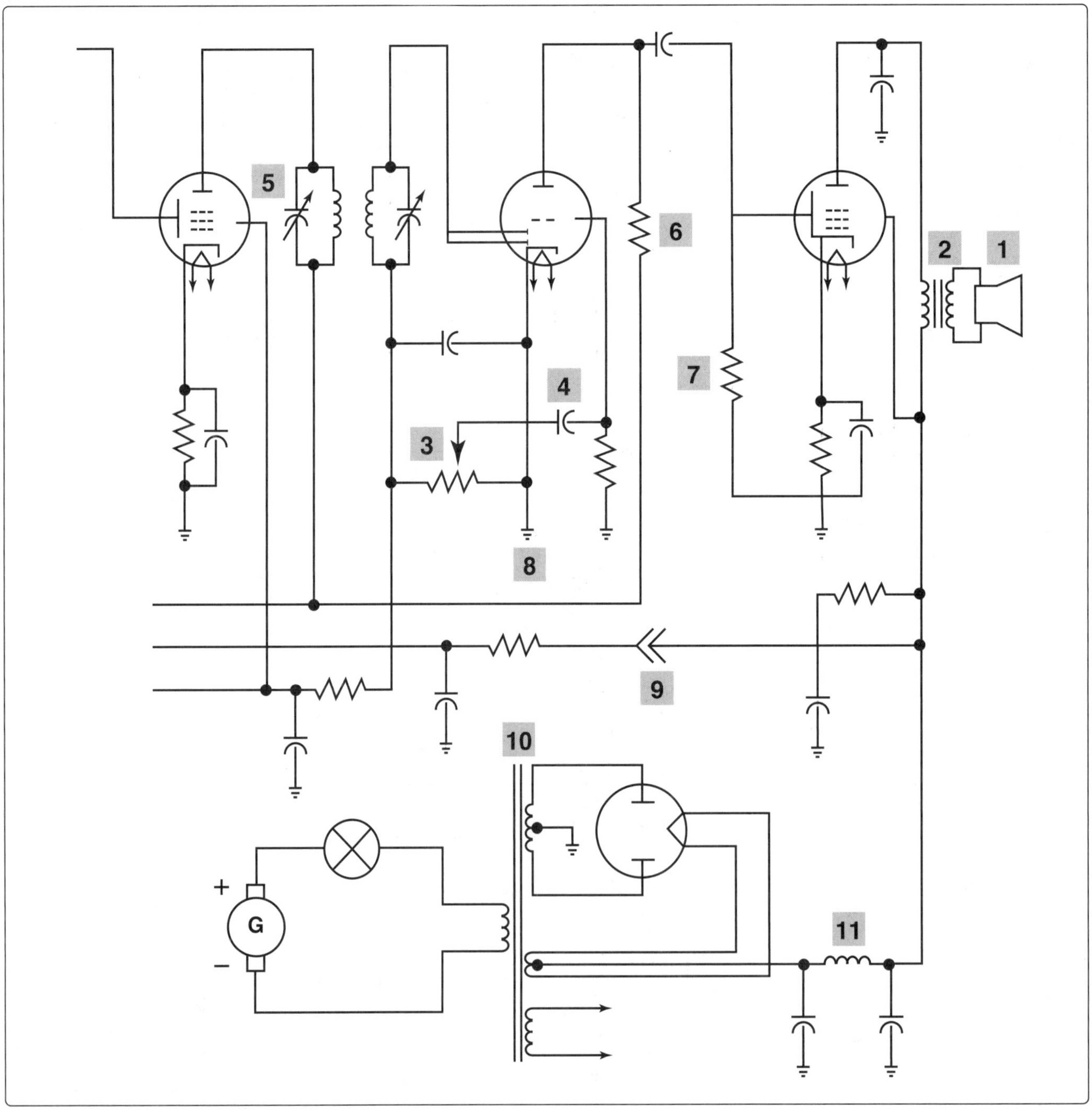

Figure 17. Electrical symbols

Answers
8065 [B] (031) AMT-G Ch 4
8066 [C] (031) AMT-G Ch 4

8067. (Refer to Figure 18.) When the landing gear is up and the throttles are retarded, the warning horn will not sound if an open occurs in wire

A—4.
B—2.
C—9.

Wire 4 is in the landing gear warning horn ground circuit. If it is open, the warning horn cannot sound when the landing gears are up and the throttles are retarded.

Wire 2 is in the red warning-light circuit and not in the warning horn circuit.

Wire 9 is in the green light circuit.

8068. (Refer to Figure 18.) The control valve switch must be placed in the neutral position when the landing gear is down to

A—permit the test circuit to operate.
B—prevent the warning horn from sounding when the throttles are closed.
C—remove the ground from the green light.

If the control-valve switch were not in the neutral position, as shown here, the landing gear warning horn would sound when either throttle is closed and both landing gears are down.

The ground for the horn would be supplied through wire 6, the closed throttle switch, wires 5 and 10, the control valve switch, wire 11, the right gear switch, wire 3, the left gear switch, and wire 14 to ground.

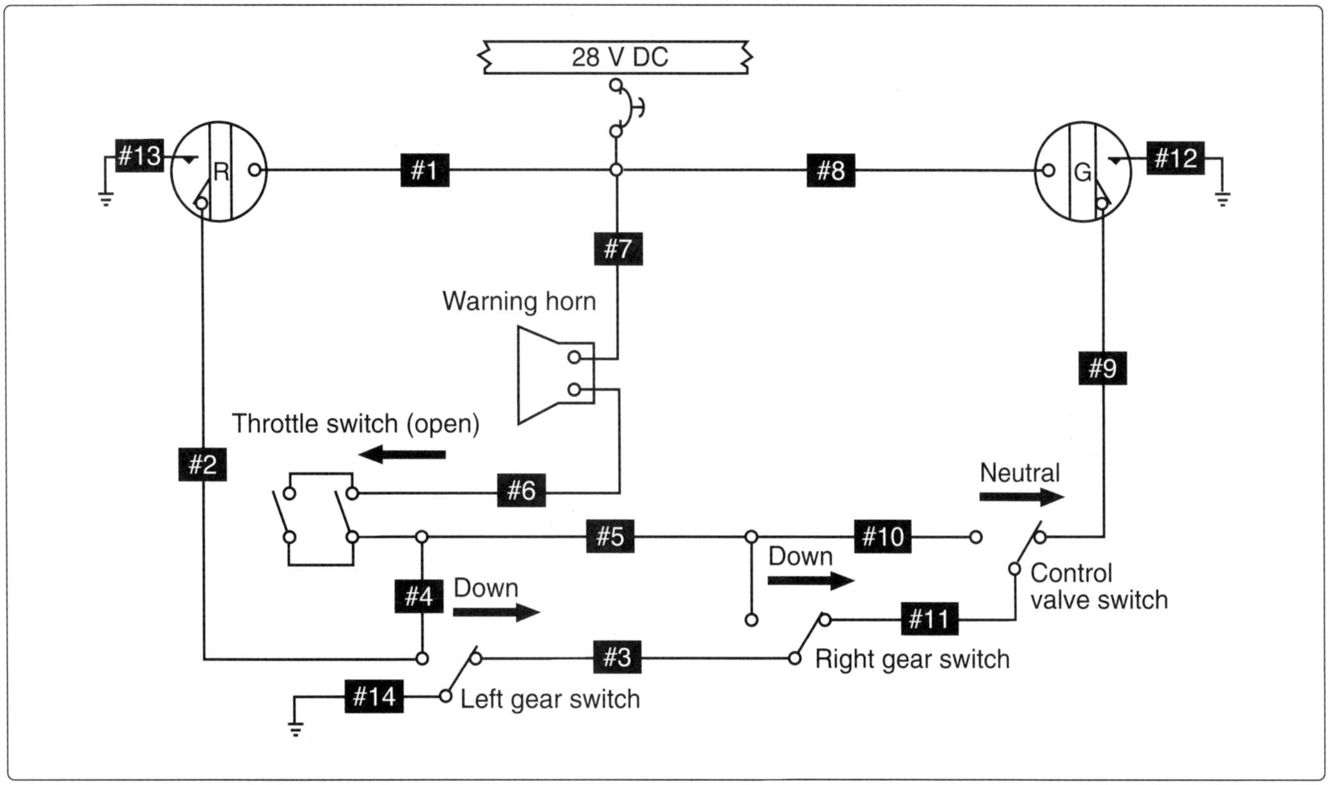

Figure 18. Landing gear circuit

Answers
8067 [A] (015) AMT-G Ch 4
8068 [B] (015) AMT-G Ch 4

8069. (Refer to Figure 19.) Under which condition will a ground be provided for the warning horn through both gear switches when the throttles are closed?

A—Right gear up and left gear down.
B—Both gears up and the control valve out of neutral.
C—Left gear up and right gear down.

A ground for the landing gear warning horn is provided through both of the gear switches only when the right landing gear is down and the left landing gear is up.

Ground current from the warning horn flows through wire 11, through a closed throttle switch, through wire 12, through the left gear switch in its UP position, through wire 5, through the right gear switch in its DOWN position, to ground.

8070. (Refer to Figure 19.) When the throttles are retarded with only the right gear down, the warning horn will not sound if an open occurs in wire

A—5.
B—13.
C—6.

Wire 5 is in the landing gear warning horn ground circuit. If there is an open in this wire, the warning horn cannot get a ground when the right landing gear is down and the left gear is not down.

Wire 13 is not in the warning horn circuit if the left landing gear is not down.

Wire 6 is in the warning horn test circuit.

8071. (Refer to Figure 19.) When the landing gears are up and the throttles are retarded, the warning horn will not sound if an open occurs in wire

A—5.
B—7.
C—6.

Wire 6 is in the ground circuit for the landing gear warning horn. The horn will not sound if there is an open in this wire when the throttles are retarded and the landing gears are up.

Wire 5 is not in the warning horn ground circuit when the right landing gear is up.

Wire 7 is not in the warning horn ground circuit.

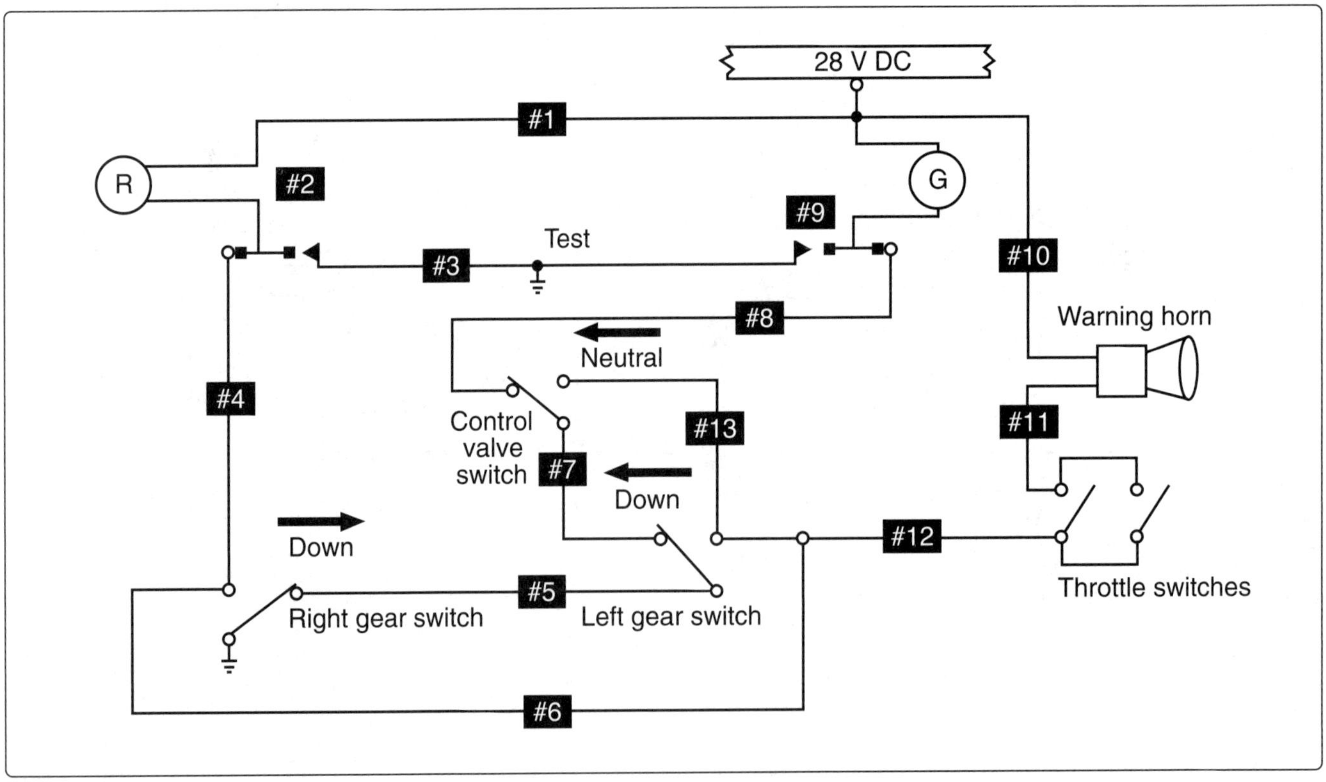

Figure 19. Landing gear circuit

Answers
8069 [C] (015) AMT-G Ch 4
8070 [A] (015) AMT-G Ch 4
8071 [C] (015) AMT-G Ch 4

8072. When referring to an electrical circuit diagram, what point is considered to be at zero voltage?

A—The circuit breaker.
B—The switch.
C—The ground reference.

The ground reference, shown on a schematic diagram as a triangular-shaped series of parallel lines, is the point considered to be at zero voltage.

All voltages, both positive and negative, are measured from this ground reference.

8072-1. What is the purpose of the ground symbol used in electrical circuit diagrams?

A—To show that there is common bus for connection of the source of electrical energy to the load.
B—To show the source of electrical energy for the load.
C—To show that there is a return path for the current between the source of electrical energy and the load.

The ground symbol used on electrical schematic diagrams indicates that there is a return path for the current between the source of electrical energy and the load.

8073. (Refer to Figure 20.) Troubleshooting an open circuit with a voltmeter as shown in this circuit will

A—permit current to flow and illuminate the lamp.
B—create a low resistance path and the current flow will be greater than normal.
C—permit the battery voltage to appear on the voltmeter.

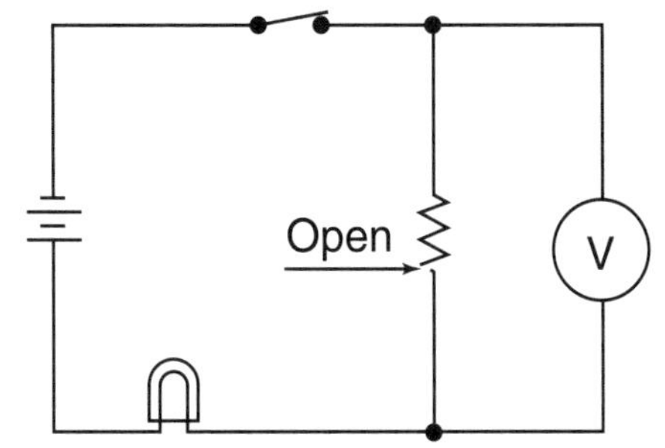

Figure 20. Circuit diagram

An open in the resistor will cause an infinite resistance. No current can flow in the circuit.

Since no current flows, there is no voltage drop across the switch or the lamp, and the entire battery voltage is read on the voltmeter.

8074. (Refer to Figure 21.) Which symbol represents a variable resistor?

A—2.
B—1.
C—3.

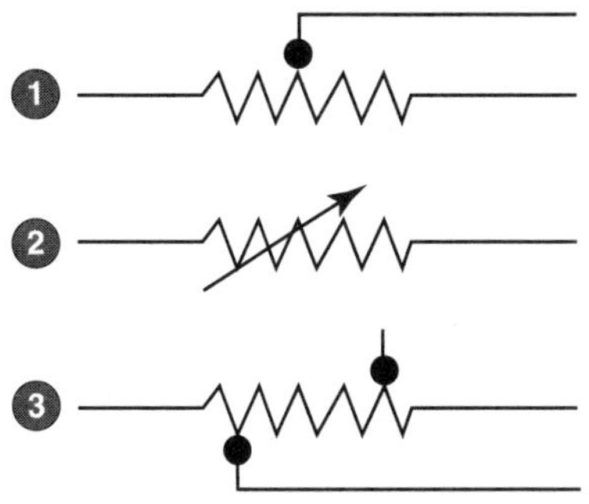

Figure 21. Electrical symbols

Symbol 2 is a variable resistor (rheostat). This is not the most widely used symbol as it can be used only for a rheostat (a variable resistor with only two connections) and not for a potentiometer.

Symbol 1 is a tapped resistor.

Symbol 3 is a tapped resistor—tapped at two places.

8075. In a P-N-P transistor application, the solid-state device is turned on when the

A—base is negative with respect to the emitter.
B—base is positive with respect to the emitter.
C—emitter is negative with respect to the base.

A P-N-P transistor conducts between the emitter and collector (is turned on) when a small amount of current flows into the base. This current flows when the emitter-base junction is forward biased. It is forward biased when the base is negative with respect to the emitter.

8076. In an N-P-N transistor application, the solid-state device is turned on when the

A—emitter is positive with respect to the base.
B—base is negative with respect to the emitter.
C—base is positive with respect to the emitter.

An N-P-N transistor conducts between the emitter and collector (is turned on) when a small amount of current flows from the base. This current flows when the emitter-base junction is forward biased. It is forward biased when the base is positive with respect to the emitter.

Answers

8072 [C] (015) AMT-G Ch 4	8072-1 [C] (031) AMT-G Ch 4	8073 [C] (015) AMT-G Ch 4	8074 [A] (031) AMT-G Ch 4
8075 [A] (031) AMT-G Ch 4	8076 [C] (031) AMT-G Ch 4		

8077. Typical application for zener diodes is as

A—full-wave rectifiers.
B—half-wave rectifiers.
C—voltage regulators.

A zener diode is a special type of semiconductor diode that is designed to operate with current flowing through it in its reverse direction. When a specific amount of inverse voltage is applied between the cathode and anode, the diode breaks down and conducts in its reverse direction. This principle is used as the voltage-sensing element in a voltage regulator.

8078. (Refer to Figure 22.) Which illustration is correct concerning bias application and current (positive charge) flow?

A—1.
B—2.
C—3.

In 1, the base of this N-P-N transistor is positive with respect to the emitter (the emitter-base junction is forward biased). Base-emitter current flows and therefore collector emitter current flows as is shown by the current-flow arrow.

In 2, the base and emitter of this N-P-N transistor have the same polarity and no emitter-base current flows. There is no flow between the emitter and the collector.

In 3, the base and emitter of this P-N-P transistor have the same polarity, and no emitter-base current flows. There is no flow between the emitter and the collector.

8079. Forward biasing of a solid-state device will cause the device to

A—conduct via zener breakdown.
B—conduct.
C—turn off.

When a solid-state device such as a diode is forward biased, the N-material is negative with respect to the P-material. A forward-biased device will conduct.

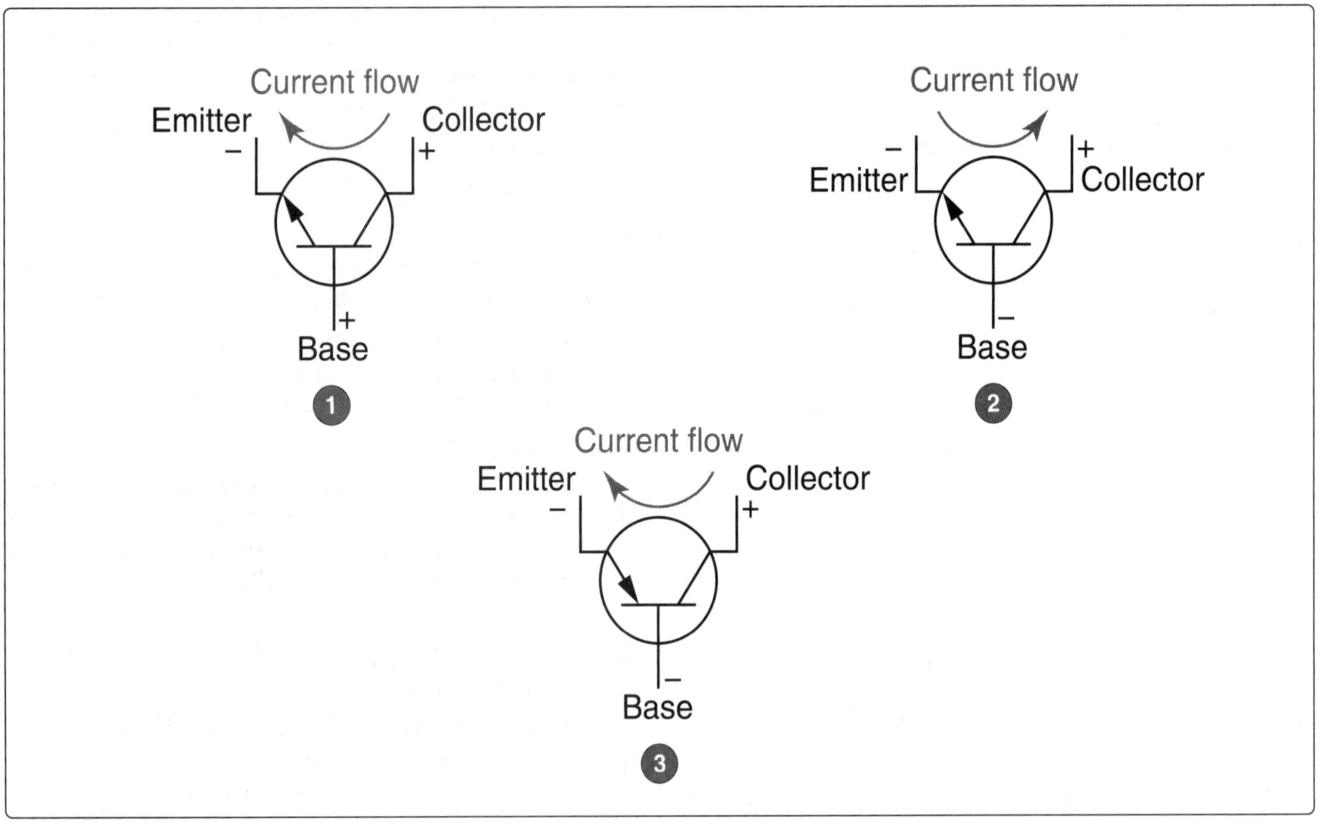

Figure 22. Transistors

Answers
8077 [C] (031) AMT-G Ch 4
8078 [A] (031) AMT-G Ch 4
8079 [B] (031) AMT-G Ch 4

8080. (Refer to Figure 23.) If an open occurs at R_1, the light

A—cannot be turned on.
B—will not be affected.
C—cannot be turned off.

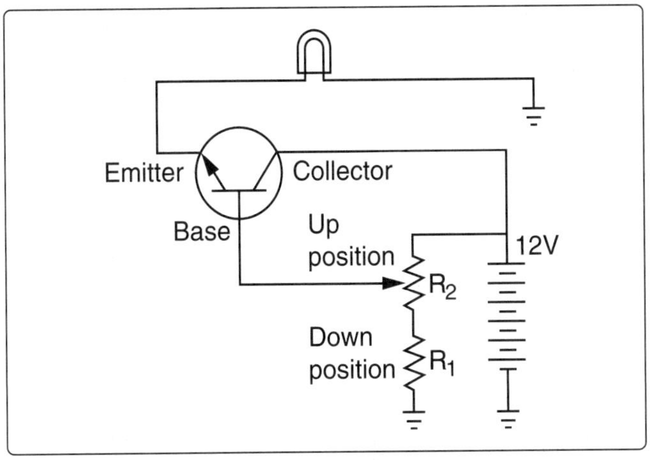

Figure 23. Transistorized circuit

If there is an open circuit in R_1, the base and the collector will have the same voltage. The base current will be maximum, and the light cannot be turned off.

8081. (Refer to Figure 23.) If R_2 sticks in the up position, the light will

A—be on full bright.
B—be very dim.
C—not illuminate.

An N-P-N transistor circuit such as this conducts the maximum amount of current between the emitter and collector (the lamp is burning brightest) when the maximum amount of current is flowing from the base. This occurs when the base is most positive with respect to the emitter. This would be the case if R_2 were stuck in the up position.

8082. (Refer to Figure 24.) Which statement concerning the depicted logic gate is true?

A—Any input being 1 will produce a 0 output.
B—Any input being 1 will produce a 1 output.
C—All inputs must be 1 to produce a 1 output.

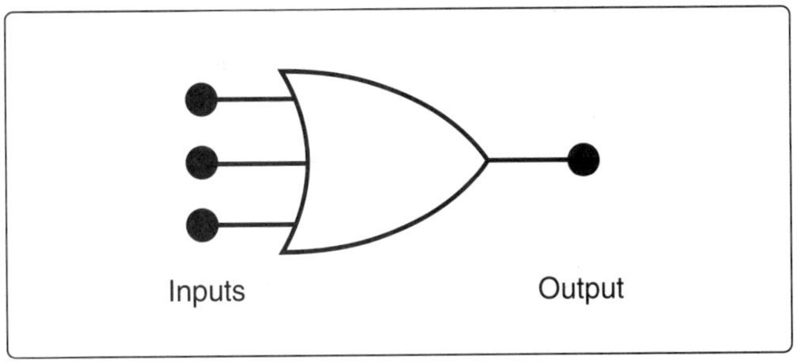

Figure 24. Logic gate

This is an OR gate. Any time there is a 1 on any of the inputs, there will be a 1 on the output.

8083. (Refer to Figure 25.) In a functional and operating circuit, the depicted logic gate's output will be 0

A—only when all inputs are 0.
B—when all inputs are 1.
C—when one or more inputs are 0.

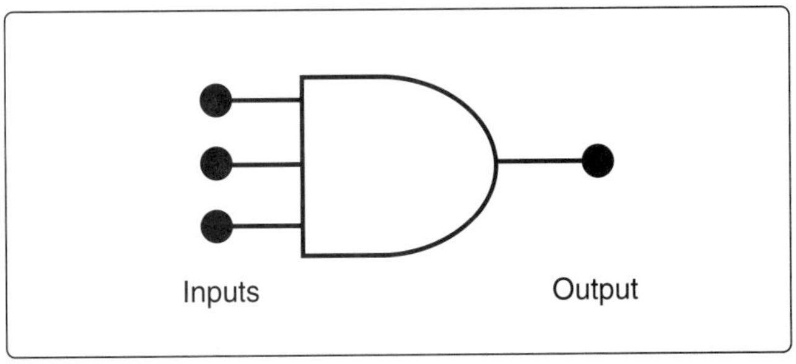

Figure 25. Logic gate

This is an AND gate. Any time one or more of the inputs do not have a 1 on them (have a 0 on them), the output will be 0. For the output to be 1, all of the inputs must be 1.

Answers

8080 [C] (015) AMT-G Ch 4 8081 [A] (015) AMT-G Ch 4 8082 [B] (015) AMT-G Ch 4 8083 [C] (015) AMT-G Ch 4

8084. (Refer to Figure 26.) Which of the logic gate output conditions is correct with respect to the given inputs?

A—1.
B—2.
C—3.

These are EXCLUSIVE OR (XOR) gates. There will be a 1 on the output when one, and only one, input has a 1 on it.

View 1 is incorrect. It has a 1 on both inputs so the output should be 0.

View 2 is correct. Only one of the inputs has a 1 on it and the output is a 1.

View 3 is incorrect. It has a 1 on one of its inputs, but the output is shown to be 0.

8084-1. Which of the following logic gates will provide an active high out only when all inputs are different?

A—XNOR.
B—NAND.
C—XOR.

The output of the XOR gate will only be at an active high when one and only one of the two inputs is high. If both inputs are low, or both inputs are high, then the output of the gate will be low.

8085. A lead-acid battery with 12 cells connected in series (no-load voltage = 2.1 volts per cell) furnishes 10 amperes to a load of 2-ohms resistance. The internal resistance of the battery in this instance is

A—0.52 ohm.
B—2.52 ohms.
C—5.0 ohms.

This battery has a no-load voltage of $12 \times 2.1 = 25.2$ *volts.*

When it supplies 10 amperes to a 2-ohm load, the loaded voltage is $10 \times 2 = 20$ *volts.*

The voltage dropped across its internal resistance is $25.2 - 20.0 = 5.2$ *volts.*

The internal resistance of the battery is found by dividing the voltage dropped across it by the load current. $5.2 \div 10 = 0.52$ *ohms.*

8086. If electrolyte from a lead-acid battery is spilled in the battery compartment, which procedure should be followed?

A—Apply boric acid solution to the affected area followed by a water rinse.
B—Rinse the affected area thoroughly with clean water.
C—Apply sodium bicarbonate solution to the affected area followed by a water rinse.

The electrolyte in a lead-acid battery is a solution of sulfuric acid and water. If any is spilled in the battery compartment, it should be neutralized with a solution of sodium bicarbonate (baking soda) and water, and the area rinsed with fresh water.

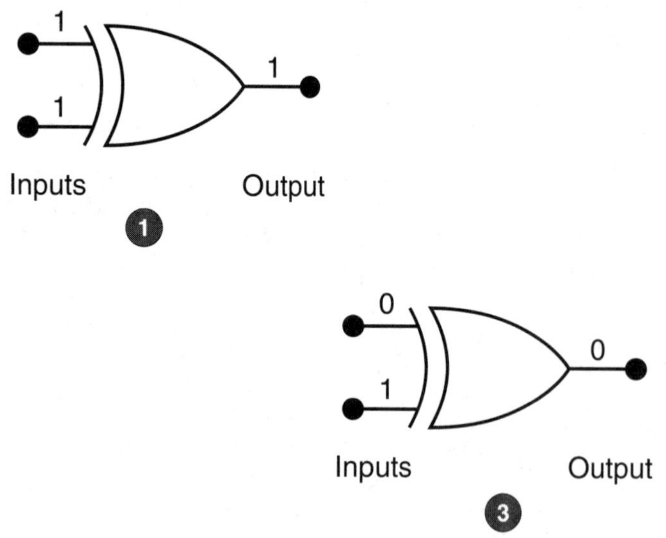

Figure 26. Logic gate

Answers
8084 [B] (015) AMT-G Ch 4
8084-1 [C] (102) AMT-G Ch 4
8085 [A] (031) AMT-G Ch 4
8086 [C] (031) AMT-G Ch 4

8087. Which statement regarding the hydrometer reading of a lead-acid storage battery electrolyte is true?

A—The hydrometer reading does not require a temperature correction if the electrolyte temperature is 80°F.
B—A specific gravity correction should be added to the hydrometer reading if the electrolyte temperature is below 59°F.
C—The hydrometer reading will give a true indication of the capacity of the battery regardless of the electrolyte temperature.

When testing the specific gravity of the electrolyte of a lead-acid battery, the temperature must be taken into consideration.

No correction is necessary when the electrolyte temperature is between 70°F and 90°F. A correction of 0.4 should be added to the specific gravity reading for each 10° above 80°F, and 0.4 should be subtracted from the specific gravity reading for each 10° below 80°F.

8088. A fully charged lead-acid battery will not freeze until extremely low temperatures are reached because

A—the acid is in the plates, thereby increasing the specific gravity of the solution.
B—most of the acid is in the solution.
C—increased internal resistance generates sufficient heat to prevent freezing.

When a lead-acid battery is charged, the sulfate radicals from both plates join with hydrogen atoms from the water in the electrolyte and form sulfuric acid.

Sulfuric acid has a much lower freezing point than water, and the electrolyte in a fully charged battery has a freezing point much lower than that of the electrolyte in a discharged battery.

8089. What determines the amount of current which will flow through a battery while it is being charged by a constant voltage source?

A—The total plate area of the battery.
B—The state-of-charge of the battery.
C—The ampere-hour capacity of the battery.

When a battery is charged by the constant-voltage method, a voltage somewhat higher than the open-circuit voltage of the battery is placed across the battery terminals.

When the battery is in a low state of charge, its voltage is low and the constant-voltage charger will put a large amount of current into it.

As the charge continues, the battery voltage rises and the current going into the battery decreases.

When the battery is fully charged, only enough current flows into it to compensate for the power lost in its internal resistance.

8090. Which of the following statements is/are generally true regarding the charging of several aircraft batteries together?

1. Batteries of different voltages (but similar capacities) can be connected in series with each other across the charger, and charged using the constant current method.
2. Batteries of different ampere-hour capacity and same voltage can be connected in parallel with each other across the charger, and charged using the constant voltage method.
3. Batteries of the same voltage and same ampere-hour capacity must be connected in series with each other across the charger, and charged using the constant current method.

A—3.
B—2 and 3.
C—1 and 2.

Batteries having different voltages, but similar capacity can be connected in series and charged by the constant-current method.

Batteries having the same voltage but different ampere-hour capacity can be connected in parallel and charged at the same time, if they are charged by the constant-voltage method.

8091. The method used to rapidly charge a nickel-cadmium battery utilizes

A—constant current and constant voltage.
B—constant current and varying voltage.
C—constant voltage and varying current.

Nickel-cadmium batteries can be charged rapidly by using constant voltage and varying current.

8092. The purpose of providing a space underneath the plates in a lead acid batter's cell container is to

A—prevent sediment buildup from contacting the plates and causing a short circuit.
B—allow for convection of the electrolyte in order to provide for cooling of the plates.
C—ensure that the electrolyte quantity ratio to the number of plates and plate area is adequate.

There is a space left below the plates in a lead acid battery cell to allow for the accumulation of sediment, thus preventing the sediment from coming in contact with the plates and causing a short circuit.

Answers

8087 [A] (031) AC 43.13-1	8088 [B] (031) AMT-G Ch 4	8089 [B] (031) AMT-G Ch 4	8090 [C] (031) AMT-G Ch 4
8091 [C] (031) AMT-G Ch 4	8092 [A] (031) AMT-G Ch 4		

8093. Which condition is an indication of improperly torqued cell link connections of a nickel-cadmium battery?

A—Light spewing at the cell caps.
B—Toxic and corrosive deposits of potassium carbonate crystals.
C—Heat or burn marks on the hardware.

Nickel-cadmium batteries are made differently from lead-acid batteries in that the individual cells are removable and are connected together with metal straps secured to the tops of the cells with nuts.

If the cell-link connections are not properly torqued, they will cause a high-resistance path for the current. They will become overheated and will show burn marks.

8094. The presence of any small amount of potassium carbonate deposits on the top of nickel-cadmium battery cells in service is an indication of

A—normal operation.
B—excessive gassing.
C—plate sulfation.

When a nickel-cadmium battery is fully charged, the battery becomes hot and the electrolyte bubbles. This causes some of the electrolyte to spew out of the top of the cell through the cell vent.

When the water evaporates from the spewed-out electrolyte, it leaves a deposit of potassium carbonate, a white powder.

8095. What is the likely result, if any, of servicing and charging nickel-cadmium and lead-acid batteries together in the same service area?

A—The electrolytes in each battery are the same, so there are no significant differences.
B—The nickel-cadmium would not be affected, but the lead-acid battery could become contaminated.
C—Contamination of both types of batteries would occur.

The chemistry of lead-acid and nickel-cadmium batteries is incompatible.

Electrolyte from one type of battery will contaminate the other. For this reason, battery shops keep the two types of batteries separated. Separate charging systems, cleaning facilities, and installation tools should be used for each type of battery.

8095-1. Which of the following best describes the operating principal in a nickel-cadmium battery installed in an aircraft?

A—At full charge, the electrolyte will be at its lowest level and should be filled.
B—To completely charge a nickel-cadmium battery, some gassing must take place; thus, some water will be used.
C—When positive plates slowly give up oxygen, which is regained by the negative plates, the battery is charging.

Toward the end of the charging cycle, the cells emit gas. This will also occur if the cells are overcharged. This gas is caused by decomposition of the water in the electrolyte into hydrogen at the negative plates and oxygen at the positive plates. To completely charge a nickel-cadmium battery, some gassing, however however slight, must take place; thus, some water will be used.

8096. The electrolyte of a nickel-cadmium battery is the lowest when the battery is

A—being charged.
B—in a discharged condition.
C—under a heavy load condition.

As a nickel-cadmium battery becomes discharged, some of the electrolyte is absorbed by the plates when the battery is fully discharged, its electrolyte level is the lowest.

8096-1. The electrolyte of a nickel cadmium battery is highest when the battery is

A—in a fully charged condition.
B—in a discharged condition.
C—under a no-load condition.

As a nickel-cadmium battery is discharged, the plates absorb some of the electrolyte and the electrolyte level is lowered. As the battery is charged, the plates give up some of the electrolyte. The level of the electrolyte is highest when the battery is in a fully charged condition.

8097. The end-of-charge voltage of a 19-cell nickel-cadmium battery, measured while still on charge,

A—must be 1.2 to 1.3 volts per cell.
B—must be 1.4 volts per cell.
C—depends upon its temperature and the method used for charging.

The end-of-charge voltage, measured while the cell is still on charge, depends upon its temperature and the method used for charging it.

A cell of a 19-cell battery being charged at room temperature at 28.5-volt constant voltage would read about

Answers

8093 [C] (031) AMT-G Ch 4	8094 [A] (031) AMT-G Ch 4	8095 [C] (031) AMT-G Ch 4	8095-1 [B] (031) AMT-G Ch 4
8096 [B] (031) AMT-G Ch 4	8096-1 [A] (031) AMT-G Ch 4	8097 [C] (031) AMT-G Ch 4	

1.5 volts at the end of charge; at a 27.5-volt constant-voltage condition, the cell would read about 1.45 volts.

Under constant-current charging conditions, this value would depend upon temperature and charge current; at the end of seven hours charging at the five-hour rate, the voltage of a cell would be about 1.58 volts, at 75°F.

8098. During discharge, nickel-cadmium batteries will show a lower liquid level than when at full charge because

A—a chemical action causes the electrolyte to evaporate through the vents.
B—current leakage from individual cells causes a rise in temperature.
C—the electrolyte becomes absorbed into the plates.

If a nickel-cadmium battery is stored for a long period of time, some of the electrolyte in the cells will be absorbed into the plates, and the level will drop.

The electrolyte level will rise when the battery is given a freshening charge before it is put into service.

8099. How can the state-of-charge of a nickel-cadmium battery be determined?

A—By measuring the specific gravity of the electrolyte.
B—By a measured discharge.
C—By the level of the electrolyte.

The specific gravity of the electrolyte of a nickel-cadmium battery does not change as the state-of-charge changes. The voltage of a nickel-cadmium battery remains relatively constant as its state-of-charge changes.

The only way to know for sure the amount of charge a nickel-cadmium battery has in it (its state-of-charge) is to completely discharge it and then to put back into it a known number of ampere-hours of charge.

8100. What may result if water is added to a nickel-cadmium battery when it is not fully charged?

A—Excessive electrolyte dilution.
B—Excessive spewing is likely to occur during the charging cycle.
C—No adverse effects since water may be added anytime.

The level of the electrolyte in a nickel-cadmium cell changes as the cell is discharged and charged. The level is lowest when the cell is discharged and highest at the end of the charging cycle.

If water is added to a cell when some of the electrolyte has been absorbed into the plates, the level will be too high when the cell is fully charged. Some of this excess liquid will likely spew out of the cell when it is near the end of its charge cycle.

8101. In nickel-cadmium batteries, a rise in cell temperature

A—causes an increase in internal resistance.
B—causes a decrease in internal resistance.
C—increases cell voltage.

One of the desirable features of a nickel-cadmium battery is its low internal resistance which gives it the ability to discharge at a high rate and to accept a high rate of charge.

The voltage and internal resistance of a nickel-cadmium cell vary inversely as the temperature. When the cell temperature increases, the voltage and internal resistance both decrease. This allows the battery to accept an excessive amount of charging current which produces more heat and can cause a thermal runaway.

8101-1. Which of the following best describes the contributing factors to thermal runaway in a nickel-cadmium battery installed in an aircraft?

A—High internal resistance intensified by high cell temperatures and a high current discharge/charge rate in a constant potential (voltage) charging system.
B—Low internal resistance intensified by high cell temperatures and a high voltage discharge/charge rate in a constant current charging system.
C—Low internal resistance intensified by high cell temperatures and a high current discharge/charge rate in a constant potential (voltage) charging system.

One of the problems with a nickel-cadmium battery is the danger of a thermal runaway. When the center cells of the battery become overheated, their resistance decreases and allows more current to flow. This increased current causes additional heating and further decreased resistance. This condition can continue until the battery is destroyed and a fire hazard is created. Thermal runaway occurs during a high current discharge/charge rate in a constant potential charging system.

8102. When a charging current is applied to a nickel cadmium battery, the cells emit gas

A—toward the end of the charging cycle.
B—throughout the charging cycle.
C—especially if the electrolyte level is high.

Gassing occurs in the cells of a nickel-cadmium battery at the end of the charging cycle when all of the oxygen has been removed from the negative plate. This gassing is caused by the decomposition of the electrolyte.

Answers

8098 [C] (015) AMT-G Ch 4	8099 [B] (031) AMT-G Ch 4	8100 [B] (031) AMT-G Ch 4	8101 [B] (031) AMT-G Ch 4
8101-1 [C] (031) AMT-G Ch 4	8102 [A] (031) AMT-G Ch 4		

Aircraft Drawings

8103. What type of line is normally used in a drawing or blueprint that indicates invisible edges or contours?

A—Medium-weight short dashes evenly spaced.
B—Medium-weight very short dashes evenly spaced.
C—Thin-weight, one long and two short dashes evenly spaced.

A medium-weight dashed line is called a hidden line and is used to show an edge or object not visible to the viewer.

A medium solid line is used as a visible outline or object line.

Alternate short and long light dashes are used to show a center line.

8104. (Refer to Figure 27.) In the isometric view of a typical aileron balance weight, identify the view indicated by the arrow.

A—1.
B—3.
C—2.

View 3 shows the aileron balance weight as seen from the direction shown by the arrow. This view shows the outline of the weight and the outline of the hole. Both of these are drawn as solid lines.

The two bolt holes are shown as light dashed lines (hidden lines), and there are also two hidden lines that show the break lines where the radius begins for the tip of the weight.

8105. (1) A detail drawing is a description of a single part.

(2) An assembly drawing is a description of an object made up of two or more parts.

Regarding the above statements,

A—only 1 is true.
B—neither 1 nor 2 is true.
C—both 1 and 2 are true.

Statement 1 is true. A detail drawing is a description of a single part that includes enough information to allow the part to be manufactured (fabricated).

Statement 2 is also true. An assembly drawing is a drawing that shows the way various detail parts are put together to form an assembly or a subassembly. Assembly drawings refer to the various parts to be assembled by the drawing number of their detail drawings.

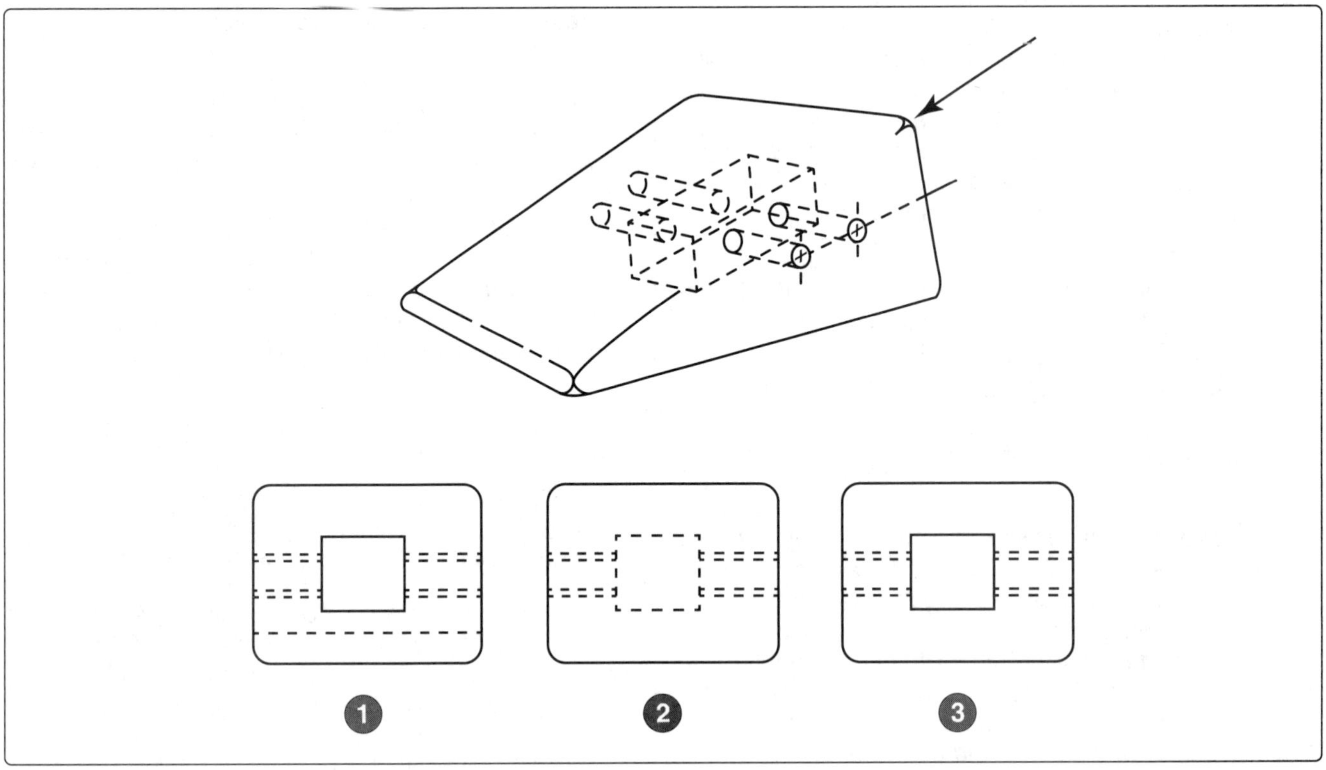

Figure 27. Object views

Answers
8103 [A] (014) AMT-G Ch 5
8104 [B] (013) AMT-G Ch 5
8105 [C] (013) AMT-G Ch 5

8106. (Refer to Figure 28.) Identify the bottom view of the object shown.

A—2.
B—3.
C—1.

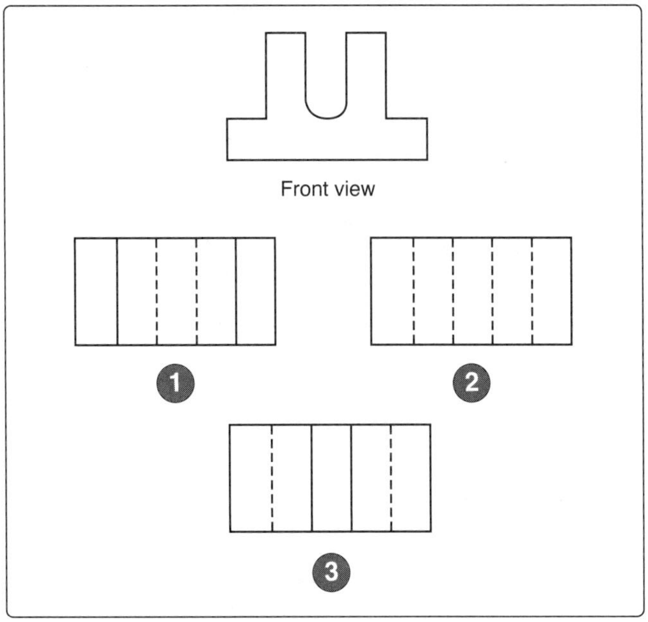

Figure 28. Object views

View 2 shows the part as it would be seen looking up at it from the bottom. The vertical lines are hidden.

View 1 is not a correct orthographic view of this part.

View 3 is not a correct orthographic view of this part.

8107. A specific measured distance from the datum or some other point identified by the manufacturer, to a point in or on the aircraft is called a

A—zone number.
B—reference number.
C—station number.

A station number is a number used to identify the number of inches from the datum or other point identified by the manufacturer to a point in or on the aircraft.

8108. Which statement is true regarding an orthographic projection?

A—There are always at least two views.
B—It could have as many as eight views.
C—One-view, two-view, and three-view drawings are the most common.

An orthographic projection can show as many as six views of an object. One-view, two-view, and three-view drawings are the most commonly used types of orthographic projections.

8109. (Refer to Figure 29.) Identify the left side view of the object shown.

A—1.
B—2.
C—3.

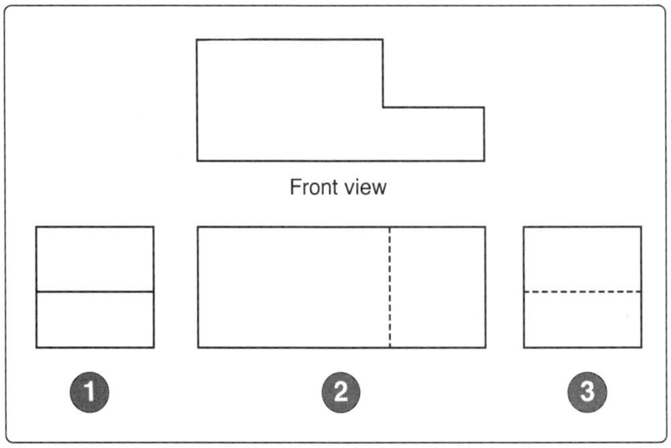

Figure 29. Object views

View 3 is the left side. The horizontal surface is shown as a hidden line.

View 1 is the right side. We see the horizontal surface as a visible line.

View 2 is the bottom view. The vertical surface is shown as a hidden line.

Answers
8106 [A] (013) AMT-G Ch 5 8107 [C] (013) AMT-G Ch 5 8108 [C] (014) AMT-G Ch 5 8109 [C] (013) AMT-G Ch 5

8110. A line used to show an edge which is not visible is a

A—phantom line.
B—hidden line.
C—break line.

A phantom line is a light line made up of an alternate long dash and two short dashes. A phantom line shows the location of a part that is used as a reference.

A hidden line is a medium-weight dashed line that shows a surface or a part that is not visible from the view in which it appears.

A break line is a wavy or a zigzag line used to show that a part has been broken off and only part of it is shown.

8110-1. What type of drawing line consists of alternating long and short lines?

A—Dimension.
B—Center.
C—Hidden.

Centerlines are made up of alternate long and short dashes. They indicate the center of an object or part of an object. Where centerlines cross, the short dashes intersect symmetrically. In the case of very small circles, the centerlines may be shown unbroken.

8111. (Refer to Figure 30.) Identify the bottom view of the object.

A—1.
B—2.
C—3.

View 1 is the bottom. The two vertical surfaces are shown as hidden lines.

View 2 is the left side. The two horizontal surfaces are shown as hidden lines.

View 3 is the top view. The two vertical surfaces are shown as visible lines.

8112. (1) Schematic diagrams indicate the location of individual components in the aircraft.

(2) Schematic diagrams indicate the location of components with respect to each other within the system.

Regarding the above statements,

A—only 1 is true.
B—both 1 and 2 are true.
C—only 2 is true.

Statement 1 is not true. Schematic diagrams do not indicate the location of individual components in the aircraft.

Statement 2 is true. Schematic diagrams do show the location of the components with respect to each other within the system.

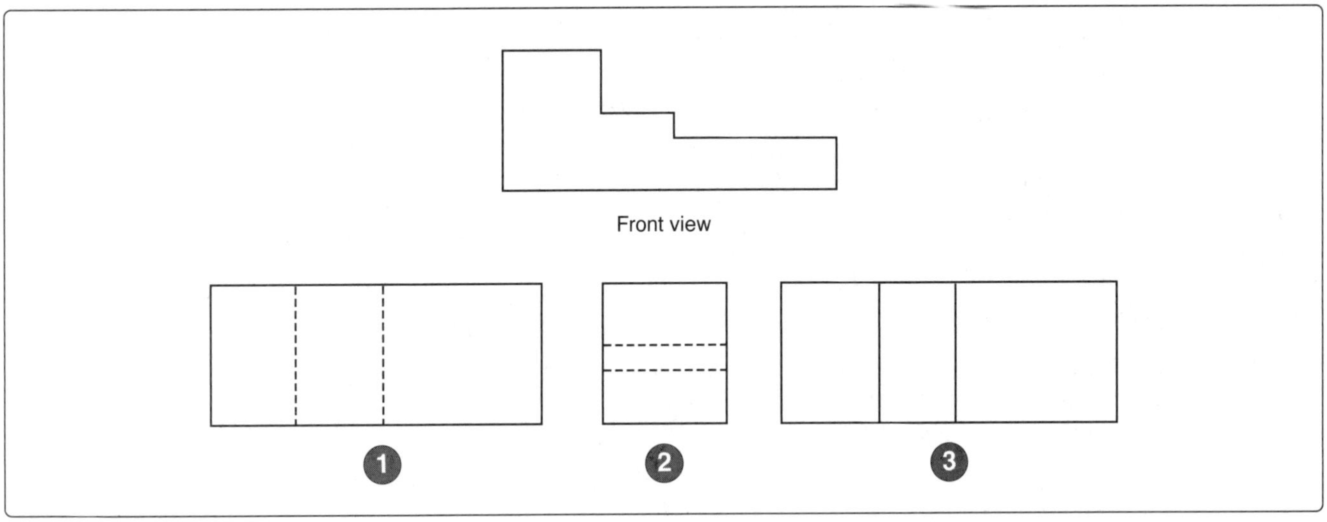

Figure 30. Object views

Answers

8110 [B] (013) AMT-G Ch 5
8110-1 [B] (014) AMT-G Ch 5
8111 [A] (013) AMT-G Ch 5
8112 [C] (014) AMT-G Ch 5

8113. (Refer to Figure 31.) What are the proper procedural steps for sketching repairs and alterations?

A—3, 1, 4, and 2.
B—4, 2, 3, and 1.
C—1, 3, 4, and 2.

An easy way to make a sketch of a repair or alteration is to:

3 Block in the space and basic shape to be used for the sketch;

1 Add details to the basic block;

4 Darken the lines that are to show up as visible lines in the finished sketch; and

2 Add dimensions and any other information that will make the sketch more usable.

8114. Which statement is applicable when using a sketch for making a part?

A—The sketch may be used only if supplemented with three-view orthographic projection drawings.
B—The sketch must show all information to manufacture the part.
C—The sketch need not show all necessary construction details.

A sketch is a simple, rough drawing made rapidly and without much detail. A sketch is frequently drawn for use in manufacturing a replacement part. Such a sketch must provide all necessary information to those persons who must manufacture the part.

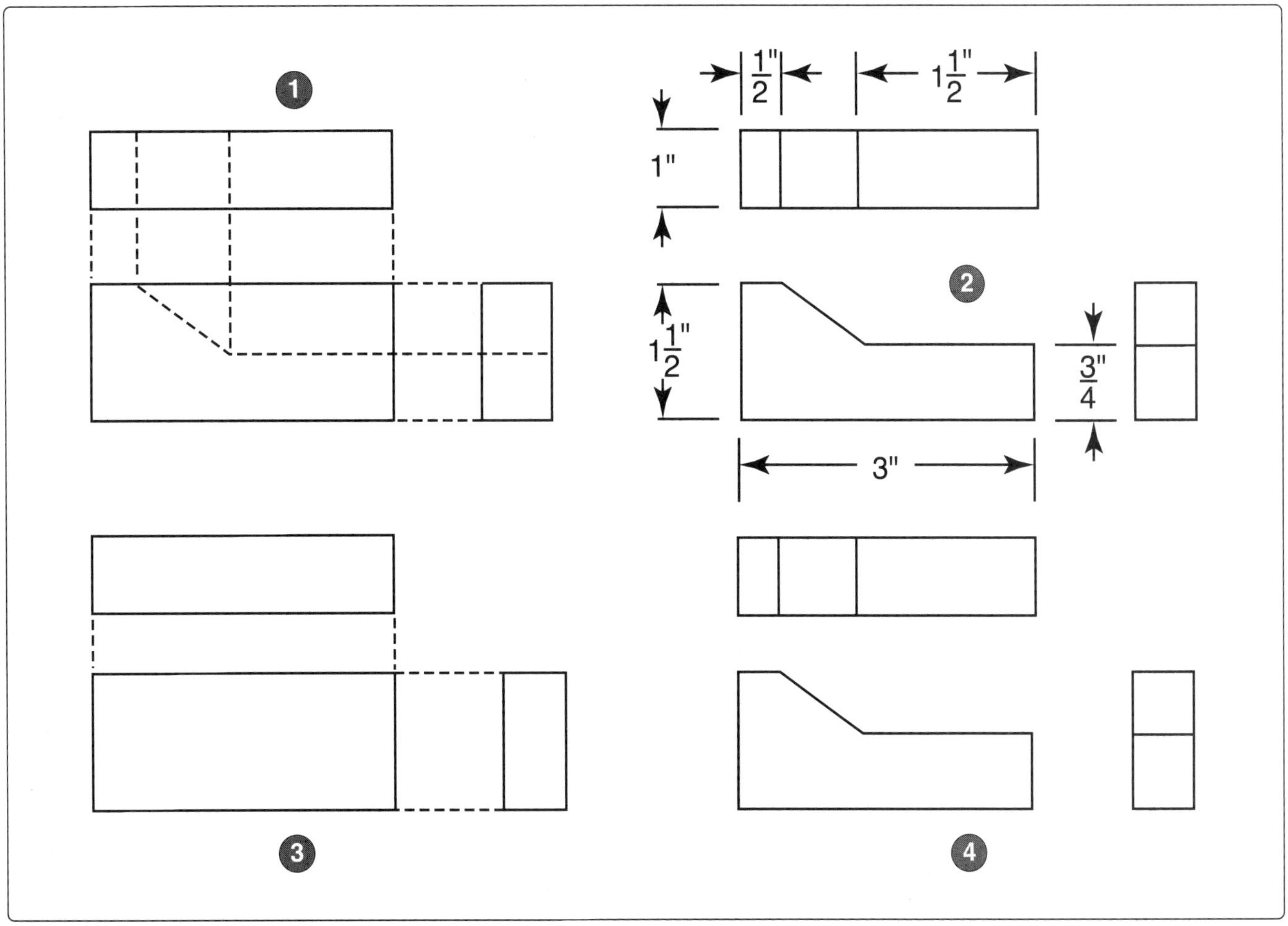

Figure 31. Sketches

Answers
8113 [A] (001) AMT-G Ch 5
8114 [B] (001) AMT-G Ch 5

8115. (Refer to Figure 32.) What is the next step required for a working sketch of the illustration?

A—Darken the object outlines.
B—Sketch extension and dimension lines.
C—Add notes, dimensions, title, and date.

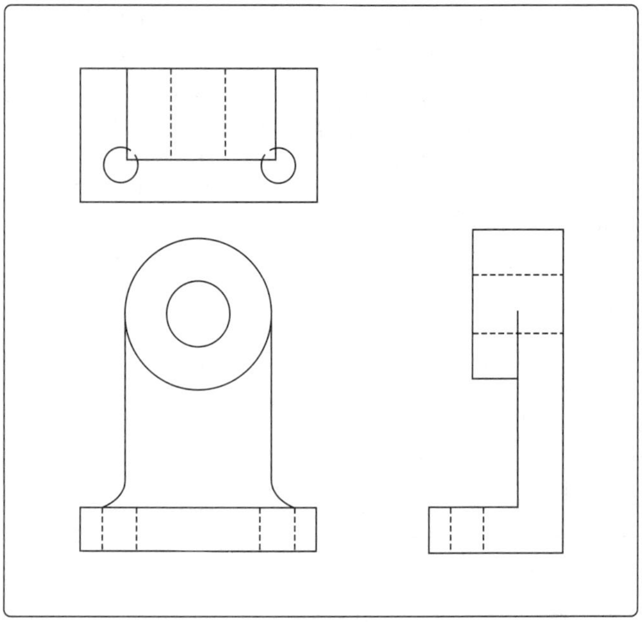

Figure 32. Sketches

In the sketch shown here, the part has already been blocked in, details have been added, the visible lines darkened, and the hidden lines added. The next step is to sketch in the extension lines and the dimension lines.

8116. For sketching purposes, almost all objects are composed of one or some combination of six basic shapes; these include the

A—angle, arc, line, plane, square, and circle.
B—triangle, circle, cube, cylinder, cone, and sphere.
C—triangle, plane, circle, line, square, and sphere.

Almost all objects are composed of one or some combination of the triangle, circle, cube, cylinder, cone, and sphere.

8116-1. In a sectional view drawing, what sections illustrate particular parts of an object?

A—Removed.
B—Revolved.
C—Half.

A removed section illustrates particular parts of an object. It is similar to revolved sections, except it is placed at one side and, to bring out pertinent details, often drawn to a larger scale than the main view on which it is indicated.

8117. What should be the first step of the procedure in sketching an aircraft wing skin repair?

A—Draw heavy guidelines.
B—Lay out the repair.
C—Block in the views.

In making a sketch of a repair, the first thing to do is to block in the views.

As you block in the views, you are able to organize the sketch so it will clearly show the most information.

8117-1. A simple way to find the center of a circle on a sketch or drawing, or a circular piece of material is to

A—draw two non-parallel chord lines across the circle and then a corresponding perpendicular bisector line across each chord line.
B—draw two parallel chord lines across the circle and then a corresponding perpendicular bisector line across each chord line.
C—draw a single chord line across the circle and then a corresponding perpendicular bisector line across each chord line.

An easy way to find the center of a circle on a sketch is to draw two non-parallel chord lines across the circle. Then, draw a perpendicular bisector of each of these chord lines. The bisector lines will cross at the center of the circle.

8118. (1) According to 14 CFR Part 91, repairs to an aircraft skin should have a detailed dimensional sketch included in the permanent records.

(2) On occasion, a mechanic may need to make a simple sketch of a proposed repair to an aircraft, a new design, or a modification.

Regarding the above statements,

A—only 1 is true.
B—only 2 is true.
C—both 1 and 2 are true.

Statement 1 is not true. Part 91 requires that maintenance records contain "a description (or reference to data acceptable to the Administrator) of the work performed..." There is no requirement in Part 91 that a detailed dimensional sketch of a repair become a part of the aircraft's permanent records.

Statement 2 is true. A simple sketch is often needed to help a mechanic make a repair, a new design, or a modification.

Answers

8115 [B] (001) AMT-G Ch 5	8116 [B] (001) AMT-G Ch 5	8116-1 [A] (013) AMT-G Ch 5	8117 [C] (001) AMT-G Ch 5
8117-1 [A] (001) AMT-G Ch 5	8118 [B] (001) AMT-G Ch 5		

8119. Working drawings may be divided into three classes. They are:

A—title drawings, installation drawings, and assembly drawings.
B—detail drawings, assembly drawings, and installation drawings.
C—detail drawings, orthographic projection drawings, and pictorial drawings.

The three classes of working drawings are: detail drawings, assembly drawings, and installation drawings.

8119-1. What is the class of working drawing that is the description/depiction of a single part?

A—Installation drawing.
B—Assembly drawing.
C—Detail drawing.

A detail drawing is a description of a single part, given in such a manner as to describe by lines, notes, and symbols the specifications as to size, shape, material, and method of manufacture that are to be used in making the part.

8120. Sketches are usually made easier by the use of

A—graph paper.
B—plain white paper.
C—artist's paper.

Sketches are easily made by using graph paper, which is available, ruled with light lines, in either four or five squares to the inch.

8120-1. (1) Sketches are usually made with the aid of drafting instruments.

(2) Sketches are usually more complicated to make when using graph paper.

Regarding the above statements,

A—Only 1 is true.
B—Only 2 is true.
C—Neither 1 nor 2 is true.

Sketches are simple drawings made without the use of tools. It is easier to do a sketch on graph paper where dimensions are easier to visualize without using tools such as a ruler.

8121. What material symbol is frequently used in drawings to represent all metals?

A—Steel.
B—Cast iron.
C—Aluminum.

If the exact specifications of a material are shown on the drawing, the easily drawn symbol for cast iron is used for the sectioning, and the material specification is listed in the bill of materials or indicated in a note.

8121-1. What is used to indicate that a surface must be machine finished?

A—Text.
B—Leader lines.
C—Finished marks.

By using finished marks a drawing identifies those surfaces that must be machine finished.

8122. (Refer to Figure 33.) Which material section-line symbol indicates cast iron?

A—1.
B—2.
C—3.

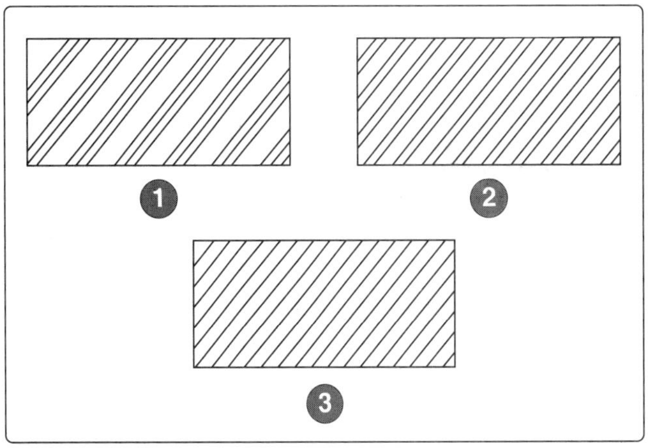

Figure 33. Material symbols

Section lines shown in 3 are for cast iron.

Section lines shown in 1 are for rubber, plastic, or electrical insulation.

Section lines shown in 2 are for steel.

Answers

8119 [B] (001) AMT-G Ch 5	8119-1 [C] (001) AMT-G Ch 5	8120 [A] (001) AMT-G Ch 5	8120-1 [C] (001) AMT-G Ch 5
8121 [B] (001) AMT-G Ch 5	8121-1 [C] (014) FAA-H-8083-30	8122 [C] (001) AMT-G Ch 5	

8123. (Refer to Figure 34.) What is the dimension of the chamfer?

A—1/16 × 37°.
B—0.3125 + .005 – 0.
C—0.0625 × 45°.

The chamfer is the tapered end of the cylindrical body of this clevis.

The drawing shows that the end is chamfered at an angle of 45°, and the chamfer extends back for 1/16 inch. One-sixteenth of an inch is 0.0625 inch.

8124. (Refer to Figure 34.) What is the maximum diameter of the hole for the clevis pin?

A—0.3175.
B—0.3130.
C—0.31255.

The hole in this clevis through which the clevis pin fits has a diameter of 0.3125 (+0.005, -0.000) inch.

The tolerance (+0.005, -0.000) allows us to make the hole anywhere between 0.3125 and 0.3175 inch in diameter.

8125. (Refer to Figure 34.) What would be the minimum diameter of 4130 round stock required for the construction of the clevis that would produce a machined surface?

A—55/64 inch.
B—1 inch.
C—7/8 inch.

The maximum diameter of the finished clevis is 7/8 (0.875) inch. To be sure that every part of this maximum diameter is machined, we would need to use a larger bar of material to make it.

55/64 inch = 0.859375 (this is too small)

1 inch (this is the correct choice)

7/8 inch = 0.875 (this is too small)

8126. (Refer to Figure 34.) Using the information, what size drill would be required to drill the clevis bolthole?

A—5/16 inch.
B—21/64 inch.
C—1/2 inch.

The drawing shows that the hole for the clevis bolt should have a diameter of 0.3125 (+.005, -0.000).

This hole could be drilled with a 5/16 drill. The decimal equivalent of 5/16 inch is 0.3125.

8127. The measurements showing the ideal or "perfect" sizes of parts on drawings are called

A—allowances.
B—dimensions.
C—tolerances.

Allowances are the difference between the nominal dimension of a part and its upper or lower limit.

Dimensions are the measurements used to describe the size of an object. It is the ideal or "perfect" size of the part.

Tolerances are the differences between the extreme allowable dimensions of a part.

8128. (Refer to Figure 35.) Identify the extension line.

A—3.
B—1.
C—4.

3 is an extension line used to show the width of the paint stripe.

1 is a visible outline.

2 is a hidden line.

4 is a center line.

Answers

8123 [C] (014) AMT-G Ch 5	8124 [A] (014) AMT-G Ch 5	8125 [B] (014) AMT-G Ch 5	8126 [A] (014) AMT-G Ch 5
8127 [B] (014) AMT-G Ch 5	8128 [A] (014) AMT-G Ch 5		

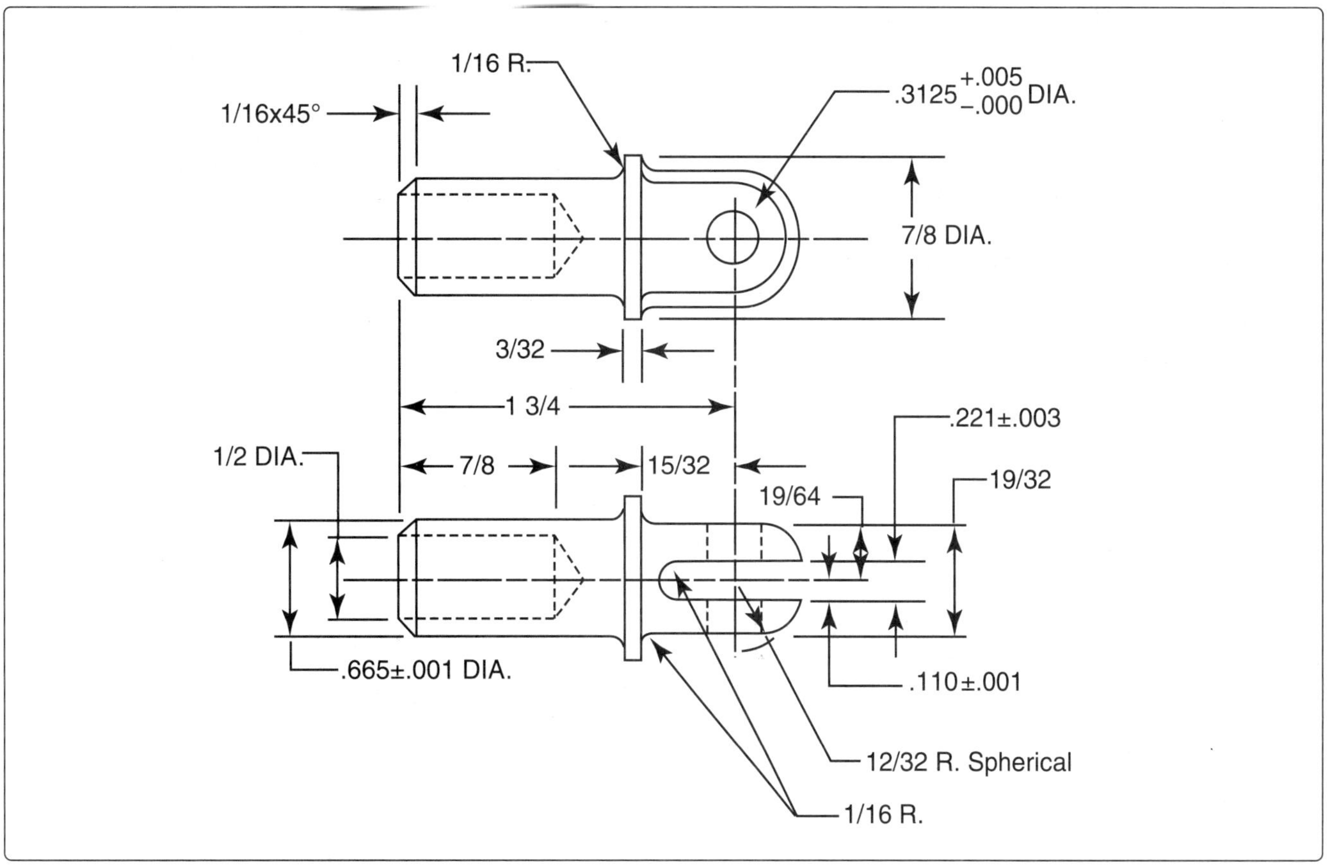

Figure 34. Aircraft drawing

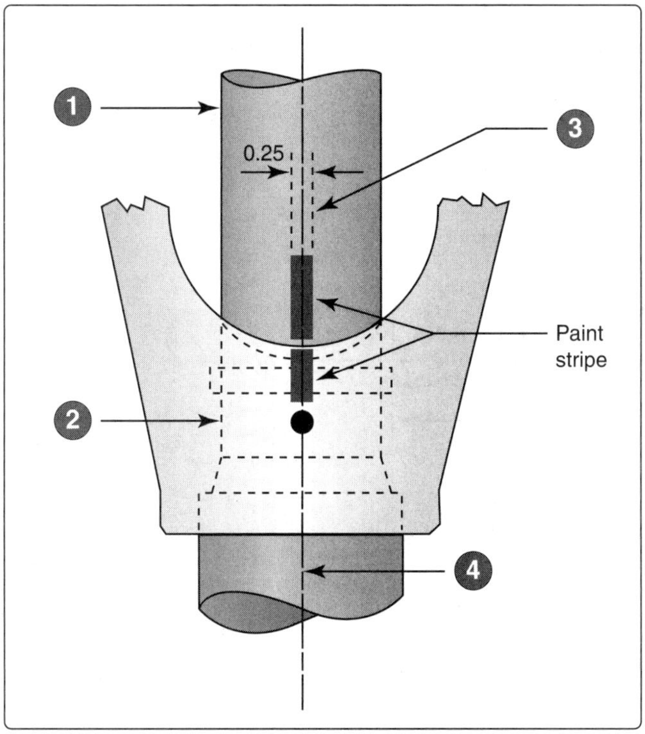

Figure 35. Aircraft drawing

8129. (Refer to Figure 36.) The diameter of the holes in the finished object is

A—3/4 inch.
B—31/64 inch.
C—1/2 inch.

The two holes in this part have a finished diameter of 1/2 inch.

They are made by first drilling them to a diameter of 31/64 inch and then reaming them to their final diameter of 1/2 inch.

This information is found in note 1.

8130. Zone numbers on aircraft blueprints are used to

A—locate parts, sections, and views on large drawings.
B—indicate different sections of the aircraft.
C—locate parts in the aircraft.

Large drawings used for manufacturing aircraft are zoned to make it easy to locate parts, sections, and views on large drawings.

Zone identifiers are placed every foot along the edge of the drawing. The identifiers along the bottom of the drawing are numbers and those up the side of the drawing are letters.

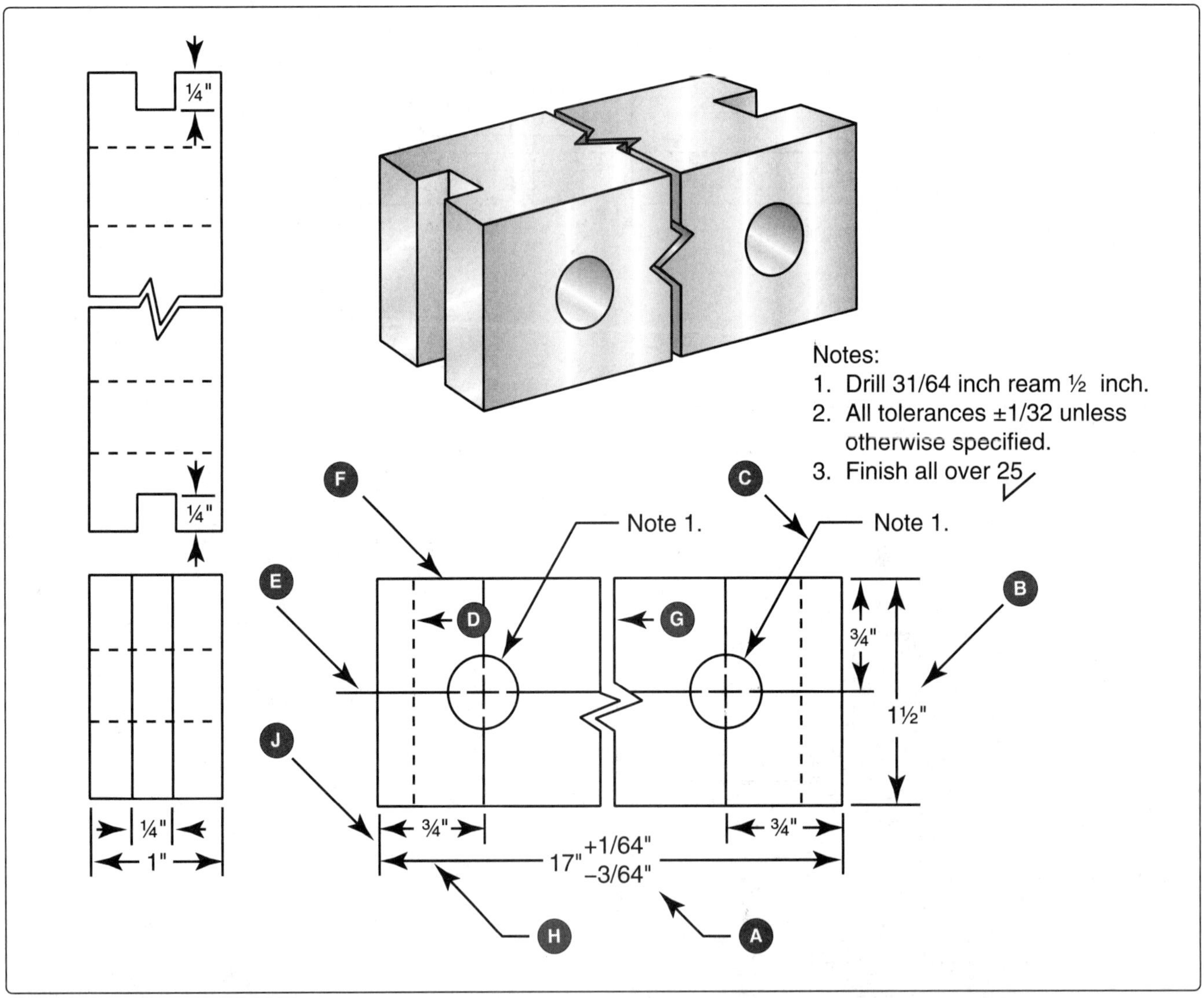

Figure 36. Aircraft drawing

Answers
8129 [C] (014) AMT-G Ch 5 8130 [A] (014) AMT-G Ch 5

8130-2. Which of the following terms is/are used to indicate specific measured distances from the datum and/or other points identified by the manufacturer, to points in or on the aircraft?

1. Zone numbers.
2. Reference numbers.
3. Station numbers.

A—1 and 3.
B—3.
C—2.

Station numbers is a numbering system used on large assemblies for aircraft to locate stations such as fuselage frames. Fuselage Frame-Sta 185 indicates the frame is 185 inches from the datum of the aircraft. The measurement is usually taken from the nose or zero station, but in some instances it may be taken from the fire wall or some other point chosen by the manufacturer.

8130-3. In order to locate wing and stabilizer frames, what numbering system is used?

A—Dimension numbers.
B—Station numbers.
C—Scale numbers.

Locations for fuselage frames in aircraft drawings are identified by station numbers.

8131. One purpose for schematic diagrams is to show the

A—functional location of components within a system.
B—physical location of components within a system.
C—size and shape of components within a system.

Schematic diagrams are used to show the functional location of components within the system by showing all of the components laid out in the way that they relate to each other in the functioning of the system.

Schematic diagrams do not show the physical location of the components within a system, nor do they show the size and shape of the components.

8132. When reading a blueprint, a dimension is given as 4.387 inches +.005 -.002. Which statement is true?

A—The maximum acceptable size is 4.390 inches.
B—The minimum acceptable size is 4.385 inches.
C—The minimum acceptable size is 4.382 inches.

The part described here has a dimension of 4.387 inches, with a tolerance of +0.005, -0.002.

The part could have a dimension of anywhere between 4.385 inches and 4.392 inches.

8133. What is the allowable manufacturing tolerance for a bushing where the outside dimensions shown on the blueprint are:

1.0625 +.0025 -.0003?

A—.0028.
B—1.0650.
C—1.0647.

The bushing described here has an outside dimension of 1.0625 inch with a tolerance of +0.0025 -0.0003.

The bushing could have an outside diameter of anywhere between 1.0622 inch and 1.0650 inch. The tolerance for this part is 0.0028 inch.

8134. A hydraulic system schematic drawing typically indicates the

A—specific location of the individual components within the aircraft.
B—direction of fluid flow through the system.
C—amount of pressure in the pressure and return lines, and in system components.

A schematic drawing of a hydraulic system would not show the specific location of any of the parts in the aircraft, nor the amount of pressure in the pressure and return lines, and in system components.

A schematic drawing shows the way all of the components are connected together to form the complete system. It also shows the direction the fluid flows through the system.

Answers

8130-2 [B] (014) AMT-G Ch 5	8130-3 [B] (014) AMT-G Ch 5	8131 [A] (014) AMT-G Ch 5	8132 [B] (014) AMT-G Ch 5
8133 [A] (014) AMT-G Ch 5	8134 [B] (014) AMT-G Ch 5		

8135. (Refer to Figure 37.) The vertical distance between the top of the plate and the bottom of the lowest 15/64-inch hole is

A—2.250.
B—2.242.
C—2.367.

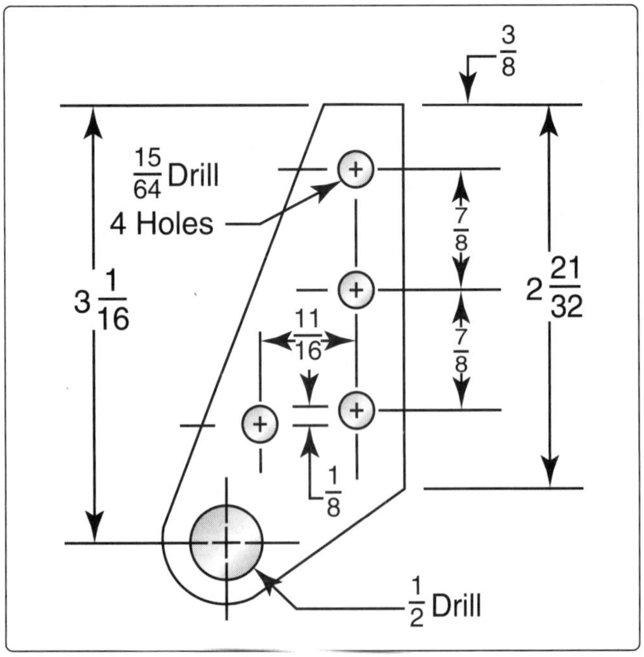

Figure 37. Aircraft drawing

The distance from the top of the plate to the center of the top hole is 3/8 inch (0.375 inch).

The distance between the center of the top hole and the center of the second hole is 7/8 inch (0.875 inch).

The distance between the center of the second hole and the center of the third hole is 7/8 inch (0.875 inch).

The distance between the center of the third hole and the center of the lowest small hole is 1/8 inch (0.125 inch).

The distance from the center of the 15/64-inch hole to its bottom edge is 15/128 inch (0.117 inch).

When all of these dimensions are added together, we find the distance from the top of the plate to the bottom of the lower small hole to be 2.367 inches.

8136. (1) A measurement should not be scaled from an aircraft print because the paper shrinks or stretches when the print is made.

(2) When a detail drawing is made, it is carefully and accurately drawn to scale, and is dimensioned.

Regarding the above statements,

A—only 2 is true.
B—both 1 and 2 are true.
C—neither 1 nor 2 is true.

Statement 1 is true. Measurements should never be scaled from an aircraft drawing because the paper shrinks and stretches. The print is seldom the exact same size as the original drawing.

Statement 2 is also true. When a detail drawing is made, it is carefully and accurately drawn to scale and is dimensioned.

8137. The drawings often used in illustrated parts manuals are

A—exploded-view drawings.
B—block drawings.
C—detail drawings.

The drawings used in illustrated parts manuals are exploded-view drawings.

8138. A drawing in which the subassemblies or parts are shown as brought together on the aircraft is called

A—an assembly drawing.
B—a detail drawing.
C—an installation drawing.

An installation drawing is one in which all of the parts and subassemblies are brought together.

8139. What type of diagram shows the wire size required for a particular installation?

A—A block diagram.
B—A schematic diagram.
C—A wiring diagram.

An electrical wiring diagram shows the wire size required for a particular installation.

Answers
8135 [C] (014) AMT-G Ch 5 8136 [B] (014) AMT-G Ch 5 8137 [A] (014) AMT-G Ch 5 8138 [C] (014) AMT-G Ch 5
8139 [C] (014) AMT-G Ch 5

8139-1. In what type of electrical diagram are images of components used instead of conventional electrical symbols?

A—A pictorial diagram.
B—A schematic diagram.
C—A block diagram.

A pictorial diagram is similar to a photograph. It shows an object as it appears to the eye, but is not satisfactory for showing complex forms and shapes.

8140. Schematic diagrams are best suited for which of the following?

A—Showing the visual details of individual components in a system.
B—Showing the overall location and appearance of components in a system.
C—Troubleshooting system malfunctions.

A schematic diagram shows the relative location of all of the parts in a system, but does not give the location of the parts in the aircraft. Schematic drawings are of great help when troubleshooting a system.

8141. In the reading of aircraft blueprints, the term "tolerance," used in association with aircraft parts or components,

A—is the tightest permissible fit for proper construction and operation of mating parts.
B—is the difference between extreme permissible dimensions that a part may have and still be acceptable.
C—represents the limit of galvanic compatibility between different adjoining material types in aircraft parts.

Tolerance is the difference between the extreme permissible dimensions of a part.

8142. (Refer to Figure 38.) An aircraft reciprocating engine has a 1,830 cubic-inch displacement and develops 1,250 brake-horsepower at 2,500 RPM. What is the brake mean effective pressure?

A—217.
B—205.
C—225.

1. *Find the 1,250-brake-horsepower vertical line at the top of the chart, and follow this line down until it intersects the diagonal line for the 1,830-cubic-inch-displacement engine.*
2. *Draw a horizontal line from this intersection point to the right until it intersects the diagonal line for 2,500 RPM.*
3. *From the intersection of the horizontal line and the RPM diagonal line, draw a line vertically downward to the BMEP scale.*
4. *You will find that the vertical line touches the BMEP scale just about on the 217 psi BMEP line.*

8143. (Refer to Figure 38.) An aircraft reciprocating engine has a 2,800 cubic-inch displacement, develops 2,000 brake-horsepower, and indicates 270 brake mean effective pressure. What is the engine speed (RPM)?

A—2,200.
B—2,100.
C—2,300.

1. *Find the 2,000-brake-horsepower vertical line along the top of the chart.*
2. *Follow this line down until it intersects the diagonal line for the 2,800-cubic-inch-displacement engine.*
3. *Draw a horizontal line from this intersection to the right of the chart.*
4. *Find the 270-BMEP vertical line at the bottom of the chart, and follow this line up until it intersects the horizontal line you just drew.*
5. *Find the diagonal line for the RPM that crosses the intersection of the two lines you have just drawn.*
6. *An R-2800 engine will need to turn at 2,100 RPM to develop 2,000 brake horsepower when it has a BMEP of 270 psi.*

8144. (Refer to Figure 38.) An aircraft reciprocating engine has a 2,800 cubic-inch displacement and develops 2,000 brake-horsepower at 2,200 RPM. What is the brake mean effective pressure?

A—257.5.
B—242.5.
C—275.0.

1. *Find the 2,000-brake-horsepower vertical line at the top of the chart and follow this line down until it intersects the diagonal line for the 2,800-cubic-inch-displacement engine.*
2. *Draw a horizontal line from this intersection point to the right until it intersects the diagonal line for 2,200 RPM.*
3. *From the intersection of the horizontal line and the RPM diagonal line, draw a line vertically downward to the BMEP scale.*
4. *You will find that the vertical line touches the BMEP scale just about on the 257-psi-BMEP line.*

Answers

8139-1 [A] (014) AMT-G Ch 5	8140 [C] (014) AMT-G Ch 5	8141 [B] (014) AMT-G Ch 5	8142 [A] (016) AMT-G Ch 5
8143 [B] (016) AMT-G Ch 5	8144 [A] (016) AMT-G Ch 5		

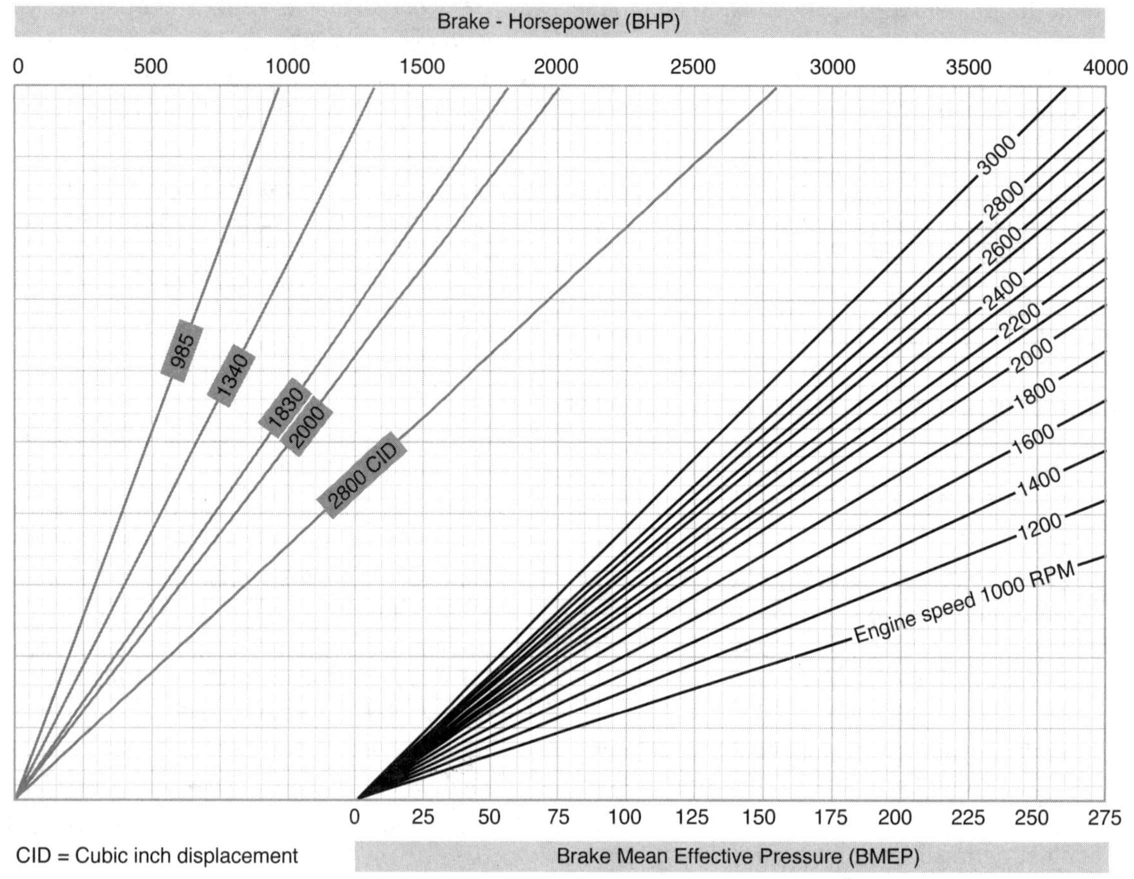

Figure 38. Performance chart

8145. (Refer to Figure 39.) Determine the cable size of a 40-foot length of single cable in free air, with a continuous rating, running from a bus to the equipment in a 28-volt system with a 15-ampere load and a 1-volt drop.

A—No. 10.
B—No. 11.
C—No. 18.

1. *Follow the 15-ampere diagonal line down until it intersects the horizontal line for 40 feet in the 28-volt column.*
2. *This intersection occurs between the vertical lines for 12-gage and 10-gage wire.*
3. *You would need a 10-gage wire (always use the larger of the two wires) to carry a 15-amp load for 40 feet and not have more than a 1-volt drop.*

8146. (Refer to Figure 39.) Determine the maximum length of a No. 16 cable to be installed from a bus to the equipment in a 28-volt system with a 25-ampere intermittent load and a 1-volt drop.

A—8 feet.
B—10 feet.
C—12 feet.

1. *Draw a diagonal line for 25 amperes midway between and parallel to the 20-ampere and the 30-ampere diagonal lines.*
2. *Follow this line down until it intersects the 16-gage vertical line.*
3. *This intersection occurs just above curve 3 on the horizontal line for 8 feet of length in the 28-volt (1-volt drop) column.*
4. *A No. 16 cable can carry an intermittent load of 25 amperes for 8 feet without exceeding a voltage drop of 1 volt.*

Answers
8145 [A] (015) AC 43.13-1 8146 [A] (015) AMT-G Ch 5

8147. (Refer to Figure 39.) Determine the minimum wire size of a single cable in a bundle carrying a continuous current of 20 amperes 10 feet from the bus to the equipment in a 28-volt system with an allowable 1-volt drop.

A—No. 12.
B—No. 14.
C—No. 16.

1. *Follow the 20-ampere diagonal line down until it intersects curve 1. This curve limits the wire sizes that can be used in a bundle.*
2. *This intersection occurs between the vertical lines for 14-gage and 12-gage wires.*
3. *A 12-gage wire is needed to carry a continuous current of 20 amps if the wire is routed in a bundle.*
4. *This wire size is chosen on the basis of the heat developed, not on the voltage drop. (If voltage drop were the limiting factor, a 16-gage wire could be used.)*

8148. (Refer to Figure 39.) Determine the maximum length of a No. 12 single cable that can be used between a 28-volt bus and a component utilizing 20 amperes continuous load in free air with a maximum acceptable 1-volt drop.

A—22.5 feet.
B—26.5 feet.
C—12.5 feet.

1. *Follow the diagonal line for 20 amperes down until it intersects the 12-gage vertical line.*
2. *Draw a line horizontally to the left from this point of intersection. This line meets the 1-volt drop column at the 26.5-foot mark.*
3. *This point of intersection is above curve 1 showing that the wire can carry this load continuously without producing too much heat.*
4. *A 12-gage wire can carry 20 amperes continuously for 26.5 feet without overheating the wire and without producing a voltage drop of more than 1 volt.*

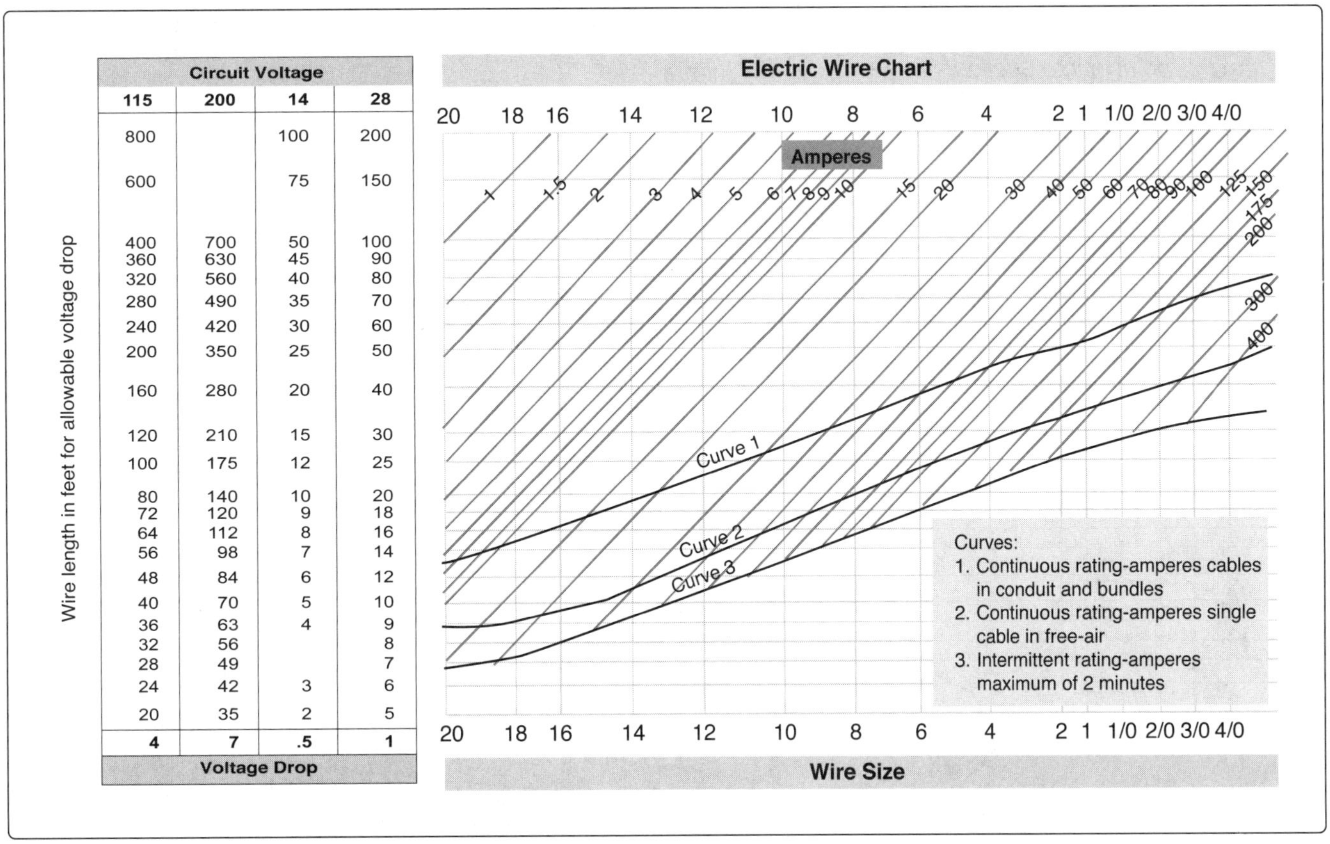

Figure 39. Electric wire chart

Answers
8147 [A] (015) AC 43.13-1
8148 [B] (015) AC 43.13-1

8149. (Refer to Figure 40.) Determine the proper tension for a 1/8-inch cable (7 × 19) if the temperature is 80°F.

A—70 pounds.
B—75 pounds.
C—80 pounds.

1. *Follow the vertical line for a temperature of 80°F upward until it intersects the curve for 1/8-inch, 7 × 19 cable.*
2. *From this point of intersection, draw a line horizontally to the right until it intersects the rigging load in pounds index. This intersection is at 70 pounds.*

8150. (Refer to Figure 40.) Determine the proper tension for a 3/16-inch cable (7 × 19 extra flex) if the temperature is 87°F.

A—135 pounds.
B—125 pounds.
C—140 pounds.

1. *Draw a line vertically upward from a temperature of 87°F until it intersects the curve for 3/16-inch, 7 × 19 cable.*
2. *From this point of intersection, draw a line horizontally to the right until it intersects the rigging load in pounds index. This intersection is at 125 pounds.*

8151. (Refer to Figure 41.) Determine how much fuel would be required for a 30-minute reserve operating at 2,300 RPM.

A—25.3 pounds.
B—35.5 pounds.
C—49.8 pounds.

1. *Follow the 2,300 RPM vertical line upward until it intersects the propeller load horsepower curve.*
2. *From the point of intersection, project a line horizontally to the left to read the brake horsepower the engine develops at 2,300 RPM. This is 110 brake horsepower.*
3. *Follow the 2,300 RPM curve upward until it intersects the propeller load brake specific fuel consumption curve.*
4. *From the point of intersection, project a line horizontally to the right to read the specific fuel consumption for 2,300 RPM. This is 0.46 pound of fuel burned per hour for each horsepower developed.*
5. *The engine burns 50.6 pounds of fuel per hour when it is developing 110 brake horsepower.*
6. *A 30-minute reserve would require one half of this, or 25.3 pounds.*

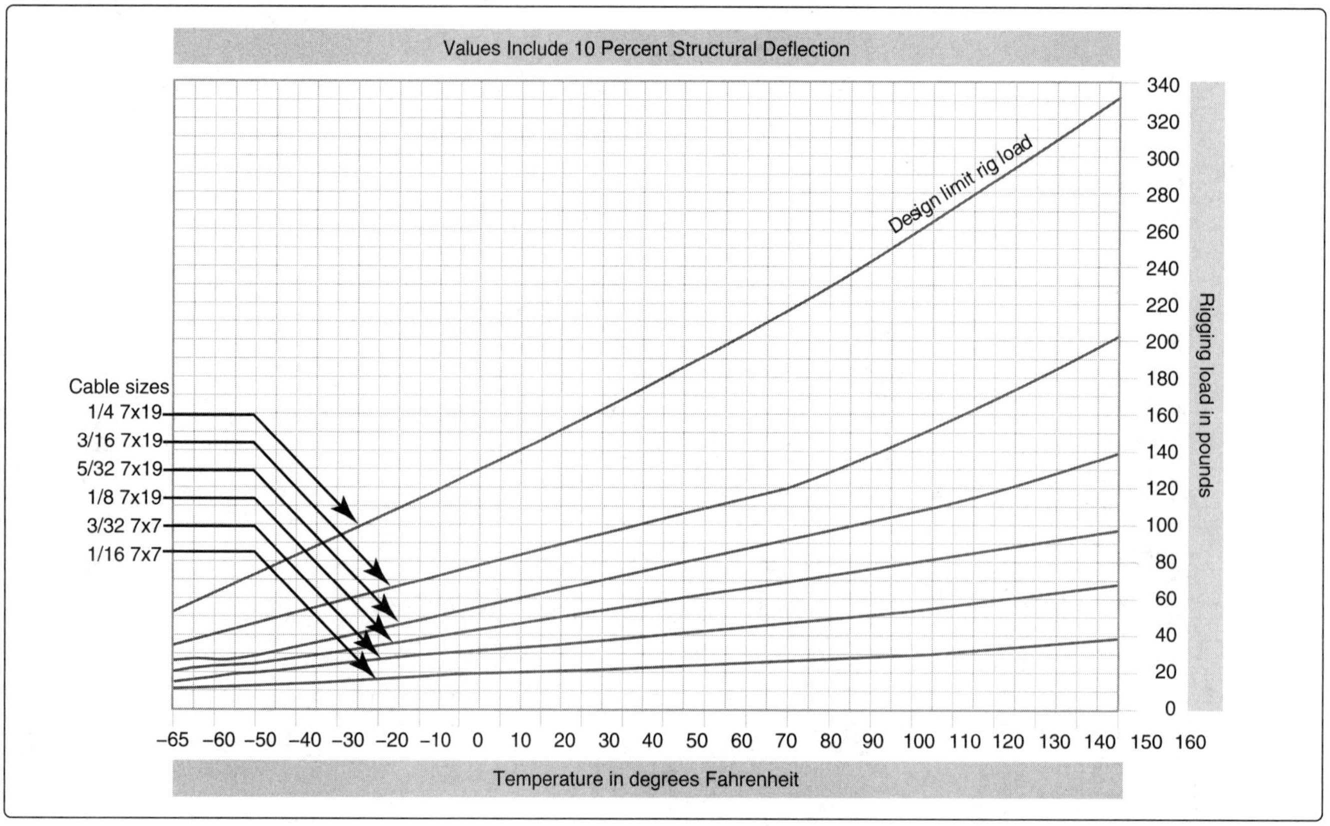

Figure 40. Cable tension chart

Answers
8149 [A] (011) AMT-STRUC
8150 [B] (011) AMT-STRUC
8151 [A] (016) AMT-G Ch 5

8152. (Refer to Figure 41.) Determine the fuel consumption with the engine operating at cruise, 2,350 RPM.

A—49.2 pounds per hour.
B—51.2 pounds per hour.
C—55.3 pounds per hour.

1. *Follow the 2,350 RPM vertical line upward until it intersects the propeller load horsepower curve.*
2. *From the point of intersection, project a line horizontally to the left to read the brake horsepower that the engine develops at 2,350 RPM. This is 118 brake horsepower.*
3. *Follow the 2,350 RPM curve upward until it intersects the propeller load brake specific fuel consumption curve.*
4. *From the point of intersection, project a line horizontally to the right to read the specific fuel consumption for 2,350 RPM. This is 0.47 pound of fuel burned per hour for each horsepower developed.*
5. *Multiply 118 by 0.47 to get 55.46, the fuel consumption in pounds per hour when the engine is developing 118 brake horsepower.*

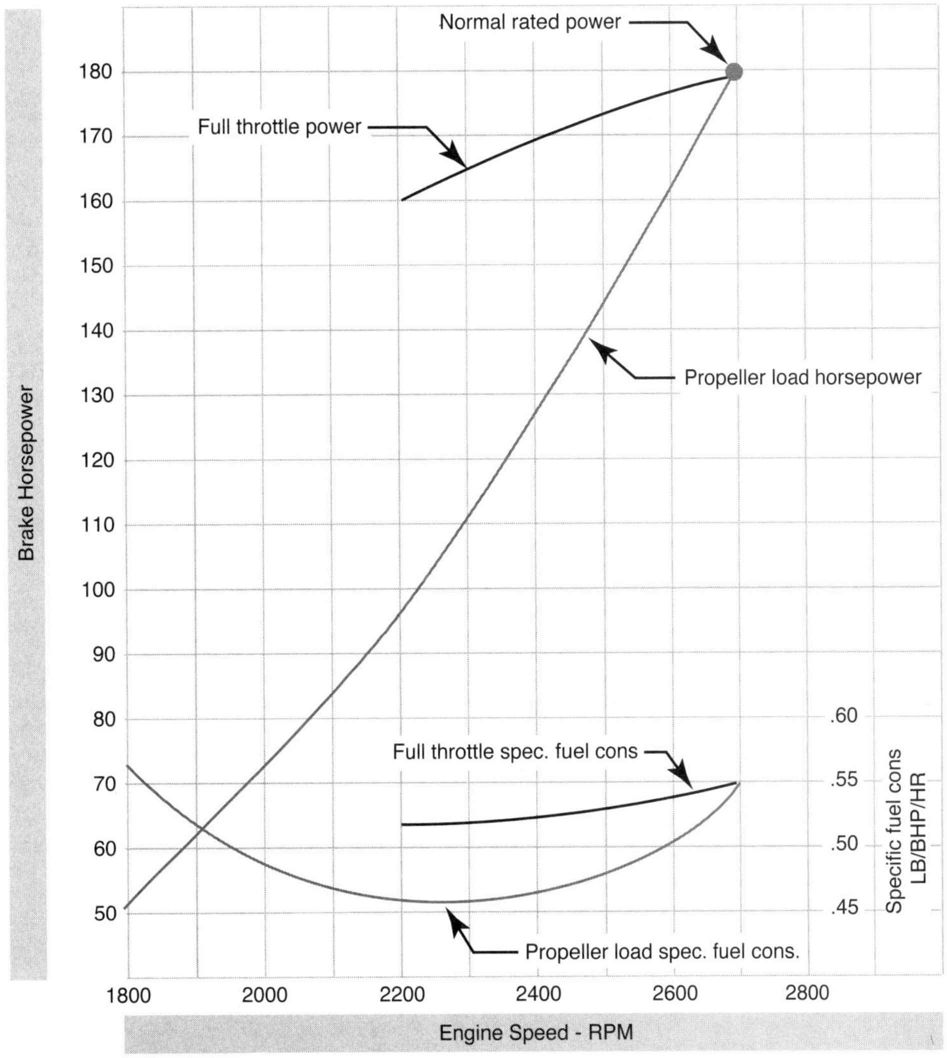

Figure 41. Performance chart

Answers
8152 [C] (016) AMT-G Ch 5

Weight and Balance

8153. When computing weight and balance, an airplane is considered to be in balance when

A—the average moment arm of the loaded airplane falls within its CG range.
B—all moment arms of the plane fall within CG range.
C—the movement of the passengers will not cause the moment arms to fall outside the CG range.

An airplane is considered to be in balance when the average moment arm of the loaded aircraft falls within its CG range.

8154. What tasks are completed prior to weighing an aircraft to determine its empty weight?

A—Remove all items except those on the aircraft equipment list; drain fuel and hydraulic fluid.
B—Remove all items on the aircraft equipment list; drain fuel, compute oil and hydraulic fluid weight.
C—Remove all items except those on the aircraft equipment list; drain fuel and fill hydraulic reservoir.

Part 23, which applies to most general aviation aircraft, defines empty weight of an aircraft. Empty weight includes fixed ballast, unusable fuel, full operating fluids including oil, hydraulic fluid and other fluids required for normal operation of airplane systems except potable water, lavatory precharge water, and water intended for injection in the engines.

When preparing an airplane for weighing, remove all items except those on the equipment list, drain the fuel, and fill the hydraulic reservoir.

8154-1. What is meant by the term "residual fuel"?

A—A known amount of fuel left in the tanks, lines, and engine.
B—The fuel remaining in the tanks, lines, and engine after draining.
C—The fuel remaining in the tank, lines, and engine before draining.

When weighing an aircraft to determine its empty weight, only the weight of residual (unusable) fuel should be included. Residual fuel is the fluid that will not normally drain out because it is trapped in the fuel lines and tanks.

8155. The useful load of an aircraft consists of the

A—crew, usable fuel, passengers, and cargo.
B—crew, usable fuel, oil, and fixed equipment.
C—crew, passengers, usable fuel, oil, cargo, and fixed equipment.

The useful load of an aircraft is the difference between its empty weight and the maximum allowable gross weight. It does not include any of the fixed or required equipment as these are part of the empty weight.

8156. Which of the following can provide the empty weight of an aircraft if the aircraft's weight and balance records become lost, destroyed, or otherwise inaccurate?

A—Reweighing the aircraft.
B—The applicable Aircraft Specification or Type Certificate Data Sheet.
C—The applicable flight manual or pilot's operating handbook.

If the aircraft weight and balance records are lost, destroyed, or otherwise inaccurate, the aircraft must be reweighed. The Aircraft Specification Sheet, Type Certificate Data Sheet, flight manual, and pilot's operating handbook do not list the empty weight of the specific aircraft.

8156-1. When calculating the new weight and balance for an aircraft, what is used to determine the operating CG range?

A—The data plate.
B—The Type Certificate Data Sheets.
C—The pilot information manual.

Some of the important weight and balance information found in a Type Certificate Data Sheet is as follows: center of gravity range, maximum weight, leveling means, number of seats and location, baggage capacity, fuel capacity, datum location, engine horsepower, oil capacity, amount of fuel in empty weight, and amount of oil in empty weight.

Answers

8153 [A] (002) AMT-G Ch 6	8154 [C] (002) AMT-G Ch 6	8154-1 [B] (003) AMT-G Ch 6	8155 [A] (002) AMT-G Ch 6
8156 [A] (002) AMT-G Ch 6	8156-1 [B] (002) AMT-G Ch 6		

8156-2. When calculating the new weight and balance for an aircraft, what is used to determine the operating CG range?

A—The Type Certificate Data Sheets.
B—The pilot information manual.
C—The data plate.

Some of the important weight and balance information found in a Type Certificate Data Sheet is as follows: center of gravity range, maximum weight, leveling means, number of seats and location, baggage capacity, fuel capacity, datum location, engine horsepower, oil capacity, amount of fuel in empty weight, and amount of oil in empty weight.

8157. In the theory of weight and balance, what is the name of the distance from the fulcrum to an object?

A—Lever arm.
B—Balance arm.
C—Fulcrum arm.

In the theory of weight and balance, the distance of any object from the fulcrum is called the lever arm.

8157-1. In the process of weighing an airplane toward obtaining the CG, the arms from the weighing points always extend

A—parallel to the centerline of the airplane.
B—straight forward from each of the landing gear.
C—directly from each weighing point to the others.

An arm, used in determining the CG of an airplane, is the horizontal distance from the datum to the center of gravity of the item. An arm is always measured parallel to the centerline of the airplane.

8157-2. Which of the following have an effect on aircraft CG results when conducting a weight and balance check?

A—Leaving the parking brake on.
B—Leaving the parking brake off.
C—Leaving the downlocks installed.

All of the required equipment must be properly installed, and there should be no equipment installed that is not included in the equipment list.

8157-3. Which of the following may cause erroneous scale readings?

A—Wheel chocks in place.
B—Parking brakes set.
C—Parking brakes not set.

When positioning an aircraft on platform-type scales for weighing, the parking brakes must be released so there will be no side load applied to the scale platform. Any side load will cause an erroneous scale reading.

8158. (1) Private aircraft are required by regulations to be weighed periodically.

(2) Private aircraft are required to be weighed after making any alteration.

Regarding the above statements,

A—neither 1 nor 2 is true.
B—only 1 is true.
C—only 2 is true.

Statement 1 is not true. No Federal Aviation Regulation requires that private aircraft be weighed periodically.

Statement 2 is not true. When a private aircraft is altered, the weight and balance records must be updated to show any change that has been made in the weight or in the empty weight CG location.

These changes are normally found mathematically rather than by actually weighing the aircraft.

8159. What FAA-approved document gives the leveling means to be used when weighing an aircraft?

A—Type Certificate Data Sheet.
B—AC 43.13-1B.
C—Manufacturer's maintenance manual.

The FAA-approved document that gives the leveling means to be used when weighing a specific aircraft is the Type Certificate Data Sheet for that aircraft.

8159-1. Which device(s) is/are used to obtain the greatest accuracy of aircraft leveling?

A—Plumb bob and chalk line.
B—Spirit level.
C—Electronic load cells.

The leveling means for determining weight and balance is specified by the aircraft manufacturer and is listed in the Type Certificate Data Sheets. Proper level may be determined with spirit levels placed across leveling lugs or along the door sill.

Answers

8156-2 [A] (002) AMT-G Ch 6	8157 [A] (002) AMT-G Ch 6	8157-1 [A] (003) AMT-G Ch 6	8157-2 [C] (003) AMT-G Ch 6
8157-3 [B] (002) AMT-G Ch 6	8158 [A] (003) AMT-G Ch 6	8159 [A] (003) AMT-G Ch 6	8159-1 [B] (002) AMT-G Ch 6

8160. To obtain useful weight data for purposes of determining the CG, it is necessary that an aircraft be weighed

A—in a level flight attitude.
B—with all items of useful load installed.
C—with no more than minimum fuel (1/12-gallon per METO horsepower) in all fuel tanks.

When an aircraft is being weighed, it must be placed in a level-flight attitude.

When the aircraft is in its level-flight attitude, the centers of gravity of all of the items are in their correct locations relative to the datum.

8161. What type of measurement is used to designate the arm in weight and balance computation?

A—Distance.
B—Weight.
C—Weight × distance.

The arm used in weight and balance computation is the distance, in inches, between the center of gravity of an object and the aircraft datum.

8162. What determines whether the value of a moment is preceded by a plus (+) or a minus (-) sign in aircraft weight and balance?

A—The location of the weight in reference to the datum.
B—The location of the weight relative to the datum and if it is being removed or added.
C—The location of the datum in reference to the aircraft CG.

A moment is a force that causes rotation about a point, and in order to specify the direction of the rotation, (+) and (-) signs are assigned to the moment.

A positive moment is one that causes the aircraft nose to go up, and a negative moment is one that causes the nose to go down.

Since a moment is the product of weight and the distance from the datum, and both of these are signed values, we have four choices for the sign of the moment:

1. *A positive weight (weight added) and a positive arm (arm behind the datum) give a positive moment.*
2. *A positive weight and a negative arm (arm ahead of the datum) give a negative moment.*
3. *A negative weight (weight removed) and a positive arm give a negative moment.*
4. *A negative weight and a negative arm gives a positive moment.*

8163. The maximum weight of an aircraft is the

A—empty weight plus crew, maximum fuel, cargo, and baggage.
B—empty weight plus crew, passengers, and fixed equipment.
C—empty weight plus useful load.

The useful load of an aircraft is found by subtracting the empty weight of the aircraft from the maximum weight. Therefore, the maximum weight is the sum of the empty weight and the useful load.

8164. Which statement is true regarding helicopter weight and balance?

A—Lateral axis CG control is not a factor in maintaining helicopter weight and balance.
B—The moment of tail-mounted components is subject to constant change.
C—Weight and balance procedures for airplanes also apply to helicopters.

When computing the weight and balance of an aircraft, it makes no difference whether the aircraft has a fixed wing or a rotary wing. The procedures are the same, but the actual effect of weight and balance is more critical for a helicopter than for a fixed-wing aircraft.

8165. What should be clearly indicated on the aircraft weighing form?

A—Minimum allowable gross weight.
B—Weight of unusable fuel.
C—Weighing points.

Since the weight and balance computations are based on the scale weights of an aircraft, the weighing form used with a specific aircraft should specify not only the leveling means, but also the location of the weighing points.

8166. If the reference datum line is placed at the nose of an airplane rather than at the firewall or some other location aft of the nose,

A—all measurement arms will be in negative numbers.
B—all measurement arms will be in positive numbers.
C—measurement arms can be either positive or negative numbers depending on the manufacturer's preference.

The reference datum used for weight and balance purposes can be located anywhere the aircraft manufacturer chooses. Current practice is to locate it on or near the nose or out ahead of the aircraft. The reason for this is that all of the arms will be positive (they will all be behind the datum).

Answers

8160 [A] (003) AMT-G Ch 6	8161 [A] (002) AMT-G Ch 6	8162 [B] (002) AMT-G Ch 6	8163 [C] (003) AMT-G Ch 6
8164 [C] (002) AMT-G Ch 6	8165 [C] (002) AMT-G Ch 6	8166 [B] (003) AMT-G Ch 6	

If all of the arms are positive, the moment of all added weight will be positive, and the moment of all removed weight will be negative. This will simplify weight and balance computations and will give less chance for error.

8167. Maximum zero fuel weight is the

A—dry weight plus the weight of full crew, passengers, and cargo.
B—basic operating weight without crew, fuel, and cargo.
C—maximum permissible weight of a loaded aircraft (passengers, crew, and cargo) without fuel.

The zero fuel weight of an aircraft is the maximum allowable weight of the loaded aircraft without fuel. The weight of the cargo, passengers, and crew are included in the zero fuel weight.

8167-1. If it is necessary to weigh an aircraft with full fuel tanks, all fuel weight must be subtracted from the scale readings

A—except minimum fuel.
B—including unusable fuel.
C—except unusable fuel.

The empty weight of an aircraft includes the weight of the unusable fuel. The weight and location of the unusable fuel are found in Note 1 in the section of the Type Certificate Data Sheets, "Data Pertinent to All Models."

8168. The empty weight of an airplane is determined by

A—adding the net weight of each weighing point and multiplying the measured distance to the datum.
B—subtracting the tare weight from the scale reading and adding the weight of each weighing point.
C—multiplying the measured distance from each weighing point to the datum times the sum of scale reading less the tare weight.

When an aircraft is to be weighed, it is placed on the scales and chocked to prevent its rolling. The weight of the chocks is called tare weight.

The empty weight of the aircraft is found by subtracting the tare weight from the scale readings, to get the net weight. The net weight from each weighing point is added to get the total net weight which is the total empty weight of the aircraft.

8169-1. When dealing with weight and balance of an aircraft, maximum weight is interpreted to mean the maximum

A—weight of the empty aircraft.
B—weight of the useful load.
C—authorized weight of the aircraft and its contents.

Maximum weight, when considering the weight and balance of an aircraft, is the maximum certificated weight of the aircraft as specified on the Type Certificate Data Sheet or in the Aircraft Specification.

8169-2. Most modern aircraft are designed so that if all seats are occupied, full baggage weight is carried, and all fuel tanks are full, what will be the weight condition of the aircraft?

A—It will be in excess of maximum takeoff weight.
B—It will be at maximum basic operating weight.
C—It will be at maximum taxi or ramp weight.

Most modern aircraft are designed so that if all seats are occupied, full baggage weight is carried, and all fuel tanks are full, the aircraft will be grossly overloaded. It will be in excess of maximum takeoff weight.

8169-3. The major source of weight change for most aircraft as they age is caused by

A—accumulation of grime and debris in hard-to-reach areas of the structure, and moisture absorption in cabin insulation.
B—repairs and alterations.
C—installation of hardware and safety wire, and added layers of primer and paint on the structure.

Changes of fixed equipment may have a major effect upon the weight of an aircraft. Many aircraft are overloaded by the installation of extra radios or instruments.

8170. The useful load of an aircraft is the difference between

A—the maximum takeoff weight and basic empty weight.
B—maximum ramp or takeoff weight as applicable, and zero fuel weight.
C—(1) the weight of an aircraft with all seats filled, full baggage/cargo, and full fuel, and (2) aircraft weight with all seats empty, no baggage/cargo, and minimum operating fuel.

The useful load of an aircraft is the difference between the maximum takeoff weight and the basic empty weight of the aircraft.

Answers

8167 [C] (003) AMT-G Ch 6	8167-1 [C] (003) FAA-H-8083-1	8168 [B] (003) AMT-G Ch 6	8169-1 [C] (003) AMT-G Ch 6
8169-2 [A] (003) AMT-G Ch 6	8169-3 [B] (003) AMT-G	8170 [A] (003) AC 43.13-1	

8171. When determining the empty weight of an aircraft, certificated under current airworthiness standards (14 CFR Part 23), the oil contained in the supply tank is considered

A—a part of the empty weight.
B—a part of the useful load.
C—the same as the fluid contained in the water injection reservoir.

The empty weight of an aircraft certificated under Part 23 includes a full supply tank of engine oil.

8172. Improper loading of a helicopter which results in exceeding either the fore or aft CG limits is hazardous due to the

A—reduction or loss of effective cyclic pitch control.
B—Coriolis effect being translated to the fuselage.
C—reduction or loss of effective collective pitch control.

If a helicopter is loaded in such a way that its CG is either too far forward or too far aft, flight will be hazardous.

The cyclic pitch control will likely not be effective enough to control the helicopter against its out-of-balance condition.

8173. The maximum weight as used in weight and balance control of a given aircraft can normally be found

A—by adding the weight of full fuel, pilot, passengers, and maximum allowable baggage to the empty weight.
B—in the Aircraft Specification or Type Certificate Data Sheet.
C—by adding the empty weight and payload.

Type Certificate Data Sheets or Aircraft Specifications include the maximum certificated gross weight of an aircraft.

8174. An aircraft with an empty weight of 2,100 pounds and an empty weight CG +32.5 was altered as follows:

1. two 18-pound passenger seats located at +73 were removed;
2. structural modifications were made at +77 increasing weight by 17 pounds;
3. a seat and safety belt weighing 25 pounds were installed at +74.5; and
4. radio equipment weighing 35 pounds was installed at +95.

What is the new empty weight CG?

A—+34.01.
B—+33.68.
C—+34.65.

Item	*Weight*	*Arm*	*Moment*
Aircraft	*2,100.*	*32.5*	*68,250.*
Seats (remove)	*36. (-)*	*73.*	*2,628. (-)*
Modification	*17.*	*77.*	*1,309.*
Seat	*25.*	*74.5*	*1,862.5*
Radio	*35.*	*95.*	*3,325.*
Total	*2,141.*	*33.68*	*72,118.5*

The new empty weight is 2,141 pounds, and the CG is located at fuselage station 33.68.

8175. The CG range in single-rotor helicopters is

A—much greater than for airplanes.
B—approximately the same as the CG range for airplanes.
C—more restricted than for airplanes.

Most helicopters have a much more restricted CG range than do airplanes. In some cases, this range is less than three inches.

8176. The amount of fuel used for computing empty weight and corresponding CG is

A—empty fuel tanks.
B—unusable fuel.
C—the amount of fuel necessary for 1/2 hour of operation.

The amount of fuel to be in the aircraft when it is weighed for purposes of finding its empty weight is only the unusable fuel.

If the aircraft is weighed with full fuel tanks, the weight of the fuel must be subtracted from the weight found by the scales.

The weight of the unusable fuel and its CG can be found in the Type Certificate Data Sheet for the aircraft.

Answers

8171 [A] (002) §23.29
8172 [A] (002) AMT-G
8173 [B] (002) AMT-G Ch 6
8174 [B] (C02) AMT-G Ch 6
8175 [C] (002) AMT-G
8176 [B] (002) §23.29

8177. An aircraft as loaded weighs 4,954 pounds at a CG of +30.5 inches. The CG range is +32.0 inches to +42.1 inches. Find the minimum weight of the ballast necessary to bring the CG within the CG range. The ballast arm is +162 inches.

A—61.98 pounds.
B—30.58 pounds.
C—57.16 pounds.

The CG of this aircraft is out of allowable range by 1.5 inches. Its CG is at fuselage station 30.5 and the forward CG limit is at station 32.0.

To find the amount of ballast needed to be attached at fuselage station 162, multiply the empty weight of the aircraft by the distance the CG is to be moved and divide this by the distance between the ballast location and the desired CG location.

$$\text{Ballast weight} = \frac{\text{Empty weight} \times \text{Distance out}}{\text{Distance ballast to new CG}}$$

$$= \frac{4954 \times 1.5}{162 - 32}$$

$$= 57.16 \text{ pounds}$$

Attaching a 57.16-pound ballast at fuselage station 162 will move the empty weight CG to fuselage station 32.0.

8178. As weighed, the total empty weight of an aircraft is 5,862 pounds with a moment of 885,957. However, when the aircraft was weighed, 20 pounds of potable water were on board at +84, and 23 pounds of hydraulic fluid are in a tank located at +101. What is the empty weight CG of the aircraft?

A—150.700.
B—151.700.
C—151.365.

When weighing an aircraft to find its empty weight, a full reservoir of hydraulic fluid is included, but the potable water is not part of the required equipment.

Item	***Weight***	***Arm***	***Moment***
Aircraft	*5,862.*	*151.13*	*885,957.*
Potable water	*20. (-)*	*84.*	*1,680. (-)*
Total	*5,842.*	*151.365*	*884,277.*

When the water is computed out of the empty weight, we find the new empty weight to be 5,842 pounds and the new empty weight CG is located at fuselage station 151.365.

8179. Two boxes which weigh 10 pounds and 5 pounds are placed in an airplane so that their distance aft from the CG are 4 feet and 2 feet respectively. How far forward of the CG should a third box, weighing 20 pounds, be placed so that the CG will not be changed?

A—3 feet.
B—2.5 feet.
C—8 feet.

In order to not change the CG of the aircraft, it is necessary that the moment of the 20-pound weight be the same but have the opposite sign as the combined moments of the 10-pound box and the 5-pound box.

The moment of the 10-pound box is 40 pound/feet.

The moment of the 5-pound box is 10 pound/feet.

The total positive moment is 50 pound/feet, and this must be balanced by a 50-pound/foot negative moment.

By dividing the required moment by the weight, we find that the 20-pound box will have to be placed 2.5 feet ahead of the CG.

8180. An aircraft with an empty weight of 1,800 pounds and an empty weight CG of +31.5 was altered as follows:

1. two 15-pound passenger seats located at +72 were removed;
2. structural modifications increasing the weight 14 pounds were made at +76;
3. a seat and safety belt weighing 20 pounds were installed at +73.5; and
4. radio equipment weighing 30 pounds was installed at +30.

What is the new empty weight CG?

A—+30.61.
B—+31.61.
C—+32.69.

Item	***Weight***	***Arm***	***Moment***
Aircraft	*1,800.*	*31.5*	*56,700.*
Seats (remove)	*30. (-)*	*72.*	*2,160. (-)*
Modification	*14.*	*76.*	*1,064.*
Seat	*20.*	*73.5*	*1,470.*
Radio	*30.*	*30.*	*900.*
Total	*1,834.*	*31.61*	*57,974.*

The alterations shown here will change the empty weight to 1,834 pounds and the empty weight CG will move to fuselage station 31.61.

Answers
8177 [C] (002) AMT-G Ch 6 8178 [C] (002) AMT-G Ch 6 8179 [B] (002) AMT-G Ch 6 8180 [B] (002) AMT-G Ch 6

8181. An aircraft had an empty weight of 2,886 pounds with a moment of 101,673.78 before several alterations were made. The alterations included:

1. removing two passenger seats (15 pounds each) at +71;
2. installing a cabinet (97 pounds) at +71;
3. installing a seat and safety belt (20 pounds) at +71; and
4. installing radio equipment (30 pounds) at +94.

The alterations caused the new empty weight CG to move

A—1.62 inches aft of the original empty weight CG.
B—2.03 inches forward of the original empty weight CG.
C—2.03 inches aft of the original empty weight CG.

Item	*Weight*	*Arm*	*Moment*
Aircraft	*2,886.*	*35.23*	*101,673.78*
Seats (remove)	*30. (-)*	*71.*	*2,130. (-)*
Cabinet	*97.*	*71.*	*6,887.*
Seat	*20.*	*71.*	*1,420.*
Radio	*30.*	*94.*	*2,820.*
Total	*3,003.*	*36.85*	*110,670.78*

The alterations shown here will change the empty weight to 3,003 pounds and the empty weight CG will move to fuselage station 36.85.

Before the alteration, the empty weight CG was at +35.23.

The new empty weight CG of +36.85 is 1.62 inches aft of the original.

8182. If a 40-pound generator applies +1400 inch-pounds to a reference axis, the generator is located

A— −35 from the axis.
B— +35 from the axis.
C— +25 from the axis.

The distance from the axis is found by dividing the moment by the weight.

$1,400 \div 40 = 35$

Since the moment is positive, the arm will also be positive. The generator is located +35 inches from the axis.

8183. In a balance computation of an aircraft from which an item located aft of the datum was removed, use

A—(-)weight × (+)arm = (-)moment.
B—(-)weight × (-)arm = (+)moment.
C—(+)weight × (-)arm = (-)moment.

A moment is a force that causes rotation about a point, and in order to specify the direction of the rotation, signs (+) and (-) are assigned to the moment.

In aircraft weight and balance, a positive moment is a moment that causes the aircraft nose to go up, and a negative moment is one that causes the nose to go down.

Since a moment is the product of weight and the distance from the datum and both of these are signed values, we have four choices for the sign of the moment:

1. *A positive weight (weight added) and a positive arm (arm behind the datum) give a positive moment.*
2. *A positive weight and a negative arm (arm ahead of the datum) give a negative moment.*
3. *A negative weight (weight removed) and a positive arm give a negative moment.*
4. *A negative weight and a negative arm give a positive moment.*

8183-1. All other things being equal, if an item of useful load located aft of an aircraft's CG is removed, the aircraft's CG change will be

A—aft in proportion to the weight of the item and its location in the aircraft.
B—forward in proportion to the weight of the item and its location in the aircraft.
C—forward in proportion to the weight of the item, regardless of its location in the aircraft.

An item located aft of an aircraft's CG has a positive arm, and when it is removed, it has a negative weight. A positive arm and a negative weight produce a negative moment (+arm x -weight = -moment). A negative moment moves the CG forward by an amount that is proportional to the weight of the item and its location in the aircraft.

Answers

8181 [A] (002) AMT-G Ch 6 | 8182 [B] (003) AMT-G Ch 6 | 8183 [A] (002) AMT-G Ch 6 | 8183-1 [B] (002) AMT-G Ch 6

8184.

Datum is forward of the main gear center point .... 30.24 inches
Actual distance between tail gear and main gear center points .... 360.26 inches
Net weight at right main gear .... 9,980 pounds
Net weight at left main gear .... 9,770 pounds
Net weight at tail gear .... 1,970 pounds

These items were in the aircraft when weighed:

1. Lavatory water tank full (34 pounds at +352).
2. Hydraulic fluid (22 pounds at -8).
3. Removable ballast (146 pounds at +380).

What is the empty weight CG of the aircraft described above?

A—62.92 inches.
B—60.31 inches.
C—58.54 inches.

We must first find the empty weight CG of the aircraft as it is weighed.

Item	*Weight*	*Arm*	*Moment*
Right main	*9,980*	*30.24*	*301,795.2*
Left main	*9,770*	*30.24*	*295,444.8*
Tail wheel	*1,970*	*390.5*	*769,285.*
Total	*21,720*	*62.91*	*1,366,525.*

Remove, by computation, the weight of the water and the removable ballast. Leave the hydraulic fluid in, as it is part of the empty weight.

Item	*Weight*	*Arm*	*Moment*
Aircraft	*21,720.*	*62.91*	*1,366,525.*
Water	*34. (-)*	*352.*	*11,968. (-)*
Ballast	*146. (-)*	*380.*	*55,480. (-)*
Total	*21,540.*	*60.31*	*1,299,077.*

The new empty weight, as corrected for the water and the ballast, is 21,540 pounds and the new empty weight CG is at fuselage station 60.31.

8185. When making a rearward weight and balance check to determine that the CG will not exceed the rearward limit during extreme conditions, the items of useful load which should be computed at their minimum weights are those located forward of the

A—forward CG limit.
B—datum.
C—rearward CG limit.

When making a rearward weight and balance check to determine that the loaded CG cannot fall behind the rearward CG limit, you should use the maximum weight of all items of the useful load whose CG is behind the rear limit and the minimum weight for all items that are ahead of the rearward CG limit.

8185-1. When, or under what condition(s) are adverse loading checks conducted?

A—At or below the maximum gross weight of the aircraft.
B—Anytime a repair or alteration causes EWCG to fall outside the CG range.
C—At specified flight hour or calendar time intervals.

When a repair or alteration of an aircraft has been made that causes the empty weight-center of gravity to fall outside the empty weight CG range, an adverse-loaded CG check should be conducted to determine whether or not it is possible to load the aircraft in such a way that its operational CG will fall outside of its allowable limits.

8185-2. When accomplishing loading computations for a small aircraft, necessary information obtained from the weight and balance records would include

A—unusable fuel weight and distance from datum.
B—weight and location of permanent ballast.
C—current empty weight and empty weight CG.

When accomplishing loading computations for a small aircraft, you must know the current empty weight and the empty weight CG of the aircraft. This information is essential to determine the loaded weight and loaded CG.

Answers
8184 [B] (002) AMT-G Ch 6
8185 [C] (002) AC 43.13-1
8185-1 [B] (002) AMT-G Ch 6, FAA-H-8083-1A
8185-2 [C] (002) AMT-G Ch 6

8186. When an empty aircraft is weighed, the combined net weight at the main gears is 3,540 pounds with an arm of 195.5 inches. At the nose gear, the net weight is 2,322 pounds with an arm of 83.5 inches. The datum line is forward of the nose of the aircraft. What is the empty weight CG of the aircraft?

A—151.1.
B—155.2.
C—146.5.

Item	*Weight*	*Arm*	*Moment*
Main wheels	*3,540.*	*195.5*	*692,070.*
Nose wheel	*2,322*	*83.5*	*193,887.*
Total	*5,862.*	*151.14*	*885,957.*

The empty weight of this aircraft is 5,862 pounds, and its empty weight CG is located at fuselage station 151.14.

8187. An aircraft with an empty weight of 1,500 pounds and an empty weight CG of +28.4 was altered as follows:

1. two 12-pound seats located at +68.5 were removed;
2. structural modifications weighing +28 pounds were made at +73;
3. a seat and safety belt weighing 30 pounds were installed at +70.5; and
4. radio equipment weighing 25 pounds was installed at +85.

What is the new empty weight CG?

A—+23.51.
B—+31.35.
C—+30.30.

Item	*Weight*	*Arm*	*Moment*
Aircraft	*1,500.*	*28.4*	*42,600.*
Seats (remove)	*24. (-)*	*68.5*	*1,644.(-)*
Modification	*28.*	*73.*	*2,044.*
Seat	*30.*	*70.5*	*2,115.*
Radio	*25.*	*85.*	*2,125.*
Total	*1,559.*	*30.30*	*47,240.*

The empty weight of this aircraft is 1,559 pounds, and its empty weight CG is located at fuselage station 30.30.

8188. The following alteration was performed on an aircraft: a model B engine weighing 175 pounds was replaced by a model D engine weighing 185 pounds at a -62.00-inch station. The aircraft weight and balance records show the previous empty weight to be 998 pounds and an empty weight CG of 13.48 inches. What is the new empty weight CG?

A—13.96 inches.
B—14.25 inches.
C—12.73 inches.

Item	*Weight*	*Arm*	*Moment*
Aircraft	*998*	*13.48*	*13,453.04*
Engine change	*10*	*62.00 (-)*	*620.00 (-)*
Total	*1,008*	*12.73*	*12,833.04*

The new empty weight is 1,008 pounds, and the new empty weight CG is at fuselage station 12.73.

8189. If the empty weight CG of an airplane lies within the empty weight CG limits,

A—it is necessary to calculate CG extremes.
B—it is not necessary to calculate CG extremes.
C—minimum fuel should be used in both forward and rearward CG checks.

If the empty weight CG of an airplane lies within the empty weight CG limits, it is not necessary to calculate the CG extremes. The airplane cannot be legally loaded in such a way that either its forward or aft CG limits can be exceeded.

8190. When computing the maximum forward loaded CG of an aircraft, minimum weights, arms, and moments should be used for items of useful load that are located aft of the

A—rearward CG limit.
B—forward CG limit.
C—datum.

When computing a maximum forward-loaded CG of an aircraft, you should use maximum weight for all items of the useful load located ahead of the forward CG limit, and the minimum weight for all items of the useful load located behind the forward CG limit.

Answers

8186 [A] (002) AC 43.13-1
8187 [C] (002) AMT-G Ch 6
8188 [C] (002) AMT-G Ch 6
8189 [B] (002) AMT-G Ch 6, FAA-H-8083-1A
8190 [B] (002) AC 43.13-1

8191. Find the empty weight CG location for the following tricycle-gear aircraft. Each main wheel weighs 753 pounds, nosewheel weighs 22 pounds, distance between nosewheel and main wheels is 87.5 inches, nosewheel location is +9.875 inches from datum, with 1 gallon of hydraulic fluid at -21.0 inches included in the weight scale.

A—+97.375 inches.
B—+95.61 inches.
C—+96.11 inches.

Item	*Weight*	*Arm*	*Moment*
Main wheels	*1,506*	*97.375*	*146,646.75*
Nosewheel	*22*	*9.875*	*217.25*
Total	*1,528*	*96.115*	*146,864.*

The empty weight of this aircraft is 1,528 pounds, and its empty weight CG is located at fuselage station 96.115.

8191-1. An aircraft's LEMAC and TEMAC are defined in terms of distance

A—from the datum.
B—from each other.
C—ahead of and behind the wing center of lift, respectively.

LEMAC is the leading edge of the mean aerodynamic chord, TEMAC is the trailing edge of the mean aerodynamic chord. These are locations measured from the datum and expressed in station numbers.

8191-2. If an aircraft CG is found to be at 24 percent of MAC, that 24 percent is an expression of the

A—distance from the TEMAC.
B—distance from the LEMAC.
C—distance from the datum.

When the CG of an aircraft is expressed as a percentage of MAC, its location is determined by finding that percent of MAC (the distance between the LEMAC and the TEMAC). The CG is located at this distance measured from the LEMAC.

Fluid Lines and Fittings

8192. Which coupling nut should be selected for use with 1/2-inch aluminum oil lines which are to be assembled using flared tube ends and standard AN nuts, sleeves, and fittings?

A—AN-818-5.
B—AN-818-16.
C—AN-818-8.

An AN-818-5 nut will fit a 5/16-inch tube. (The last dash number is the tube diameter in 1/16-inch increments.)

An AN-818-16 nut will fit a 1-inch tube.

An AN-818-8 nut will fit a 1/2-inch tube.

8193. Metal tubing fluid lines are sized by wall thickness and

A—outside diameter in 1/16 inch increments.
B—inside diameter in 1/16 inch increments.
C—outside diameter in 1/32 inch increments.

Metal tubing used in aircraft fluid power installations is sized by its outside diameter, which is measured fractionally in sixteenths of an inch.

Answers
8191 [C] (002) AMT-G Ch 6
8191-1 [A] (002) AMT-G Ch 6
8191-2 [B] (002) AMT-G Ch 6
8192 [C] (017) AMT-G Ch 9
8193 [A] (036) AMT-G Ch 9

8193-1. Rolling-type flaring tools are used to flare __________, __________, and __________ tubing.

A—Stainless steel, hard copper, mild steel.
B—Titanium, soft copper, corrosion resistant steel.
C—Soft copper, aluminum, brass.

Use rolling-type flaring tools only to flare soft copper, aluminum, and brass tubing. Do not use with corrosion resistant steel or titanium.

8194. From the following sequences of steps, indicate the proper order you would use to make a single flare on a piece of tubing:

1. Place the tube in the proper size hole in the flaring block.
2. Project the end of the tube slightly from the top of the flaring tool, about the thickness of a dime.
3. Slip the fitting nut and sleeve on the tube.
4. Strike the plunger several light blows with a lightweight hammer or mallet and turn the plunger one-half turn after each blow.
5. Tighten the clamp bar securely to prevent slippage.
6. Center the plunger or flaring pin over the tube.

A—1, 3, 5, 2, 4, and 6.
B—3, 1, 6, 2, 5, and 4.
C—3, 1, 2, 6, 5, and 4.

The correct sequence for making a single flare on a piece of tubing is:

(3) Slip the fitting nut and sleeve on the tube.

(1) Place the tube in the proper size hole in the flaring block.

(6) Center the plunger or flaring pin over the tube.

(2) Project the end of the tube slightly from the tip of the flaring tool, about the thickness of a dime.

(5) Tighten the clamp bar securely to prevent slippage.

(4) Strike the plunger several light blows with a lightweight hammer or mallet. Turn the plunger one-half turn after each blow.

8195. Hydraulic tubing, which is damaged in a localized area to such an extent that repair is necessary, may be repaired

A—by cutting out the damaged area and utilizing a swaged tube fitting to join the tube ends.
B—only by replacing the tubing section run (connection to connection) using the same size and material as the original.
C—by cutting out the damaged section and soldering in a replacement section of tubing.

If a piece of high-pressure hydraulic tubing is damaged in a localized area, the damage can be cut out and a new piece of tubing cut to replace the damaged section. Swage-type splice fittings are slipped over each end of the tubing, and the fittings are swaged to the tube ends.

8196. What is an advantage of a double flare on aluminum tubing?

A—Ease of construction.
B—More resistant to damage when the joint is tightened.
C—Can be applied to any size and wall-thickness of tubing.

Tubing made of 5052-O and 6061-T aluminum alloy in sizes from 1/8- to 3/8-inch OD should be flared with a double flare. Double flares are smoother than single flares and are more concentric. Also, the extra metal makes the flare more resistant to the shearing effect when the fittings are torqued.

8197. A certain amount of slack must be left in a flexible hose during installation because, when under pressure, it

A—expands in length and diameter.
B—expands in length and contracts in diameter.
C—contracts in length and expands in diameter.

When flexible hose is installed in an aircraft, it must be given a certain amount of slack because when pressure is applied to the hose, it contracts in length and expands in diameter.

8198. The term "cold flow" is generally associated with

A—the effects of low temperature gasses or liquids flowing in hose or tubing.
B—impressions left in natural or synthetic rubber hose material.
C—flexibility characteristics of various hose materials at low ambient temperatures.

Cold flow describes the deep, permanent impression left in a natural or synthetic rubber hose by the pressure of hose clamps or supports.

8199. What is the color of an AN steel flared-tube fitting?

A—Black.
B—Blue.
C—Red.

Steel AN flared tube fittings are colored black. Aluminum alloy AN fittings are colored blue.

Answers

8193-1 [C] (017) FAA-H-8083-30	8194 [B] (017) AMT-G Ch 9	8195 [A] (036) AMT-G Ch 9	8196 [B] (036) AMT-G Ch 9
8197 [C] (036) AMT-G Ch 9	8198 [B] (036) AMT-G Ch 9	8199 [A] (017) AMT-G Ch 9	

8200. Which of the following statements is/are correct in reference to flare fittings?

1. AN fittings have an identifying shoulder between the end of the threads and the flare cone.
2. AC and AN fittings are considered identical except for material composition and identifying colors.
3. AN fittings are generally interchangeable with AC fittings of compatible material composition

A—1.
B—1 and 3.
C—1, 2, and 3.

AN flare fittings have a shoulder between the end of the threads and the flare cone. In AC fittings the threads go all the way to the cone. AN fittings are dyed blue or black and AC fittings are gray or yellow. The threads on an AN fitting are coarser than those on an AC fitting. AN and AC fittings are not interchangeable.

8201. Flexible lines must be installed with

A—a slack of 5 to 8 percent of the length.
B—a slack of at least 10 to 12 percent of the length.
C—enough slack to allow maximum flexing during operation.

When flexible lines are installed in a fluid power system, they should be between 5 percent and 8 percent longer than the space between the fittings.

This extra length (this slack) makes allowance for expansion in the system due to heat and for the fact that a hose contracts in its length when it is pressurized.

8202. The maximum distance between end fittings to which a straight hose assembly is to be connected is 50 inches. The minimum hose length to make such a connection should be

A—54-1/2 inches.
B—51-1/2 inches.
C—52-1/2 inches.

When a flexible line is installed in a fluid power system, it should be between 5 percent and 8 percent longer than the space between the fittings.

If the distance between the fittings is 50 inches, the hose should be at least 5 percent longer than this, or 52-1/2 inches long.

8203. Excessive stress on fluid or pneumatic metal tubing caused by expansion and contraction due to temperature changes can best be avoided by

A—using short, straight sections of tubing between fixed parts of the aircraft.
B—using tubing of the same material as the majority of the adjoining structure.
C—providing bends in the tubing.

Never select a path for a rigid fluid line that does not require bends in the tubing. Bends are necessary to permit the tubing to expand and contract under temperature changes and to absorb vibration.

8204. The material specifications for a certain aircraft require that a replacement oil line be fabricated from 3/4-inch 0.072 5052-0 aluminum alloy tubing. What is the inside dimension of this tubing?

A—0.606 inch.
B—0.688 inch.
C—0.750 inch.

Find the inside diameter of a tube by subtracting two times the wall thickness from its outside diameter.

$$0.750 - 2(0.072) = 0.606 \text{ inch}$$

The inside diameter is 0.606 inch.

8205. In most aircraft hydraulic systems, two-piece tube connectors consisting of a sleeve and a nut are used when a tubing flare is required. The use of this type connector eliminates

A—the flaring operation prior to assembly.
B—the possibility of reducing the flare thickness by wiping or ironing during the tightening process.
C—wrench damage to the tubing during the tightening process.

There are two types of flare fittings that can be used in aircraft hydraulic systems. One type is the single-piece AN817 nut, and the other is the two-piece MS20819 sleeve and an AN818 nut.

The AN818 nut and sleeve are preferred over the single-piece fitting because it eliminates the possibility of reducing the thickness of the flare by the wiping or ironing action when the nut is tightened.

With the two-piece fitting, there is no relative motion between the fitting and the flare when the nut is being tightened.

Answers

8200 [A]	(017)	AMT-G Ch 9	8201 [A]	(037)	AMT-G Ch 9	8202 [C]	(036)	AC 43.13-1	8203 [C]	(036)	AC 65-9A
8204 [A]	(017)	AMT-G Ch 9	8205 [B]	(036)	AMT-G Ch 9						

8206. During installation, MS flareless fittings

A—are normally tightened by turning the nut a specified amount, unless the manufacturer lists torque values.
B—should be assembled by applying an anti-seize compound to both surfaces of the fitting and flare.
C—are normally tightened by applying torque in small increments to prevent over-heating the tube mating surfaces.

MS flareless fittings are attached to the end of a metal tube by presetting the fitting on the tube.

Presetting consists of putting enough pressure on the fitting to deform the ferrule and cause it to cut into the outside of the tube. Presetting is done by lubricating the threads of the presetting tool and the nut with hydraulic fluid, assembling the nut and ferrule on the tube, putting it in the presetting tool, and tightening the nut by hand until resistance is felt, then turning it with a wrench from 1 to 1-1/4 turns.

When installing the fitting in an aircraft hydraulic system, tighten the nut by hand until resistance is felt and then turn it 1/6 to 1/3 of a turn (one hex to two hexes) with a wrench.

8207. When flaring aluminum tubing for use with AN fittings, the flare angle must be

A—37°.
B—39°.
C—45°.

The flare angle used with AN fittings is 37°.

8208. Scratches or nicks on the straight portion of aluminum alloy tubing may be repaired if they are no deeper than

A—20 percent of the wall thickness.
B—1/32 inch or 20 percent of wall thickness, whichever is less.
C—10 percent of the wall thickness.

Scratches or nicks are allowed in a piece of aluminum alloy tubing provided it is no deeper than 10 percent of the wall thickness of the tube, and it is not in the heel of a bend.

Scratches and nicks should be burnished out of the tube, to prevent stress concentrations.

8209. Flexible hose used in aircraft systems is classified in size according to the

A—outside diameter.
B—wall thickness.
C—inside diameter.

The size of flexible hose is determined by its inside diameter.

Sizes are in 1/16-inch increments and relate to corresponding sizes of rigid tubing with which it can be used.

8209-1. When a Teflon hose has been in service for a time, what condition may have occurred and/or what precaution should be taken when it is temporarily removed from the aircraft?

A—The hose interior must be kept wet with the fluid carried to prevent embrittlement/deterioration.
B—The hose may become stiff and brittle if not flexed or moved regularly.
C—The hose may have developed a set, or have been manufactured with a pre-set shape, and must be supported to maintain its shape.

Teflon hoses develop a permanent set after having been in use for an extended period of time or may have been manufactured with a permanent set for the particular function, thus is should be supported to maintain its shape and prevent inadvertent straightnening.

8210. A scratch or nick in aluminum tubing can be repaired provided it does not

A—appear in the heel of a bend.
B—appear on the inside of a bend.
C—exceed 10 percent of the tube OD on a straight section.

Scratches or nicks not deeper than 10 percent of the wall thickness in aluminum alloy tubing, that are not in the heel of a bend, may be repaired by burnishing (forcing the displaced metal back into the nick or scratch) with a polished steel burnishing hand tool.

8211. Which of the following hose materials are compatible with phosphate-ester base hydraulic fluids?

A—Butyl and Teflon.
B—Neoprene and Teflon.
C—Teflon and Buna-N.

Butyl is not suitable for use with petroleum products, but is an excellent inner liner for phosphate-ester base hydraulic fluids.

Teflon hose is unaffected by any fuel, petroleum, or synthetic-base oils, alcohol, coolants, or solvents commonly used in aircraft.

Buna-N should not be used with phosphate-ester base hydraulic fluids.

Neoprene is not suitable for use with phosphate-ester base hydraulic fluids.

Answers

8206 [A] (017) AMT-G Ch 9
8207 [A] (017,036) AMT-G Ch 9
8208 [C] (017,036) AMT-G Ch 9
8209 [C] (037) AMT-G Ch 9
8209-1 [C] (037) AMT-G Ch 9
8210 [A] (036) AMT-G Ch 9
8211 [A] (037) AMT-G Ch 9

8212. Which tubings have the characteristics (high strength, abrasion resistance) necessary for use in a high-pressure (3,000 PSI) hydraulic system for operation of landing gear and flaps?

A—2024-T or 5052-0 aluminum alloy.
B—Corrosion-resistant steel annealed or 1/4H.
C—1100-1/2H or 3003-1/2H aluminum alloy.

Rigid tubing made of corrosion-resistant steel, either annealed or 1/4 hard, is used in high-pressure hydraulic or pneumatic systems where high strength and abrasion resistance are important.

8213. When installing bonded clamps to support metal tubing,

A—paint removal from tube is not recommended as it will inhibit corrosion.
B—paint clamp and tube after clamp installation to prevent corrosion.
C—remove paint or anodizing from tube at clamp location.

When a piece of metal tubing is installed in a bonded clamp, any paint or anodizing oxide film must be removed from the portion of the tube where the clamp is to fit.

Both paint and the oxide film are electrical insulators.

8214. In a metal tubing installation,

A—rigid straight line runs are preferable.
B—tension is undesirable because pressurization will cause it to expand and shift.
C—a tube may be pulled in line if the nut will start on the threaded coupling.

When making an installation of rigid metal tubing, each run of the tubing must have at least one bend in it to allow for the shifting of the line as it is pressurized.

There must be no tension on the line (the flare in both ends of the tube should rest squarely on the flare cones of the fittings and not have to be pulled into place with the nut).

8214-1. Which of the following tools is best to use when cutting soft aluminum tubing?

A—Hand operated wheel-type tubing cutter.
B—Angle grinder with cut-off wheel.
C—Circular-saw equipped with an abrasive cutting wheel.

A hand operated wheel-type tubing cutter is the best tool to use when cutting aluminum tubing, or any tubing of moderately soft metal.

8214-2. The primary purpose of providing suitable bends in fluid and pneumatic metal tubing runs is to

A—clear obstacles and make turns in aircraft structures.
B—provide for access within aircraft structures.
C—prevent excessive stress on the tubing.

When making an installation of rigid metal tubing, each run of the tubing must have at least one bend in it to allow for the shifting of the line as it is pressurized. This prevents excessive stress on the tubing.

8214-3. Which of the following statements is true regarding minimum allowable bend radii for 1.5 inches OD or less aluminum alloy and steel tubing of the same size?

A—The minimum radius for steel is greater than for aluminum.
B—The minimum radius for steel is less than for aluminum.
C—The minimum radius is the same for both steel and aluminum.

The minimum allowable bend radius for a 1.5 inch OD aluminum tubing is 5 inches. The minimum allowable bend radius for the same diameter steel tubing is 5.25 inches. Steel tubing in sizes smaller than 1.5 inch OD require a greater minimum bend radius than aluminum alloy tubing of the same size.

8215. A gas or fluid line marked with the letters PHDAN is

A—a dual-purpose pneumatic and/or hydraulic line for normal and emergency system use.
B—used to carry a hazardous substance.
C—a pneumatic or hydraulic system drain or discharge line.

The marking PHDAN on a fluid line indicates that the fluid carried in the line is physically hazardous and dangerous to personnel.

8215-1. Which statement is true regarding the variety of symbols utilized on the identifying color-code bands that are currently used on aircraft plumbing lines?

A—Symbols are composed of various single colors according to line content.
B—Symbols are always black against a white background regardless of line content.
C—Symbols are composed of one to three contrasting colors according to line content.

The fluid carried in fluid lines in an aircraft is identified by a series of color-coded bands around the line. These bands have from one to three contrasting colors. There is also a white band with black geometric symbols for the benefit of color-blind personnel.

Answers

8212 [B] (042) AMT-G Ch 9	8213 [C] (036) AMT-G Ch 9	8214 [B] (036) AMT-G Ch 9	8214-1 [A] (036) AMT-G Ch 9
8214-2 [C] (036) AMT-G Ch 9	8214-3 [A] (036,042) AC 43.13-1	8215 [B] (010) AMT-G Ch 9	8215-1 [B] (010) AMT-G Ch 9

8215-2. If a flared tube coupling nut is overtightened, where is the tube most likely to be weakened/damaged?

A—Along the entire length of the sleeve and tube interface.
B—At the edge of the sleeve and straight portion of the tube.
C—At the sleeve, fitting nut, or tube flare.

Overtightening a flared tube coupling nut will likely weaken or damage the tube and it is most likely to fail at the sleeve, fitting nut, or tube flare.

8215-3. When installing a castle nut, and the nut castellation does not align with the cotter pin hole in the bolt within the torque range, the acceptable practice is to

A—back the nut off and align it to the nearest hole.
B—continue tightening the nut to the next hole.
C—change the nut or washer and try again.

When tightening castellated nuts on bolts, the cotter pin holes may not line up with the slots in the nuts for the range of recommended values. Except in cases of highly-stressed engine parts, the nut may not be over-torqued. Remove hardware and realign the holes.

8216. Which statement concerning Bernoulli's principle is true?

A—The pressure of a fluid increases at points where the velocity of the fluid increases.
B—The pressure of a fluid decreases at points where the velocity of the fluid increases.
C—It applies only to gases and vaporized liquids.

Bernoulli's principle is one of the most useful principles we have to explain the behavior of fluid (either liquid or gas) in motion.

Bernoulli's principle tells us that if we neither add energy nor take any energy from fluid in motion, an increase in the velocity of the fluid (its kinetic energy) will result in a corresponding decrease in its pressure (its potential energy).

8217. (1) Bonded clamps are used for support when installing metal tubing.

(2) Unbonded clamps are used for support when installing wiring.

Regarding the above statements,

A—only 1 is true.
B—both 1 and 2 are true.
C—neither 1 nor 2 is true.

Statement 1 is true. Bonded clamps (clamps in which the tube is contacted with a piece of bare metal) are used when installing metal tubing in an aircraft. Bonded clamps keep the tube at the same electrical potential as the aircraft structure.

Statement 2 is also true. Unbonded (cushion) clamps are used when securing wire bundles to the aircraft structure. The soft cushion in the clamp prevents abrasion wearing away the insulation on the wire.

8217-1. Which statement is true regarding flattening of tubing in bends?

A—The small diameter of the flattened portion must not be less than 65 percent of the original outside diameter.
B—The small diameter of the flattened portion must not be less than 75 percent of the original outside diameter.
C—The small diameter portion in the bend cannot exceed more than 75 percent of the diameter of straight tubing.

Tubing in the bend is often deformed, and the bend is not satisfactory if its small diameter is less than 75 percent of the outside diameter of the straight tubing.

8218. A 3/8 inch aircraft high pressure flexible hose as compared to 3/8 inch metal tubing used in the same system will

A—have higher flow capabilities.
B—have equivalent flow characteristics.
C—usually have interchangeable applications.

Flexible hose may be used in any part of an aircraft fluid system where it has been proven by the aircraft manufacturer to be suitable.

The hose must be able to carry the pressure, withstand the vibration, and pass the required fluid flow.

The size of a flexible hose is approximately its inside diameter in 1/16-inch increments. This refers to the outside diameter of a rigid tube that has the equivalent flow characteristics.

Answers

8215-2 [C] (036) AMT-G Ch 9	8215-3 [C] (017) AMT-G Ch 9	8216 [B] (027) AMT-G Ch 3	8217 [B] (017) AMT-G Ch 9
8217-1 [B] (036) AMT-G Ch 9	8218 [B] (037,042) AMT-G Ch 9		

Materials and Processes

8219. Magnetic particle inspection is used primarily to detect

A—distortion.
B—deep subsurface flaws.
C—flaws on or near the surface.

Magnetic particle inspection is used to detect flaws in ferromagnetic material on or near the surface.

These flaws form north and south magnetic poles when the part is magnetized. Iron oxide suspended in a fluid pumped over the part is attracted to and held by the magnetism and it outlines the flaw.

8220. Liquid penetrant inspection methods may be used on which of the following?

A—Ferrous metals and nonporous plastics.
B—Porous and nonporous plastics and nonferrous metals.
C—Ferrous and nonferrous metals and nonporous plastics.

Liquid penetrant inspection methods may be used to detect faults that extend to the surface on both ferrous and nonferrous metals and nonporous plastics.

8221. Which of these nondestructive testing methods is suitable for the inspection of most metals, plastics, and ceramics for surface and subsurface defects?

A—Eddy current inspection.
B—Magnetic particle inspection.
C—Ultrasonic inspection.

Ultrasonic inspection uses high-frequency sound waves to detect faults in a material. It can be used on a wide variety of materials such as ferrous and nonferrous metals, plastics and ceramics. It can detect subsurface as well as surface defects.

8221-1. Which of the following defects are not acceptable for metal lines?

A—Scratches or nicks on the inside of a bend less than 10% of wall thickness.
B—Dents in straight section that are 10% of tube diameter.
C—Dents in straight section that are 20% of tube diameter.

Scratches or nicks less than 10% of the wall thickness of the tube are repairable if they are not in the heel of the bend, as are dents that are 10% of tube diameter. A dent of more than 20% of the tube diameter is not acceptable.

8222. What nondestructive testing method requires little or no part preparation, is used to detect surface or near-surface defects in most metals, and may also be used to separate metals or alloys and their heat-treated conditions?

A—Eddy current inspection.
B—Ultrasonic inspection.
C—Magnetic particle inspection.

Eddy current inspection requires relatively little preparation of the part being inspected. It induces a magnetic field into the part which causes eddy currents to flow. Variations in the magnitude of the eddy currents affect this magnetic field, and when it is analyzed electronically, it gives information regarding such structural characteristics as flaws, discontinuities, thickness, and alloy or heat-treated condition of the material. Eddy current inspection is used to locate defects both on the surface and below the surface.

8223. What method of magnetic particle inspection is used most often to inspect aircraft parts for invisible cracks and other defects?

A—Residual.
B—Inductance.
C—Continuous.

The continuous method of magnetic particle inspection is used for most aircraft parts because it provides the strongest magnetic field to attract the oxide from the fluid.

In the continuous method of magnetic particle inspection, the part is either placed between the heads of the magnetizing machine or held inside the solenoid (coil). Magnetizing current flows while the fluid is pumped over the part.

In the residual method of magnetic particle inspection, used for some smaller parts, the parts are magnetized and the magnetizing current is shut off. Only residual magnetism is left in the part to attract the oxide.

Answers

8219 [C] (024) AMT-G Ch 7	8220 [C] (024) AMT-G Ch 7	8221 [C] (024) AC 43-3	8221-1 [C] (036) AC 43.13-1
8222 [A] (024) AC 43-3	8223 [C] (024) AMT-G Ch 7		

8224. Which of the following factors are considered essential knowledge for X-ray exposure?

A—Processing of the film and its characteristics.
B—Material thickness and density and the type of defect to be detected.
C—Processing of the film, characteristics of X-ray machine used, and film characteristics.

The factors of radiographic exposure are so interdependent that it is necessary to consider all factors for any particular radiographic exposure. These factors include, but are not limited to, the following:

1. *Material thickness and density.*
2. *Shape and size of the object.*
3. *Type of defect to be detected.*
4. *Characteristics of X-ray machine used.*
5. *Exposure distance.*
6. *Exposure angle.*
7. *Film characteristics.*
8. *Type of intensifying screen, if used.*

8225. The testing medium that is generally used in magnetic particle inspection utilizes a ferromagnetic material that has

A—high permeability and low retentivity.
B—low permeability and high retentivity.
C—high permeability and high retentivity.

The testing medium used to indicate the presence of a fault in magnetic particle inspection is a finely ground iron oxide that has a high permeability and low retentivity, and is nontoxic. It is usually suspended in a light oil such as kerosine.

8226. Which statement relating to the residual magnetizing inspection method is true?

A—Subsurface discontinuities are made readily apparent.
B—It is used in practically all circular and longitudinal magnetizing procedures.
C—It may be used with steels which have been heat treated for stressed applications.

In the residual method of magnetic particle inspection, the part is magnetized and removed from the magnetic field before the oxide-carrying fluid is pumped over it.

Steel that has a high retentivity (retains its magnetism after the magnetizing force has been removed) can be inspected by the residual method.

Steel that has been heat-treated for stressed applications has a high retentivity and it can be inspected by the residual method.

8227. A mechanic has completed a bonded honeycomb repair using the potted compound repair technique. What nondestructive testing method is used to determine the soundness of the repair after the repair has cured?

A—Eddy current test.
B—Metallic ring test.
C—Ultrasonic test.

After a bonded honeycomb repair has been made using the potted-compound repair technique, the soundness of the repair can be tested by using the metallic ring test.

The repaired surface is tested by tapping it with the edge of a coin. If the repair is sound, the tapping will produce a metallic ringing sound. If there is any void in the material, the tapping will produce a dull, thudding sound.

8228. What two types of indicating mediums are available for magnetic particle inspection?

A—Iron and ferric oxides.
B—Wet and dry process materials.
C—High retentivity and low permeability material.

The magnetic medium used for magnetic particle inspection can be applied either as a dry oxide powder dusted over the surface or (as is more commonly done) suspended in a light oil such as kerosine and pumped over the surface.

The iron oxide used as the indicating medium is often treated with a fluorescent dye that causes it to glow with a green light when an ultraviolet light (black light) is shone on it.

8229. Which of the following materials may be inspected using the magnetic particle inspection method?

A—Copper alloys.
B—Aluminum alloys.
C—Iron alloys.

In order for a part to be inspected by the magnetic particle method, it must be magnetizable. The only magnetizable metals listed are iron alloys.

Answers

8224 [B] (024) AMT-G Ch 7	8225 [A] (024) AMT-G	8226 [C] (024) AMT-G Ch 7	8227 [B] (024) AMT-G Ch 7
8228 [B] (024) AMT-G Ch 7	8229 [C] (024) AMT-G Ch 7		

8230. One way a part may be demagnetized after magnetic particle inspection is by

A—subjecting the part to high voltage, low amperage AC.
B—slowly moving the part out of an AC magnetic field of sufficient strength.
C—slowly moving the part into an AC magnetic field of sufficient strength.

A steel part is magnetized by holding it in a strong, steady magnetic field that aligns all of the magnetic domains in the material.

It is demagnetized by placing it in an AC magnetic field that continually reverses its polarity. This causes the domains to continually reverse their direction. As the domains are reversing, the part is slowly moved from the field so the domains remain in a disoriented state when the demagnetizing force is removed.

8231. Which type crack can be detected by magnetic particle inspection using either circular or longitudinal magnetization?

A—45°.
B—Longitudinal.
C—Transverse.

Longitudinal magnetization produces a magnetic field that extends lengthwise in the material. It is used to detect faults that extend across the part, perpendicular to the lines of magnetic flux.

Circular magnetization produces a magnetic field that extends across the material. It can detect faults that are oriented along the length of the part.

Either type of magnetization can detect a fault that runs at 45° to the length of the part.

8232. Which of the following methods may be suitable to use to detect cracks open to the surface in aluminum forgings and castings?

A—Dye penetrant inspection and eddy current inspection.
B—Dye penetrant inspection and magnetic particle inspection.
C—Magnetic particle inspection and metallic ring inspection.

Dye penetrant, eddy current, ultrasonic, and visual inspections may be used on aluminum forgings and castings. Magnetic particle inspection can only be used on ferrous metals, and the metallic ring inspection is used to check for delaminations in bonded composite structural materials.

8233. To detect a minute crack using dye penetrant inspection usually requires

A—that the developer be applied to a flat surface.
B—a longer-than-normal penetrating time.
C—the surface to be highly polished.

The amount of penetrant that can enter a small crack is determined by both the length of time the penetrant is allowed to remain on the surface and the temperature of the part.

When looking for very small cracks, the part can be heated (but not enough to cause the penetrant to evaporate from the surface), and the penetrant can be allowed to stay on the surface for a longer than normal time before it is washed off.

8233-1. Which of the following is a main determinant of the dwell time to use when conducting a dye or fluorescent penetrant inspection?

A—The size and shape of the discontinuities being looked for.
B—The size and shape of the part being inspected.
C—The type and/or density of the part material.

The dwell time (the time the penetrant is allowed to remain on the surface) is determined by the size and shape of the discontinuity being looked for.

8234. When checking an item with the magnetic particle inspection method, circular and longitudinal magnetization should be used to

A—reveal all possible defects.
B—evenly magnetize the entire part.
C—ensure uniform current flow.

Since longitudinal magnetization detects faults that lie across a part, and circular magnetization detects faults that lie parallel to its length, a complete inspection that will show up all possible defects requires that the part be magnetized twice, longitudinally and circularly, and given two separate inspections.

8235. In magnetic particle inspection, a flaw that is perpendicular to the magnetic field flux lines generally causes

A—a large disruption in the magnetic field.
B—a minimal disruption in the magnetic field.
C—no disruption in the magnetic field.

In order to locate a defect in a part by the magnetic particle inspection method, it is essential that the magnetic lines of force pass approximately perpendicular to the defect. This causes the maximum disruption of the magnetic field and forms magnetic poles which attract the indicating medium across the defect.

Answers

8230 [B] (024) AMT-G Ch 7
8231 [A] (019,024) AMT-G Ch 7
8232 [A] (019) AMT-G Ch 7
8233 [B] (019,024) AMT-G Ch 7
8233-1 [A] (019,024) AMT-G Ch 7
8234 [A] (019,024) AMT-G Ch 7
8235 [A] (024) AMT-G Ch 7

8236. If dye penetrant inspection indications are not sharp and clear, the most probable cause is that the part

A—was not correctly degaussed before the developer was applied.
B—has no appreciable damage.
C—was not thoroughly washed before the developer was applied.

After the penetrant has been on the surface of a part for the correct dwell time, the surface must be thoroughly washed to remove all traces of the penetrant. When the surface is clean and dry, the developer is sprayed or dusted on.

Any penetrant left on the surface or in the pores of the material will stain the developer and faults will not show up as sharp and clear marks.

8237. (1) An aircraft part may be demagnetized by subjecting it to a magnetizing force from alternating current that is gradually reduced in strength.

(2) An aircraft part may be demagnetized by subjecting it to a magnetizing force from direct current that is alternately reversed in direction and gradually reduced in strength.

Regarding the above statements,

A—both 1 and 2 are true.
B—only 1 is true.
C—only 2 is true.

Statement 1 is true. A part is demagnetized by placing it in an AC magnetic field whose strength is gradually reduced while it continually reverses its polarity. This leaves the domains in a disoriented state when the demagnetizing force is removed.

Statement 2 is also true. A DC magnetic field whose direction is continually reversed and the strength is gradually reduced may be used to demagnetize an aircraft part that has been inspected by the magnetic particle inspection method.

8238. The pattern for an inclusion is a magnetic particle buildup forming

A—a fernlike pattern.
B—a single line.
C—parallel lines.

Inclusions are impurities trapped inside a piece of metal when it was cast.

When the part is inspected by magnetic particle inspection, the inclusion does not show up as a clearly defined fault but the indication is fuzzy.

Rather than sharply defined poles, there are several sets of poles that cause the oxide to form in a series of parallel lines.

8239. A part which is being prepared for dye penetrant inspection should be cleaned with

A—a volatile petroleum-base solvent.
B—the penetrant developer.
C—water-base solvents only.

It is important when performing a dye penetrant inspection that the surface of the part be as clean as possible.

Volatile petroleum-based solvents such as Stoddard solvent and naphtha are widely used for cleaning parts to be inspected.

8240. Under magnetic particle inspection, a part will be identified as having a fatigue crack under which condition?

A—The discontinuity pattern is straight.
B—The discontinuity is found in a nonstressed area of the part.
C—The discontinuity is found in a highly stressed area of the part.

Fatigue cracks usually show up in areas that have been subjected to high concentrations of stresses. They are likely to form where the cross-sectional area of the part changes sharply.

8241. In performing a dye penetrant inspection, the developer

A—seeps into a surface crack to indicate the presence of a defect.
B—acts as a blotter to produce a visible indication.
C—thoroughly cleans the surface prior to inspection.

To perform a dye penetrant inspection, the part to be inspected is thoroughly cleaned and soaked in a liquid penetrant which seeps into any cracks or defects that extend to the surface. After the part is soaked for the required dwell time, the penetrant is washed from the surface, and the surface is covered with a developer which, acting as a blotter, pulls the penetrant from the fault. The penetrant pulled out by the developer shows up as a visible indication.

8242. What defects will be detected by magnetizing a part using continuous longitudinal magnetization with a cable?

A—Defects perpendicular to the long axis of the part.
B—Defects parallel to the long axis of the part.
C—Defects parallel to the concentric circles of magnetic force within the part.

A part magnetized longitudinally by current flowing through a cable wrapped around it will show up defects that are perpendicular (at right angles) to the long axis of the part.

Answers
8236 [C] (019,024) AMT-G Ch 7
8237 [A] (019,024) AMT-G Ch 7
8238 [C] (024) AMT-P Ch 9
8239 [A] (024) AC 43.13-1
8240 [C] (024) AMT-P Ch 9
8241 [B] (024) AMT-G Ch 7
8242 [A] (019,024) AMT-G Ch 7

8243. Circular magnetization of a part can be used to detect which defects?

A—Defects parallel to the long axis of the part.
B—Defects perpendicular to the long axis of the part.
C—Defects perpendicular to the concentric circles of magnetic force within the part.

A part magnetized circularly by the magnetizing current flowing lengthwise through it, will show up defects parallel to the long axis of the part.

8244. (1) In nondestructive testing, a discontinuity may be defined as an interruption in the normal physical structure or configuration of a part.

(2) A discontinuity may or may not affect the usefulness of a part.

Regarding the above statements,

A—only 1 is true.
B—only 2 is true.
C—both 1 and 2 are true.

Statement 1 is true. In nondestructive testing, a discontinuity may be defined as an interruption in the normal physical structure or configuration of a part.

Statement 2 is also true. A discontinuity may or may not affect the usefulness of a part.

8245. What type of corrosion may attack the grain boundaries of aluminum alloys when the heat treatment process has been improperly accomplished?

A—Concentration cell.
B—Intergranular.
C—Fretting.

An aluminum alloy part is heat-treated by being heated in an oven and then removed and immediately quenched in cold water.

If there is a delay between the time the part is removed from the oven and the time it is quenched, the grains in the metal will grow. Because of this, there is a good probability that intergranular corrosion will develop along the boundaries of the grains within the metal.

8246. Which of the following describe the effects of annealing steel and aluminum alloys?

A—Decreasing internal stresses and softening of the metal.
B—Softening of the metals and improved corrosion resistance.
C—Improved corrosion resistance.

Steel and aluminum alloys may be annealed to decrease internal stresses and soften the metal. Annealing does not improve corrosion resistance.

8247. Which heat-treating process of metal produces a hard, wear-resistant surface over a strong, tough core?

A—Case hardening.
B—Annealing.
C—Tempering.

Case hardening is a heat treatment process for steel in which the surface is hardened to make it wear resistant, but the inside of the metal remains strong and tough.

Annealing is a heat treatment process for either ferrous or nonferrous metal that makes the metal softer.

Tempering is a method of heat treatment in which some of the hardness is removed from a hardened metal. Removing some of the hardness makes the metal less brittle.

8248. Which heat-treating operation would be performed when the surface of the metal is changed chemically by introducing a high carbide or nitride content?

A—Tempering.
B—Normalizing.
C—Case hardening.

In case hardening, the surface of the metal is changed chemically by introducing a high carbide or nitride content. The core is unaffected chemically. When heat-treated, the surface responds to hardening while the core remains tough.

8249. Normalizing is a process of heat treating

A—aluminum alloys only.
B—iron-base metals only.
C—both aluminum alloys and iron-base metals.

Normalizing is a heat treating process in which an iron-base metal is heated to a temperature above its critical temperature and allowed to cool in still air. Normalizing reduces the stresses in the metal that were put there by the fabrication process.

Answers

8243 [A] (024) AMT-P Ch 9	8244 [C] (019,024) AMT-G Ch 7	8245 [B] (019,042) AMT-G Ch 7	8246 [A] (019,042) AMT-G Ch 7
8247 [A] (019,042) AMT-G Ch 7	8248 [C] (019) AMT-G Ch 7	8249 [B] (019,042) AMT-G Ch 7	

8250. Which of the following occurs when a mechanical force such as rolling, hammering, or bending is repeatedly applied to most metals at room temperature?

A—The metals become artificially aged.
B—The metals become stress corrosion cracked.
C—The metals become strain or work hardened or cold worked.

When a mechanical force such as rolling, hammering, or bending is repeatedly applied to most metals at room temperature, the metals become strain or work hardened or cold worked. They may become so hard and brittle that they break.

8251. The reheating of a heat treated metal, such as with a welding torch

A—has little or no effect on a metal's heat treated characteristics.
B—has a cumulative enhancement effect on the original heat treatment.
C—can significantly alter a metal's properties in the reheated area.

When a heat-treated metal is reheated with a welding torch there is no close control of the temperature and the metal's properties in the reheated area may be significantly altered.

8252. Why is steel tempered after being hardened?

A—To increase its hardness and ductility.
B—To increase its strength and decrease its internal stresses.
C—To relieve its internal stresses and reduce its brittleness.

Steel is tempered after it is hardened to remove some of the internal stresses and make it less brittle. Tempering is done by heating it to a temperature quite a way below its critical temperature and allowing it to cool in still air.

8253. What aluminum alloy designations indicate that the metal has received no hardening or tempering treatment?

A—3003-F.
B—5052-H36.
C—6061-O.

In the temper designations used with aluminum alloy, these letters have the following meanings:

F means "as fabricated." There has been no control over its temper.

H36 means the metal is nonheat-treatable, but it has been strain-hardened and stabilized to its 3/4 hard state.

O means the metal has been annealed.

8254. Which material cannot be heat treated repeatedly without harmful effects?

A—Unclad aluminum alloy in sheet form.
B—6061-T9 stainless steel.
C—Clad aluminum alloy.

Clad aluminum alloy sheets have a core of high-strength aluminum alloy onto whose surface have been rolled a thin layer of pure aluminum.

When clad sheets are heated in the process of heat treatment, some of the pure aluminum diffuses into the core alloy and weakens the sheet.

The manufacturer of the aluminum specifies the number of times clad sheets can be heat-treated. Typically, they allow the sheet to be heat-treated only one to three times.

8255. What is descriptive of the annealing process of steel during and after it has been annealed?

A—Rapid cooling; high strength.
B—Slow cooling; low strength.
C—Slow cooling; increased resistance to wear.

Annealing of steel is accomplished by heating the metal to just above the upper critical point, soaking at that temperature and cooling very slowly in the furnace.

Annealing of steel produces a fine-grained, soft, ductile metal without internal stresses or strains. In the annealed state steel has its lowest strength.

8256. Torque values for aircraft bolts normally consider

A—the threads to be clean and dry.
B—tightening the bolt head.
C—lubricating the threads.

The amount of torque used to screw a nut onto a bolt is critical in determining the integrity of a bolted joint.

For torque to be uniform and to allow the torque specified by the manufacturer to be duplicated in the field, the following rule applies: Unless it is specified otherwise, the values given in a torque chart relate to clean, dry threads.

8257. What is generally used in the construction of aircraft exhaust collectors, stacks, and manifolds?

A—Stainless steel.
B—Titanium.
C—Aluminum.

The material most generally used for firewalls, exhaust collectors, stacks, and manifolds on aircraft is stainless steel at least 0.015 inch thick. Mild steel, at least 0.018 inch thick and protected from corrosion, terneplate at least 0.018 inch thick, and Monel at least 0.018 inch thick may also be used.

Answers

8250 [C] (019) AMT-G Ch 7	8251 [C] (019) AMT-G Ch 7	8252 [C] (019,042) AMT-G Ch 7	8253 [A] (019,042) AMT-G Ch 7
8254 [C] (019) AMT-G Ch 7	8255 [B] (042) AMT-G Ch 7	8256 [A] (017) AMT-G Ch 7	8257 [A] (020) AMT-G Ch 7

8257-1. What metal has special short-time heat properties and is used in the construction of aircraft firewalls?

A—Stainless steel.
B—Chrome molybdenum alloy steel.
C—Titanium alloy.

Titanium has some merit for short-time exposure up to 3,000°F where strength is not important. Aircraft firewalls demand this requirement.

8258. Unless otherwise specified or required, aircraft bolts should be installed so that the bolthead is

A—upward, or in a rearward direction.
B—upward, or in a forward direction.
C—downward, or in a forward direction.

An accepted rule of thumb for installing bolts in an aircraft structure is to have the bolt head up, forward, or outboard.

When the bolt is installed in this way, it is least likely to fall out if the nut should ever back off.

8259. Alclad is a metal consisting of

A—aluminum alloy surface layers and a pure aluminum core.
B—pure aluminum surface layers on an aluminum alloy core.
C—a homogeneous mixture of pure aluminum and aluminum alloy.

Alclad is the registered trade name for an aluminum alloy sheet that has pure aluminum rolled onto its surfaces.

The pure aluminum protects the alloy core from corrosion.

8260. A fiber-type, self-locking nut must never be used on an aircraft if the bolt is

A—under shear loading.
B—under tension loading.
C—subject to rotation.

Fiber-type, self-locking nuts depend upon the fiber insert in the end of the nut gripping the bolt threads tight enough to prevent the nut backing off.

Since there is no mechanical lock between the nut and the bolt, the FAA recommends that a fiber-type self-locking nut not be used in any installation in which the fastener is subject to rotation.

8260-1. Self-locking nuts may be used on aircraft provided that

A—the head of the bolt is safety wired.
B—they are installed with a lock washer.
C—the bolt or nut is not subject to rotation.

Self-locking nuts are used on aircraft to provide tight connections which will not shake loose under severe vibration. Do not use self-locking nuts at joints that subject either the nut or bolt to rotation.

8261. The Society of Automotive Engineers (SAE) and the American Iron and Steel Institute use a numerical index system to identify the composition of various steels. In the number "4130" designating chromium molybdenum steel, the first digit indicates the

A—percentage of the basic element in the alloy.
B—percentage of carbon in the alloy in hundredths of a percent.
C—basic alloying element.

In the SAE four-digit numbering system for identifying the composition of steel, the first two digits identify the basic alloy, and the second two digits show the percentage of carbon in hundredths of a percent.

8262. (Refer to Figure 42.) Which of the bolthead code markings shown identifies an AN corrosion resistant steel bolt?

A—1.
B—2.
C—3.

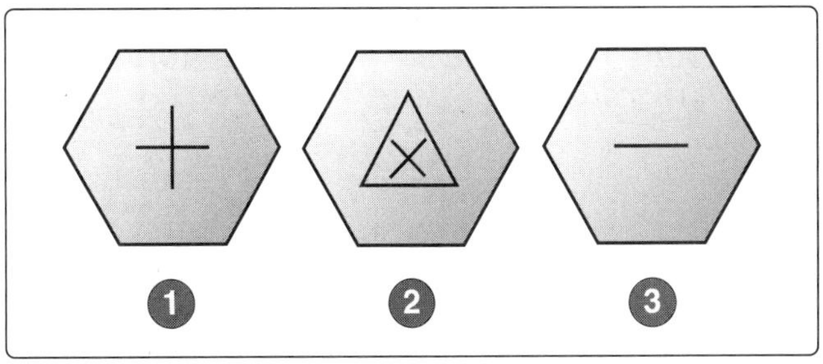

Figure 42. Aircraft hardware

The single dash on the head of a bolt identifies it as a standard bolt made of corrosion-resistant steel.

The cross on the head of a bolt identifies it as a standard AN bolt made of nickel alloy steel.

The cross inside a triangle identifies the bolt as an NAS close-tolerance bolt.

Answers

8257-1 [C] (020) AMT-G Ch 7
8258 [B] (017) AMT-G Ch 7
8259 [B] (019,020) AMT-G Ch 7
8260 [C] (017) AC 43.13-1
8260-1 [C] (017) AMT-G Ch 7
8261 [C] (019) AMT-G Ch 7
8262 [C] (017) AC 43.13-1

8263. Aircraft bolts with a cross or asterisk marked on the bolthead are

A—made of aluminum alloy.
B—close tolerance bolts.
C—standard steel bolts.

A cross or asterisk on the head of a bolt identifies it as a standard AN bolt made of nickel alloy steel.

8264. Which statement regarding aircraft bolts is correct?

A—When tightening castellated nuts on drilled bolts, if the cotter pin holes do not line up, it is permissible to overtighten the nut to permit alignment of the next slot with the cotter pin hole.
B—In general, bolt grip lengths should equal the material thickness.
C—Alloy steel bolts smaller than 1/4-inch diameter should not be used in primary structure.

Bolts for installation in an aircraft structure should be selected so that their grip length (the length of the unthreaded shank) is equal to the thickness of the material being joined.

8265. Generally speaking, bolt grip lengths should be

A—equal to the thickness of the material which is fastened together, plus approximately one diameter.
B—equal to the thickness of the material which is fastened together.
C—one and one half times the thickness of the material which is fastened together.

Bolts for installation in an aircraft structure should be selected so that their grip length (the length of the unthreaded shank) is equal to the thickness of the material being joined.

8266. When the specific torque value for nuts is not given, where can the recommended torque value be found?

A—AC 43.13-1B.
B—Technical Standard Order.
C—AC 43.13-2A.

A list of recommended torque values for nut-bolt combinations (without lubrication) are found in the AC 43.13-1B.

8267. (Refer to Figure 43.) Identify the clevis bolt illustrated.

A—1.
B—3.
C—2.

The bolt shown in View 3 is a clevis bolt.

The bolt shown in View 1 is a drilled-head, hex-head bolt.

The bolt shown in View 2 is an eyebolt.

8268. A particular component is attached to the aircraft structure by the use of an aircraft bolt and a castle tension nut combination. If the cotter pin hole does not align within the recommended torque range, the acceptable practice is to

A—exceed the recommended torque range by no more than 10 percent.
B—tighten below the torque range.
C—change washers and try again.

When tightening castle nuts on bolts, the cotter pin holes may not line up with the slots in the nuts at maximum recommended torque, plus friction drag. If the hole and nut castellation do not align, change washers and try again. Exceeding the maximum recommended torque is not recommended.

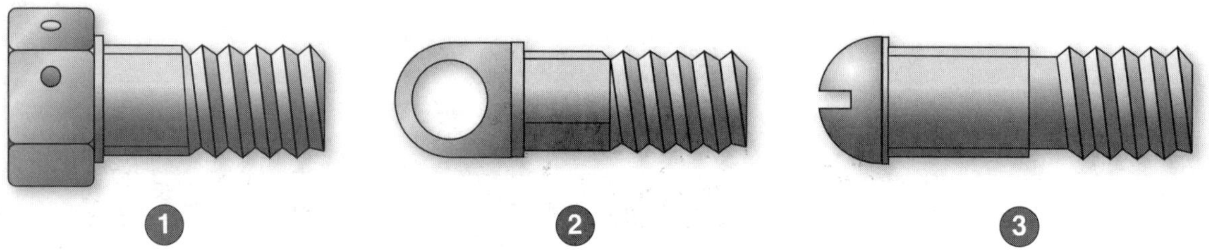

Figure 43. Aircraft hardware

Answers

8263 [C] (017) AMT-G Ch 7	8264 [B] (017) AC 43.13-1	8265 [B] (017) AC 43.13-1	8266 [A] (017) AC 43.13-1
8267 [B] (017) AMT-G Ch 7	8268 [C] (017) AC 43.13-1		

8269. A bolt with a single raised dash on the head is classified as an

A—AN corrosion-resistant steel bolt.
B—NAS standard aircraft bolt.
C—NAS close tolerance bolt.

An AN corrosion-resistant steel bolt is identified by a single raised dash on its head.

8270. How is a clevis bolt used with a fork-end cable terminal secured?

A—With a shear nut tightened to a snug fit, but with no strain imposed on the fork and safetied with a cotter pin.
B—With a castle nut tightened until slight binding occurs between the fork and the fitting to which it is being attached.
C—With a shear nut and cotter pin or a thin self-locking nut tightened enough to prevent rotation of the bolt in the fork.

When a clevis bolt is used to secure a fork-end cable terminal, a shear castle nut should be used on the clevis bolt.

The nut should be tightened until it is snug, but there must be no strain on the fork.

The nut is secured to the clevis bolt with a cotter pin.

8271. Where is an AN clevis bolt used in an airplane?

A—For tension and shear load conditions.
B—Where external tension loads are applied.
C—Only for shear load applications.

A clevis bolt should be used only where the load to which the bolt is applied is a shear load. A clevis bolt is not designed to take any type of tensile load.

The threaded portion of a clevis bolt is short and there is a groove between the threads and the shank. The head of a clevis bolt has a screwdriver slot rather than flats for the use of a wrench.

8272. A bolt with an X inside a triangle on the head is classified as an

A—NAS standard aircraft bolt.
B—NAS close tolerance bolt.
C—AN corrosion-resistant steel bolt.

An NAS close-tolerance bolt has a cross or an X inside a triangle on its head.

An NAS or an AN standard aircraft bolt has a raised cross or asterisk on its head.

An AN corrosion-resistant steel bolt has a single raised dash on its head.

8273. The core material of Alclad 2024-T4 is

A—heat-treated aluminum alloy, and the surface material is commercially pure aluminum.
B—commercially pure aluminum, and the surface material is heat-treated aluminum alloy.
C—strain-hardened aluminum alloy, and the surface material is commercially pure aluminum.

Alclad 2024-T4 is a type of sheet metal that has a core of 2024-T4 solution-heat-treated aluminum alloy. Commercially pure aluminum is rolled onto the surfaces of the sheet for corrosion protection.

The name Alclad is a registered trade name.

8274. The aluminum code number 1100 identifies what type of aluminum?

A—Aluminum alloy containing 11 percent copper.
B—Aluminum alloy containing zinc.
C—99 percent commercially pure aluminum.

Aluminum identified by the code number 1100 is 99 percent commercially pure aluminum.

8275. Aircraft bolts are usually manufactured with a

A—class 1 fit for the threads.
B—class 2 fit for the threads.
C—class 3 fit for the threads.

A class-3 fit is a medium fit. It is used on almost all standard aircraft bolts.

A class-1 fit is a loose fit. This is used for coarse-thread stove bolts and square nuts.

A class-2 fit is a free fit. It is used on some machine screws.

8276. In the four-digit aluminum index system number 2024, the first digit indicates

A—the major alloying element.
B—the number of major alloying elements used in the metal.
C—the percent of alloying metal added.

In the four-digit numbering system for identifying aluminum alloys, the first digit shows the major alloy used with the aluminum.

The 1000 series is commercially pure aluminum.

The 2000 series has copper as the main alloy.

The 3000 series has manganese as the main alloy.

The 4000 series has silicon as the main alloy.

The 5000 series has magnesium as the main alloy.

The 6000 series has magnesium and silicon in it.

The 7000 series has zinc as the main alloy.

Answers

8269 [A] (017) AMT-G Ch 7	8270 [A] (017) AMT-G Ch 7	8271 [C] (017) AMT-G Ch 7	8272 [B] (017) AC 43.13-1
8273 [A] (019) AMT-G Ch 7	8274 [C] (019) AMT-G Ch 7	8275 [C] (017) AMT-G Ch 7	8276 [A] (019,020) AMT-G Ch 7

8277. How is the locking feature of the fiber-type locknut obtained?

A—By the use of an unthreaded fiber locking insert.
B—By a fiber insert held firmly in place at the base of the load carrying section.
C—By making the threads in the fiber insert slightly smaller than those in the load carrying section.

A fiber-type lock nut is held firmly on the threads of a bolt by pressure caused by an unthreaded fiber insert locked into a recess in the end of the nut.

When the bolt is screwed through the nut, it forces its way through the unthreaded fiber. The fiber grips the threads and applies a downward force between the threads in the nut and those on the bolt. This force prevents the nut vibrating loose.

8277-1. Why should an aircraft maintenance technician be familiar with weld nomenclature?

A—So that accurate visual (pictorial) comparisons can be made.
B—In order to gain familiarity with the welding technique, filler material, and temperature range used.
C—In order to compare welds with written (non-pictorial) description standards.

It is extremely important to make a weld repair equal to the original weld. Identifying the kind of metal to be welded, identifying the kind of welding process used in building the part originally, and determining the best way to make welded repairs are of utmost importance.

8278. (Refer to Figure 44.) Identify the weld caused by an excessive amount of acetylene.

A—4.
B—1.
C—3.

The weld in view 3 has been made with a flame that had an excess of acetylene. There are bumps along the center of the bead and craters at the edge of the weld. Cross checks are apparent where the body of the weld is sound. If this weld were cross-sectioned, it would show pockets and porosity.

The weld in view 1 was made too rapidly. The long and pointed appearance of the ripples was caused by an excessive amount of heat or by an oxidizing flame. If this weld were cross-sectioned, it would probably show gas pockets, porosity, and slag inclusions.

The weld in view 2 has improper penetration and cold laps caused by insufficient heat. It appears rough and irregular and its edges are not feathered into the base metal.

The weld in view 4 has considerable variations in depth of penetration. It often has the appearance of a cold weld.

8279. (Refer to Figure 44.) Select the illustration which depicts a cold weld.

A—3.
B—2.
C—4.

The weld in view 2 is a cold weld. It has improper penetration and cold laps caused by insufficient heat. It appears rough and irregular and its edges are not feathered into the base metal.

8280. Why is it considered good practice to normalize a part after welding?

A—To relieve internal stresses developed within the base metal.
B—To increase the hardness of the weld.
C—To remove the surface scale formed during welding.

When a part is welded, it has expanded and been fused to another part. When it cools, stresses inside it try to deform it.

After a part has been welded, it should be normalized by heating it to a temperature above its critical temperature and allowed to cool in still air.

This heating relieves the stresses in the metal, and the part is not so likely to crack in service.

8281. Holes and a few projecting globules are found in a weld. What action should be taken?

A—Reweld the defective portions.
B—Remove all the old weld, and reweld the joint.
C—Grind the rough surface smooth, inspect, and reweld all gaps/holes.

Blow holes and projecting globules are indications of a poor weld. All of the old weld bead should be removed and the material rewelded.

8282. Which condition indicates a part has cooled too quickly after being welded?

A—Cracking adjacent to the weld.
B—Discoloration of the base metal.
C—Gas pockets, porosity, and slag inclusions.

Heat causes metal to expand. Cooling causes it to contract. If a metal is cooled too quickly after it is welded, it will contract unevenly and stresses will remain in the metal. These stresses produce cracks adjacent to the weld.

Answers

8277 [A] (017) AMT-G Ch 7	8277-1 [B] (098) AC 43.13-1	8278 [C] (098) AMT-G Ch 7	8279 [B] (098) AMT-G Ch 7
8280 [A] (098) AMT-G Ch 7	8281 [B] (098) AC 43.13-1	8282 [A] (098) AMT-STRUC 2	

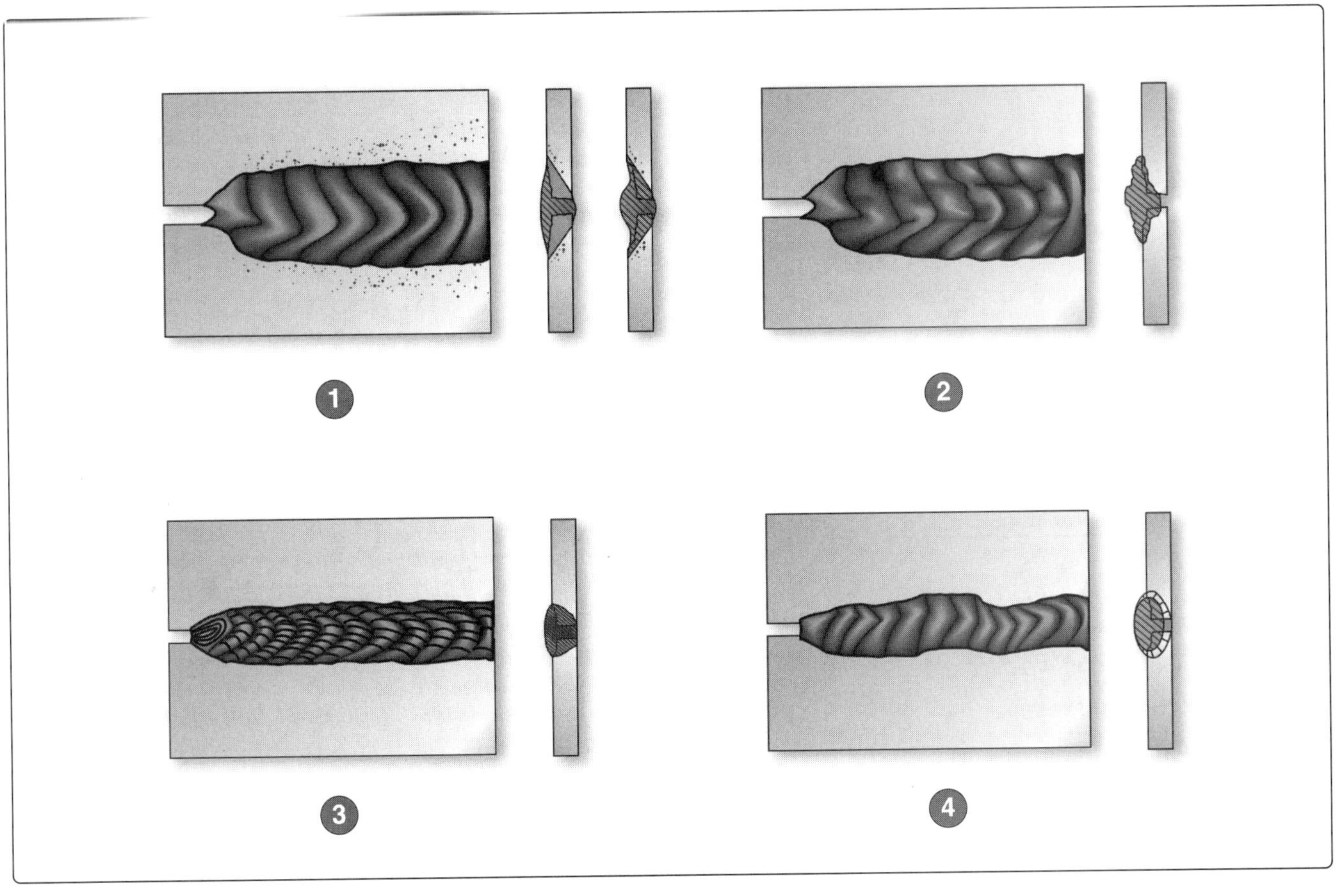

Figure 44. Welds

8283. Select a characteristic of a good gas weld.

A—The depth of penetration shall be sufficient to ensure fusion of the filler rod.
B—The height of the weld bead should be 1/8 inch above the base metal.
C—The weld should taper off smoothly into the base metal.

The bead of a gas weld that has good penetration and good fusion is uniform and straight. It has a slightly crowned surface that tapers off smoothly into the base metal.

8284. One characteristic of a good weld is that no oxide should be formed on the base metal at a distance from the weld of more than

A—1/2 inch.
B—1 inch.
C—1/4 inch.

When making a good weld, the heat should be concentrated in the area being welded.

The oxides that form on the base metal give an indication of the amount of heat put into the metal.

Oxides formed for a distance of much more than 1/2 inch from the weld show that too much heat was put into the metal. The metal may have been weakened.

8284-1. In examining and evaluating a welded joint, a mechanic should be familiar with

A—likely ambient exposure conditions and intended use of the part, along with type of weld and original part material composition.
B—the welding technique, filler material, and temperature range used.
C—the parts, proportions, and formation of a weld.

It is important when evaluating a welded joint that you are familiar with the likely ambient conditions to which the part will be exposed, the intended use of the part, the type of weld, and the material of which the part is made.

Answers
8283 [C] (098) AMT-STRUC 2 8284 [A] (098) AC 43.13-1 8284-1 [A] (098) AMT-G Ch 7

8285. (Refer to Figure 45.) What type weld is shown at A?

A—Fillet.
B—Butt.
C—Lap.

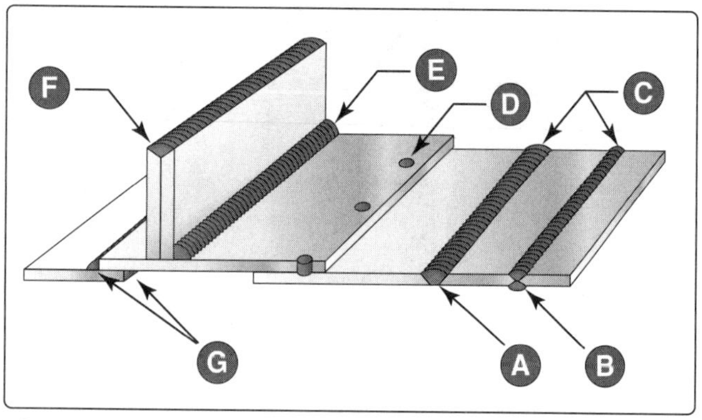

Figure 45. Welds

Weld A is a single butt weld.

Weld B is a double butt weld.

Welds C are both butt welds.

Weld D is a rosette weld.

Weld E is a fillet weld.

Weld F is an edge weld.

Welds G are lap welds.

8286. (Refer to Figure 45.) What type weld is shown at B?

A—Butt.
B—Double butt.
C—Fillet.

Weld B is a double butt weld. Both sides of the material have been ground in a V and a bead is formed on both sides of the sheet.

8287. (Refer to Figure 45.) What type weld is shown at G?

A—Lap.
B—Butt.
C—Joint.

The two welds shown at G are lap welds. When both edges are welded as is done here, the joint is called a double lap joint.

8288. On a fillet weld, the penetration requirement includes what percentage(s) of the base metal thickness?

A—100 percent.
B—25 to 50 percent.
C—60 to 80 percent.

A properly made fillet weld has a penetration of 25 to 50 percent of the thickness of the base metal.

8289. Which tool can be used to measure the alignment of a rotor shaft or the plane of rotation of a disk?

A—Dial indicator.
B—Shaft gauge.
C—Protractor.

A dial indicator is used to measure the alignment of a rotor shaft.

The dial indicator is clamped to the structure, the contact finger is placed against the surface of the shaft, and the indicator is zeroed. The shaft is rotated and the dial indicator measures the amount the shaft is out of alignment.

The plane of rotation of a disk may also be measured with a dial indicator.

8290. (Refer to Figure 46.) The measurement reading on the illustrated micrometer is

A—0.2851
B—0.2911
C—0.2901

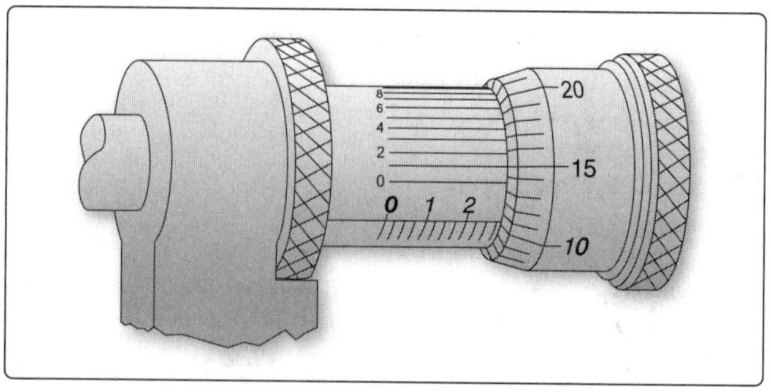

Figure 46. Precision measurement

The thimble has been screwed out more than 0.275 inch (the third mark beyond the 2 is visible).

The thimble has rotated just a bit more than ten hundredths of the way around, as is shown by the line on the sleeve. It is just beyond the 10 on the thimble. This means that 0.010 is added to the 0.275 on the sleeve.

The vernier line on the barrel for 1 is lined up with one of the marks on the thimble, and this means that we add 0.0001 inch to the two other numbers we have.

The total reading of this vernier micrometer is 0.275 + 0.010 + 0.0001 = 0.2851 inch.

Answers

8285 B] (098) AMT-STRUC 2
8286 [B] (098) AMT-STRUC 2
8287 [A] (098) AMT-STRUC 2
8288 [B] (098) AMT-G Ch 7
8289 [A] (057) DAT
8290 [A] (057) AMT-G Ch 7

8291. Identify the correct statement.

A—An outside micrometer is limited to measuring diameters.
B—Tools used on certificated aircraft must be an approved type.
C—Dividers do not provide a reading when used as a measuring device.

Dividers do not provide a reading when they are used as a measuring device. They are used by placing their points at the locations between which the measurement is to be taken. Then the distance between the points is measured with a steel machinist's scale.

8292. (Refer to Figure 47.) What is the measurement reading on the vernier caliper scale?

A—1.411 inches.
B—1.436 inches.
C—1.700 inches.

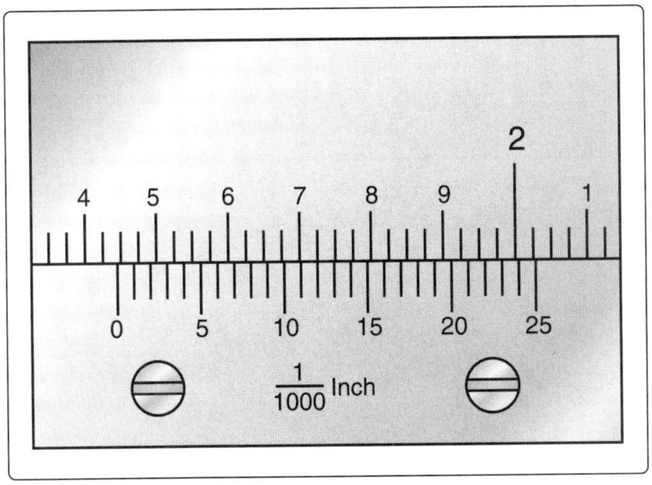

Figure 47. Precision measurement

The zero on the vernier scale is beyond the 1. This shows the measurement is more than 1 inch.

It is beyond the 4. This shows it is more than 1.4 inch.

It is beyond the first 0.025 mark on the bar. This shows that it is more than 1.425 inch.

The 11 line on the vernier scale lines up with one of the marks on the bar. This 0.011 is added to the reading we have.

The total reading is 1.425 + 0.011 = 1.436 inches.

8293. Which tool is used to measure the clearance between a surface plate and a relatively narrow surface being checked for flatness?

A—Depth gauge.
B—Thickness gauge.
C—Dial indicator.

A part is checked for flatness by putting it on a surface plate and sliding a thickness gauge (a feeler gauge) between the part and the surface plate.

The thickness of the feeler gauge that will slip between the part and the surface plate is the amount the part lacks being flat.

8294. Which number represents the vernier scale graduation of a micrometer?

A—.00001
B—.001
C—.0001

The vernier scale (the series of parallel lines on the sleeve) on a vernier micrometer caliper is used to give an indication of one ten thousandth of an inch (0.0001 inch) of spindle movement.

8295. Which tool is used to find the center of a shaft or other cylindrical work?

A—Combination set.
B—Dial indicator.
C—Micrometer caliper.

The center of a shaft or other circle can be found with the center head of a combination set.

A combination set consists of a steel scale that has three heads that can be moved to any position on the scale and locked in place.

The three heads are a stock head that measures 90° and 45° angles, a protractor head that can measure any angle between the head and the blade, and the center head that uses one side of the blade as the bisector of a 90° angle.

The center head is placed against the circumference of the circle and a diameter is drawn along the edge of the blade. The head is moved about a quarter of the way around the circle and another diameter is drawn. The two diameters cross in the center of the circle.

Answers

8291 [C] (057) AMT-G Ch 7	8292 [B] (057) AMT-G Ch 7	8293 [B] (057) AMT-G Ch 7	8294 [C] (057) AMT-G Ch 7
8295 [A] (057) AMT-G Ch 7			

8296. (Refer to Figure 48.) What does the micrometer read?

A—.2974
B—.3004
C—.3108

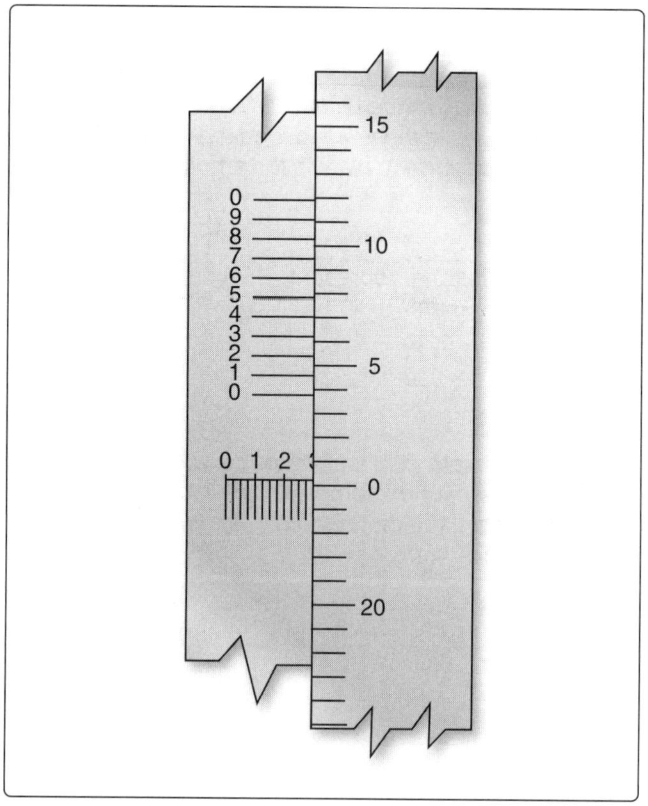

Figure 48. Precision measurement

The thimble has been screwed out slightly more than 0.300 inch (the line by the 3 is just barely visible).

The thimble has rotated just a bit beyond the zero line on the sleeve. The vernier line on the barrel for 4 is lined up with one of the marks on the thimble, and this means that we add 0.0004 inch to the other numbers we have.

The total reading of this vernier micrometer is 0.300 + 0.0004 = 0.3004 inch.

8297. If it is necessary to accurately measure the diameter of a hole approximately 1/4 inch in diameter, the mechanic should use a

A—telescoping gauge and determine the size of the hole by taking a micrometer reading of the adjustable end of the telescoping gauge.
B—0- to 1-inch inside micrometer and read the measurement directly from the micrometer.
C—small-hole gauge and determine the size of the hole by taking a micrometer reading of the ball end of the gauge.

The diameter of a small hole is measured by placing a ball-type, small-hole gauge in the hole and expanding it until its outside diameter is exactly the same size as the inside diameter of the hole.

Remove the small-hole gauge from the hole and measure its outside diameter with a micrometer caliper.

8298. (Refer to Figure 49.) The measurement reading on the micrometer is

A—.2758
B—.2702
C—.2792

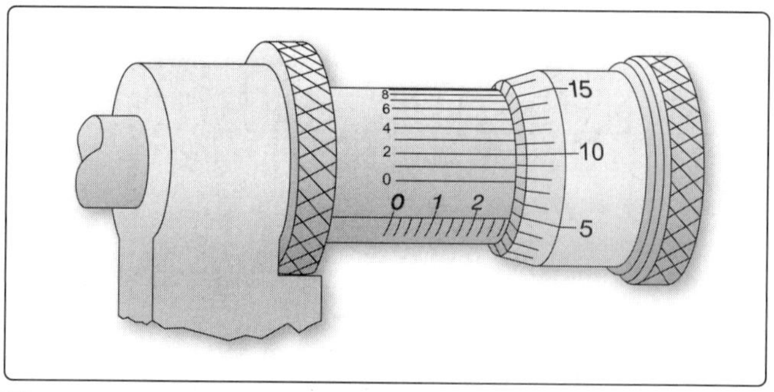

Figure 49. Precision measurement

The thimble has moved out beyond two tenths of an inch (0.200 inch).

It has moved out to a point that is beyond the third twenty-five thousandths of an inch mark. (0.075 inch.)

The 4 mark on the thimble has just passed the scale on the sleeve (0.075 + 0.004 inch = 0.079).

The 2 line on the vernier scale lines up with a number on the thimble. This adds 0.0002 inch.

The total measurement is 0.2792 inch.

Answers

8296 [B] (057) AMT-G Ch 7
8297 [C] (057) AMT-G Ch 7
8298 [C] (057) AMT-G Ch 7

8299. What tool is generally used to set a divider to an exact dimension?

A—Machinist scale.
B—Surface gauge.
C—Dial indicator.

Dividers are set with a machinist's scale.

One of the points of the dividers is placed at the one-inch mark on the scale. The other point is moved out until it touches the mark for the distance you want between the points.

8300. What tool is generally used to calibrate a micrometer or check its accuracy?

A—Gauge block.
B—Dial indicator.
C—Machinist scale.

Micrometer calipers are checked for accuracy by using gauge blocks.

A 0- to 1-inch micrometer is checked with the thimble screwed down against the anvil. No gauge block is used.

A 1- to 2-inch micrometer uses a 1-inch gauge block.

A 2- to 3-inch micrometer uses a 2-inch gauge block.

8301. What precision measuring tool is used for measuring crankpin and main bearing journals for out-of-round wear?

A—Dial gauge.
B—Micrometer caliper.
C—Depth gauge.

A vernier micrometer caliper is used to measure a crankpin and a main bearing journal for an out-of-round condition.

Two measurements are made at right angles to each other. The difference between the two readings is the amount the shaft is out-of-round.

8302. The side clearances of piston rings are measured with a

A—micrometer caliper gauge.
B—thickness gauge.
C—dial gauge.

A thickness gauge is used to measure the side clearance of a piston ring in its ring groove.

The ring is installed in the groove and its outside edge is held flush with the side of the piston. A thickness gauge is placed between the side of the piston ring and the edge of the ring groove to measure the amount of clearance between the ring and the groove.

8303. How can the dimensional inspection of a bearing in a rocker arm be accomplished?

A—Depth gauge and micrometer.
B—Thickness gauge and push-fit arbor.
C—Telescopic gauge and micrometer.

A dimensional inspection of a bearing in a rocker arm can be made by expanding a telescopic gauge inside the bushing (bearing) until its length is exactly the same as the inside diameter of the bushing.

Remove the gauge and measure it with a vernier micrometer caliper.

Measure the rocker arm shaft with the same vernier micrometer caliper.

The difference between the diameter of the shaft and that of the hole is the fit of the shaft in its bushing.

8304. The twist of a connecting rod is checked by installing push-fit arbors in both ends, supported by parallel steel bars on a surface plate. Measurements are taken between the arbor and the parallel bar with a

A—dial gauge.
B—height gauge.
C—thickness gauge.

Connecting rod twist is measured by fitting a thickness gauge between the ends of arbors and the parallel bars.

8306. What may be used to check the stem on a poppet-type valve for stretch?

A—Dial indicator.
B—Micrometer.
C—Telescoping gauge.

The stem of a poppet valve is checked for stretch by using a vernier micrometer caliper to measure the stem diameter in the center of the stem and at the spring end. If the center diameter is less than the diameter at the spring end, the valve stem has been stretched.

8307. Which tool can be used to determine piston pin out-of-round wear?

A—Telescopic gauge.
B—Micrometer caliper.
C—Dial indicator.

Piston pin out-of-round can be measured with a vernier micrometer caliper.

Measure each end of the pin in two directions at right angles to each other. The difference in the two readings is the amount the pin is out-of-round.

Answers

8299 [A] (057) AMT-G Ch 7	8300 [A] (057) AMT-G Ch 7	8301 [B] (057) AMT-P Ch 9	8302 [B] (057) AMT-P Ch 9
8303 [C] (057) AMT-P	8304 [C] (057) AMT-P Ch 9	8306 [B] (057) AMT-G Ch 7	8307 [B] (057) AMT-G

Ground Operation and Servicing

8308. During starting of a turbine powerplant using a compressed air starter, a hung start occurred. Select the proper procedure.

A—Shut off the fuel.
B—Re-engage the starter.
C—Shut the engine down.

A hung start of a turbojet engine is a start in which the engine lights off as it should, but does not accelerate to a speed that allows it to operate without help from the starter.

Anytime a hung start occurs, the engine should be shut down and the cause of the problem found and corrected.

8309. A hung start in a jet engine is often caused by

A—malfunctions in the ignition system.
B—the starter cutting off too soon.
C—an excessively rich fuel/air mixture.

A hung, or false, start is often the result of insufficient power to the starter or the starter cutting off before the engine reaches its self-accelerating speed.

8310. Which statement below reflects a typical requirement when towing some aircraft?

A—Discharge all hydraulic pressure to prevent accidental operation of the nosewheel steering mechanism.
B—Tailwheel aircraft must be towed backwards.
C—If the aircraft has a steerable nosewheel, the torque-link lock should be set to full swivel.

When towing a tricycle-gear airplane, the nose wheel torque-link lock should either be disconnected or set to full swivel, whichever the aircraft manufacturer recommends.

If this is not done, there is a good possibility that the tow bar can turn the nose wheel enough to break the steering stops.

8311. Which statement is true regarding tiedown of small aircraft?

A—The aircraft should be headed downwind in order to eliminate or minimize wing lift.
B—Leave the nosewheel or tailwheel unlocked.
C—Nylon or dacron rope is preferred to manila rope.

Manila (hemp) rope has the tendency to shrink, not stretch, when it gets wet. Nylon and dacron rope are both superior to manila because they are stronger, and neither of them shrink when they are wet.

The airplanes should be pointed as nearly into the wind as practicable and the tail wheel or nosewheel should be locked in their straight ahead position to prevent the wind slewing the aircraft around.

8312. When approaching the front of an idling jet engine, the hazard area extends forward of the engine approximately

A—10 feet.
B—15 feet.
C—25 feet.

It is extremely dangerous to approach an operating turbojet engine from either ahead or behind.

The hazard area extends out ahead of an idling turbojet engine for about 25 feet.

8313. Which of the following is the most satisfactory extinguishing agent for use on a carburetor or intake fire?

A—Dry chemical.
B—A fine, water mist.
C—Carbon dioxide.

Carbon dioxide (CO_2) is the most satisfactory fire-extinguishing agent to use for putting out an induction system fire in an aircraft engine.

CO_2 does not damage the engine, and it does not leave any residue to clean up.

Answers

8308 [C] (095) AMT-G Ch 10
8309 [B] (045,094) AMT-G Ch 10
8310 [C] (045) AMT-G Ch 10
8311 [C] (045) AMT-G Ch 10
8312 [C] (045) AMT-G Ch 10
8313 [C] (045) AMT-G Ch 10

8314. (Refer to Figure 50.) Identify the signal to engage rotor on a rotorcraft.

A—1.
B—3.
C—2.

Figure 50. Marshalling signals

Signal 3 means to engage the rotor.

Signal 1 means to start the engine.

Signal 2 means to stop the rotor.

8315. If a radial engine has been shut down for more than 30 minutes, the propeller should be rotated through at least two revolutions to

A—check for hydraulic lock.
B—check for leaks.
C—prime the engine.

A radial engine that has been shut down for some time should be turned through by hand for at least two revolutions to check for a hydraulic lock.

A hydraulic lock is a condition in a reciprocating engine in which oil has leaked past the piston rings into a cylinder below the center of the engine.

If the engine fires when there is oil in any of its cylinders, it will sustain major structural damage.

8316. The priming of a fuel injected horizontally opposed engine is accomplished by placing the fuel control lever in the

A—IDLE-CUTOFF position.
B—AUTO-RICH position.
C—FULL-RICH position.

When starting a horizontally opposed aircraft engine equipped with a fuel-injection system, prime the engine by placing the mixture control in the FULL-RICH position and turning on the fuel boost pump until there is an indication of fuel flow on the flow meter.

After some fuel has flowed through the injector nozzles, the mixture control is returned to the IDLE-CUTOFF position and the engine is started.

As soon as the engine starts, the mixture control is again placed in the FULL-RICH position.

8317. The most important condition to be monitored during start after fuel flow begins in a turbine engine is the

A—EGT, TIT, or ITT.
B—RPM.
C—oil pressure.

When starting a turbine engine, the most critical instrument to watch after the fuel flow begins is the EGT, TIT, or ITT to be sure that the engine lights off properly and the temperature does not rise above its allowable limits.

8317-1. Which of the following conditions has the most potential for causing engine damage when starting or attempting to start a turbine engine?

A—Hung start.
B—Cold start.
C—Hot start.

A hot start is one in which the EGT or TIT rises above its allowable limit. An engine can be seriously damaged by a hot start.

8318. How is a flooded engine, equipped with a float-type carburetor, cleared of excessive fuel?

A—Crank the engine with the starter or by hand, with the mixture control in cutoff, ignition switch off, and the throttle fully open, until the fuel charge has been cleared.
B—Turn off the fuel and the ignition. Discontinue the starting attempt until the excess fuel has cleared.
C—Crank the engine with the starter or by hand, with the mixture control in cutoff, ignition switch on, and the throttle fully open, until the excess fuel has cleared or until the engine starts.

A flooded reciprocating engine can be cleared of excessive fuel by placing the mixture control in the CUTOFF position to shut off all flow of fuel to the cylinders. Turn the ignition off, open the throttle and crank the engine with the starter or by hand until the fuel charge in the cylinders has been cleared.

Answers

8314 [B] (045) AMT-G Ch 10
8315 [A] (045) AMT-G Ch 10
8316 [C] (058) AMT-G Ch 10
8317 [A] (095) AMT-G Ch 10
8317-1 [C] (095) AMT-G Ch 10
8318 [A] (094) AMT-G Ch 10

8319. (Refer to Figure 51.) Which marshalling signal should be given if a taxiing aircraft is in imminent danger of striking an object?

A—1 or 3.
B—2.
C—3.

Figure 51. Marshalling signals

Signal 3 calls for an emergency stop.

If the aircraft is in imminent danger of striking an object, the signal shown in 3 should be used.

Signal 1 means to stop.

Signal 2 means to come ahead.

8320. Generally, when an induction fire occurs during starting of a reciprocating engine, the first course of action should be to

A—discharge carbon dioxide from a fire extinguisher into the air intake of the engine.
B—continue cranking and start the engine if possible.
C—close the throttle.

If an induction system fire occurs when starting a reciprocating engine, the best procedure is to continue cranking and start the engine if possible. When the engine starts, the air flowing into the engine will extinguish the fire.

8320-1. If a fire develops in an engine during the starting procedure, you should

A—discontinue the start attempt and allow the fireguard to extinguish the fire.
B—continue cranking to start the engine and extinguish the fire.
C—continue cranking and allow the fireguard to extinguish the fire.

If an engine fire develops during the starting procedure, continue cranking to start the engine and blow out the fire. If the engine does not start and the fire continues to burn, discontinue the start attempt. The fireguard should extinguish the fire using the available equipment.

8321. When starting and ground operating an aircraft's engine, the aircraft should be positioned to head into the wind primarily

A—to aid in achieving and maintaining the proper air flow into the engine induction system.
B—for engine cooling purposes.
C—to help cancel out engine torque effect.

Position the aircraft to head into the prevailing wind to ensure adequate air flow over the engine for cooling purposes.

8322. When approaching the rear of an idling turbojet or turbofan engine, the hazard area extends aft of the engine approximately

A—200 feet.
B—100 feet.
C—50 feet.

The hazard area extends aft of an idling turbojet or turbofan engine for approximately 100 feet.

8323. If a hot start occurs during starting of a turbine powerplant, what is the likely cause?

A—The starting unit overheated.
B—The ambient air temperature was too high (over 100°F).
C—The fuel/air mixture was excessively rich.

A hot start of a turbojet engine is one in which the engine starts normally but the exhaust-gas temperature exceeds its allowable limits.

Hot starts are usually caused by too rich a fuel/air mixture. (There was too much fuel for the amount of air being moved through the engine by the compressor.)

Answers

8319 [C] (045) AMT-G Ch 10
8320 [B] (045) AMT-G Ch 10
8320-1 [B] (094) AMT-G Ch 10
8321 [B] (045) AMT-G Ch 10
8322 [B] (045,096) AMT-G Ch 10
8323 [C] (094,095) AMT-G Ch 10

8324. What effect, if any, will aviation gasoline mixed with jet fuel have on a turbine engine?

A—No appreciable effect.
B—The tetraethyl lead in the gasoline forms deposits on the turbine blades.
C—The tetraethyl lead in the gasoline forms deposits on the compressor blades.

Many aviation gas turbine engine manufacturers allow the use of some aviation gasoline as a fuel when turbine fuel is not available.

The manufacturer limits the amount of time aviation gasoline can be used for two reasons: (1) The tetraethyl lead in the aviation gasoline causes deposits to form on the turbine blades. (2) Aviation gasoline does not have the lubricating properties of kerosine. Using too much gasoline can cause excessive wear on the fuel control.

8325. (1) Jet fuel is of higher viscosity than aviation gasoline and therefore holds contaminants more readily.

(2) Viscosity has no relation to contamination of fuel.

Regarding the above statements,

A—only 1 is true.
B—both 1 and 2 are true.
C—neither 1 nor 2 is true.

Statement 1 is true. Jet fuel has a higher viscosity than gasoline and it holds contaminants more readily (better) than gasoline.

Statement 2 is not true. Viscosity does have a great deal to do with the fact that jet fuel holds more contaminants than gasoline. The higher the viscosity, the fewer contaminants will settle out of the fuel.

8326. When towing a large aircraft

A—a person should be in the cockpit to watch for obstructions.
B—persons should be stationed at the nose, each wingtip, and the empennage at all times.
C—a person should be in the cockpit to operate the brakes.

When a large aircraft is being towed, there should be a person in the cockpit to operate the brakes in the event of an emergency.

8327. Weathervaning tendency is greatest when taxiing

A—both nosewheel and tailwheel-type airplanes in a quartering tailwind.
B—a tailwheel-type airplane in a direct crosswind.
C—a nosewheel-type airplane in a quartering headwind.

Weathervaning tendency is more prevalent in the tailwheel-type because the airplane's surface area behind the main landing gear is greater than in nosewheel-type airplanes. The tendency of a tailwheel-type airplane to weather vane is greatest while taxiing directly crosswind. It is difficult to prevent the airplane from turning into any wind of considerable velocity since the airplane's rudder capability may be inadequate to counteract the crosswind.

8328. When taxiing an airplane with a quartering tailwind, the elevators and

A—upwind aileron should be held in the up position.
B—upwind aileron should be held in the down position.
C—both ailerons should be kept in the neutral position.

When taxiing with a quartering tailwind, the elevator should be held in the DOWN position, and the upwind aileron, DOWN. Since the wind is striking the airplane from behind, these control positions reduce the tendency of the wind to get under the tail and the wing and to nose the airplane over.

8329. When taxiing (or towing) an aircraft, a flashing red light from the control tower means

A—stop and wait for a green light.
B—move clear of the runway/taxiway immediately.
C—return to starting point.

The meanings of the light signals that are used by control towers to control the operation of aircraft on the ground are:

Flashing red—Taxi clear of the runway or taxiway

Steady red—Stop

Steady green—OK to taxi

Alternating red and green—OK to taxi, but exercise extreme caution

Flashing white—Return to starting point

Answers

8324 [B]	(040)	AMT-G Ch 10	8325 [A]	(040)	AMT-G Ch 10	8326 [C]	(045)	AMT-G Ch 10	8327 [B]	(045)	FAA-H-8083-3
8328 [B]	(045)	8083-3	8329 [B]	(045)	AMT-G Ch 10						

8330. A person should approach or leave a helicopter in the pilot's field of vision whenever the engine is running in order to avoid

A—the tail rotor.
B—the main rotor.
C—blowing dust or debris caused by rotor downwash.

When approaching or leaving a helicopter whose engine is running, you should remain within the pilot's field of vision to avoid an encounter with the tail rotor.

8331. When taxiing (or towing) an aircraft, a flashing white light from the control tower means

A—move clear of the runway/taxiway immediately.
B—OK to proceed but use extreme caution.
C—return to starting point.

The meanings of the light signals that are used by control towers to control the operation of aircraft on the ground are:

Steady red—Stop

Flashing red—Taxi clear of the runway or taxiway

Steady green—OK to taxi

Alternating red and green—OK to taxi, but exercise extreme caution

Flashing white—Return to starting point

8332. When taxiing (or towing) an aircraft, an alternating red and green light from the control tower means

A—move clear of the runway/taxiway immediately.
B—OK to proceed but use extreme caution.
C—return to starting point.

The meanings of the light signals that are used by control towers to control the operation of aircraft on the ground are:

Steady red—Stop

Flashing red—Taxi clear of the runway or taxiway

Steady green—OK to taxi

Alternating red and green—OK to taxi, but exercise extreme caution

Flashing white—Return to starting point

8333. When stopping a nosewheel-type airplane after taxiing, the nosewheel should be left

A—unlocked and pointed straight ahead.
B—turned at a small angle towards uphill if the parking area is not perfectly flat.
C—pointed straight ahead.

When stopping an airplane that is equipped with a nosewheel, the nosewheel should be left straight ahead to relieve any strain on the nose gear and to make it easier to start moving straight ahead.

8334. When first starting to move an aircraft while taxiing, it is important to

A—test the brakes.
B—closely monitor the instruments.
C—notify the control tower.

When first starting to taxi an airplane, test the brakes for proper operation. If braking action is unsatisfactory, the engine should be shut down immediately.

8335. The color of 100LL fuel is

A—blue.
B—colorless or straw.
C—red.

Low-lead 100-octane aviation gasoline is dyed blue.

Turbine fuel is normally colorless or straw colored.

Grade 80 aviation gasoline is dyed red.

8336. How are aviation fuels, which possess greater antiknock qualities than 100 octane, classified?

A—According to the milliliters of lead.
B—By reference to normal heptane.
C—By performance numbers.

Aviation fuel whose antidetonation characteristics are better than those of the reference fuel (100-octane) are rated in performance numbers.

8337. Why is ethylene dibromide added to aviation gasoline?

A—To remove zinc silicate deposits from the spark plugs.
B—To scavenge lead oxide from the cylinder combustion chambers.
C—To increase the antiknock rating of the fuel.

Tetraethyl lead is added to aviation gasoline to improve its antidetonation characteristics (to raise its critical pressure and temperature), but deposits left inside the cylinders from the tetraethyl lead foul spark plugs and cause corrosion. In order to get rid of the residue from the tetraethyl lead, ethylene dibromide is mixed with the gasoline.

When the gasoline burns, the ethylene dibromide combines with the lead and forms volatile lead bromides that go out the exhaust and do not form solid contaminants inside the cylinder.

Answers

8330 [A] (045) AMT-G Ch 10	8331 [C] (045) AMT-G Ch 10	8332 [B] (045) AMT-G Ch 10	8333 [C] (045) FAA-H-8083-3
8334 [A] (045) 8083-3	8335 [A] (040) AMT-G Ch 10	8336 [C] (040) AMT-G Ch 10	8337 [B] (040) AMT-G Ch 10

8338. Both gasoline and kerosene have certain advantages for use as turbine fuel. Which statement is true in reference to the advantages of each?

A—Kerosene has a higher heat energy/value per unit weight than gasoline.
B—Gasoline has a higher heat energy/value per unit volume than kerosene.
C—Kerosene has a higher heat energy/value per unit volume than gasoline.

Gasoline has a higher heat energy per pound than kerosine (nominally 20,000 Btu per pound for gasoline versus about 18,500 Btu per pound for kerosine).

Kerosine, however, weighs more than gasoline (about 6.7 pounds per gallon for kerosine compared with about 6.0 pounds per gallon for gasoline).

Because there are more pounds of kerosine per gallon, there are more Btu's in a gallon of kerosine than in a gallon of gasoline.

8339. What must accompany fuel vaporization?

A—An absorption of heat.
B—A decrease in vapor pressure.
C—A reduction in volume.

When fuel changes from a liquid into a vapor, it absorbs heat from the surrounding air. This absorption of heat drops the temperature of the air enough that moisture can condense out and freeze. This is the main cause of carburetor ice.

8340. Characteristics of detonation are

A—cylinder pressure remains the same, excessive cylinder head temperature, and a decrease in engine power.
B—rapid rise in cylinder pressure, excessive cylinder head temperature, and a decrease in engine power.
C—rapid rise in cylinder pressure, cylinder head temperature normal, and a decrease in engine power.

Detonation is an uncontrolled burning, or explosion, of the fuel/air mixture within the cylinder of a reciprocating engine.

The fuel/air mixture ignites and burns normally. But as it burns, it compresses and heats the mixture ahead of the flame front. When the heated and compressed mixture reaches its critical pressure and temperature, it releases its energy almost instantaneously (it explodes).

It is the explosions inside the cylinder that cause the cylinder-head temperature to go up, the cylinder pressure to go up, and the engine power to decrease.

8341. A fuel that vaporizes too readily may cause

A—hard starting.
B—detonation.
C—vapor lock.

If a fuel vaporizes too readily, it has a high vapor pressure. It requires a high pressure to keep the vapors in the fuel.

Vapors that form in a fuel line can prevent liquid fuel flowing through the line and can stop the engine because of fuel exhaustion. This is a vapor lock.

8342. Jet fuel number identifiers are

A—performance numbers to designate the volatility of the fuel.
B—performance numbers and are relative to the fuel's performance in the aircraft engine.
C—type numbers and have no relation to the fuel's performance in the aircraft engine.

Jet engine fuel identification numbers (JP-4, JP-5, Jet A, Jet A1, and Jet B) are identification numbers only and do not relate in any way to the performance of the fuel in the engine.

8343. The main differences between grades 100 and 100LL fuel are

A—volatility and lead content.
B—volatility, lead content, and color.
C—lead content and color.

The main difference between grades 100 and 100LL aviation gasoline is the content of tetraethyl lead and the color. Their antiknock characteristics are the same.

Grade 100 is allowed to have a maximum of 3.0 milliliter of TEL per gallon, and it is dyed green.

Grade 100LL is allowed to have a maximum of 2.0 milliliter of TEL per gallon, and it is dyed blue.

8344. Characteristics of aviation gasoline are

A—high heat value, high volatility.
B—high heat value, low volatility.
C—low heat value, low volatility.

Aviation gasoline is suitable as a fuel for reciprocating engines because it has a high heat value (nominally 20,000 Btu per pound) and a high volatility. It readily changes from a liquid into a vapor so that it can be burned.

Answers

8338 [C] (040)	AMT-G Ch 10	8339 [A] (040)	AMT-G Ch 10	8340 [B] (040)	AMT-G Ch 10	8341 [C] (040)	AMT-G Ch 10
8342 [C] (040)	AMT-G Ch 10	8343 [C] (040)	AMT-G Ch 10	8344 [A] (040)	AMT-G Ch 10		

8345. Tetraethyl lead is added to aviation gasoline to

A—retard the formation of corrosives.
B—improve the gasoline's performance in the engine.
C—dissolve the moisture in the gasoline.

Tetraethyl lead is added to aviation gasoline to increase its critical pressure and temperature.

The higher critical pressure and temperature allow the engine to operate with higher cylinder pressures without the fuel/air mixture detonating.

8346. A fuel that does not vaporize readily enough can cause

A—vapor lock.
B—detonation.
C—hard starting.

An ideal fuel for an aircraft reciprocating engine must vaporize (change from a liquid into a vapor) easily, yet it must not vaporize so easily that it will form vapor locks in the fuel system.

Liquid fuel will not burn, so for it to burn, it must be changed into a fuel vapor. If the fuel does not vaporize readily enough, it will cause the engine to be hard to start.

Cleaning and Corrosion Control

8347. A primary reason why ordinary or otherwise non-approved cleaning compounds should not be used when washing aircraft is because their use can result in

A—hydrogen embrittlement in metal structures.
B—hydrogen embrittlement in nonmetallic materials.
C—a general inability to remove compound residues.

Some nonapproved commercial cleaning compounds can cause a chemical reaction with some of the metals used in aircraft structure. This reaction releases hydrogen gas that can be absorbed into the metal and cause hydrogen embrittlement which weakens the metal and can cause cracking and failure.

8348. How may magnesium engine parts be cleaned?

A—Soak in a 20 percent caustic soda solution.
B—Spray with methyl ethyl ketone (MEK).
C—Wash with a commercial solvent, decarbonize, and scrape or grit blast.

Magnesium engine parts are cleaned by washing them with a commercial solvent such as naphtha or Stoddard solvent, then soaking them in a decarbonizer that has been proven safe for magnesium.

Any hard deposits that are not removed by this treatment can be removed with a scraper or with a grit blast.

8349. When an anodized surface coating is damaged in service, it can be partially restored by

A—applying a thin coat of zinc chromate primer.
B—chemical surface treatment.
C—use of a suitable mild cleaner.

An anodized coating is an electrolytically deposited film of oxide that covers the surface of the metal and keeps air and moisture away from it. If this coating is damaged, the metal can corrode.

Damaged anodized coating can be repaired by treating the damaged area with a chemical conversion coating material such as Alodine. This chemical treatment forms a hard oxide film on the surface much like the anodized surface.

8349-1. For which of the following reasons would a water break test be conducted?

A—To make certain that a newly alodized aluminum surface is sufficiently coated.
B—To make certain that a bare metal surface is thoroughly clean.
C—To make certain that an anodizing coating has been sufficiently removed before an electrical bonding connection can be made.

Alodine can be applied to a surface after all traces of corrosion have been removed. The surface should be chemically cleaned until it supports an unbroken water film. Any breaks in the film of rinse water show that there some wax, grease, or oil on the surface, and further cleaning must be done.

Answers

8345 [B] (040) AMT-G Ch 10	8346 [C] (040) AMT-G Ch 10	8347 [A] (009) AC 43-4	8348 [C] (009) AMT-G Ch 8
8349 [B] (009) AMT-G Ch 8	8349-1 [B] (009) AMT-G Ch 8		

8350. Select the solvent recommended for wipedown of cleaned surfaces just before painting.

A—Aliphatic naptha.
B—Dry-cleaning solvent.
C—Aromatic naptha.

Aliphatic naptha is a petroleum product between gasoline and kerosine in its characteristics. It is well suited for use as a cleaning agent for removing fingerprints, dust, and oily deposits that have settled on a surface to prepare the surface for painting.

Dry-cleaning solvent, such as Stoddard solvent, leaves a slight residue on the surface that can interfere with the adhesion of the paint.

Aromatic naptha is a coal tar derivative that is toxic and attacks acrylics and rubber products. It is not suitable for wiping down a surface before painting.

8351. Nickel-cadmium battery cases and drain surfaces which have been affected by electrolyte should be neutralized with a solution of

A—boric acid.
B—sodium bicarbonate.
C—potassium hydroxide.

An area that has been affected by the electrolyte from a nickel-cadmium battery should be washed and neutralized with ammonia or a boric acid solution, allowed to dry thoroughly, then painted with an alkali-resisting varnish.

8352. Which of the following are acceptable to use when utilizing chemical cleaning agents on aircraft?

A—Cotton fiber wiping cloths when using a flammable agent and atomizing spray equipment.
B—Microfiber wiping cloths when using a flammable agent and atomizing spray equipment.
C—Synthetic fiber wiping cloths when using a flammable agent.

When cleaning and/or depainting an aircraft surface with a flammable agent, use only a cotton wiping cloth or a natural bristle brush. Synthetic fibers like microfiber tend to create unsafe charges of static electricity that could ignite the flammable agent. Emulsion-type cleaning agents may be applied to a surface with atomizing spray equipment. After the agent has penetrated the dirt or exhaust residue, it should be scrubbed with a natural bristle brush and washed from the surface.

8353. Select the solvent used to clean acrylics and rubber.

A—Aliphatic naphtha.
B—Methyl ethyl ketone.
C—Aromatic naphtha.

Aliphatic naphtha is the only one of the three materials listed here that will not damage rubber or acrylic plastic.

Be sure that aromatic naphtha (a coal tar derivative) is not used.

8354. Fayed surfaces cause concern in chemical cleaning because of the danger of

A—forming passive oxides.
B—entrapping corrosive materials.
C—corrosion by imbedded iron oxide.

Fayed surfaces are the parts of a structure that are covered in a lap joint.

It is important when a structure is chemically cleaned that the fayed surfaces be protected so that corrosive materials do not seep between the sheets in the lap joints. This would cause corrosion to form in an area where it is hard to detect.

8355. Caustic cleaning products used on aluminum structures have the effect of producing

A—passive oxidation.
B—improved corrosion resistance.
C—corrosion.

Aluminum alloys such as those used in an aircraft structure are reactive metals. This means that they are likely to react with chemicals to form salts (corrosion).

Many caustic cleaning products react with aluminum alloy and cause them to corrode.

8356. Fretting corrosion is most likely to occur

A—when two surfaces fit tightly together but can move relative to one another.
B—only when two dissimilar metals are in contact.
C—when two surfaces fit loosely together and can move relative to one another.

Fretting corrosion is a form of corrosion that forms between closely fitting assembled parts that have a slight amount of relative motion.

When sheets of aluminum alloy are riveted together, there should be no relative motion between the sheets or between the sheets and the rivets. But if there is a slight bit of movement, the protective oxide coating will be rubbed off of the metal and a new oxide coating will form. The material that has been rubbed off acts as an abrasive and accelerates the wear.

Answers

8350 [A] (009) AMT-G Ch 8	8351 [A] (009) AMT-G Ch 8	8352 [A] (009) AMT-G Ch 8	8353 [A] (009) AMT-G Ch 8
8354 [B] (009) AMT-G Ch 8	8355 [C] (009) AMT-G Ch 8	8356 [A] (012) AMT-G Ch 8	

8357. The rust or corrosion that occurs with most metals is the result of

A—a tendency for them to return to their natural state.
B—blocking the flow of electrons in homogenous metals, or between dissimilar metals.
C—electron flow in or between metals from cathodic to anodic areas.

Corrosion is a natural phenomenon which attacks metal by chemical or electrochemical action and converts it into a metallic compound, such as an oxide, hydroxide, or sulfate. Corrosion occurs because of the tendency for metals to return to their natural state. Noble metals like gold and platinum do not corrode since they are chemically uncombined in their natural state.

8358. Which of the following are the desired effects of using Alodine on aluminum alloy?

A—A smooth painting surface and increased corrosion resistance.
B—Relieved surface stresses.
C—A slightly rough surface and increased corrosion resistance.

Alodine is a conversion coating used to prepare aluminum alloys for painting. It etches the surface providing a microscopically rough surface and forms an oxide film on the surface to increase the corrosion resistance.

8359. Which of the listed conditions is NOT one of the requirements for corrosion to occur?

A—The presence of an electrolyte.
B—Electrical contact between an anodic area and a cathodic area.
C—The presence of a passive oxide film.

A passive oxide film is used as a corrosion preventive.

There are four conditions that must exist before corrosion can occur:

1. *The presence of a metal that will corrode, the anode.*
2. *Presence of a dissimilar conductive material, the cathode, which has less tendency to corrode.*
3. *Presence of a conductive liquid, the electrolyte.*
4. *Electrical contact between the anode and cathode.*

8360. The lifting or flaking of the metal at the surface due to delamination of grain boundaries caused by the pressure of corrosion residual product buildup is called

A—brinelling.
B—granulation.
C—exfoliation.

Exfoliation corrosion is a severe form of intergranular corrosion that normally forms in extruded metal.

When metal is extruded, its grain structure is basically arranged in a series of layers. If an extrusion is improperly heat-treated, the grains are enlarged to the extent that intergranular corrosion can form along the grain boundaries within the metal.

Severe intergranular corrosion in an extruded material causes it to delaminate (the layers of the metal to push apart). The surface of the metal lifts or flakes off.

8361. A nonelectrolytic chemical treatment for aluminum alloys to increase corrosion resistance and paint-bonding qualities is called

A—anodizing.
B—alodizing.
C—dichromating.

Alodizing is the depositing of an oxide film on the surface of aluminum alloy by the application of the patented chemical, Alodine. The generic term for this type of non-electrolytic corrosion protection is conversion coating.

Anodizing is a method of electrolytically depositing a hard film of aluminum hydroxide on the surface of the metal.

8362. Which of the following are acceptable to use in cleaning anodized surfaces?

A—Steel wool, aluminum wool, and fiber bristle brushes.
B—Brass wire brushes and stainless steel wire brushes.
C—Aluminum wool and fiber bristle brushes.

Anodized surfaces should never be cleaned with anything that could scratch through the anodizing and expose the untreated alloy, or that could contaminate the surface. For this reason only aluminum wool or fiber bristle brushes are suitable for cleaning these surfaces.

Answers

8357 [A] (012) AC 43-4A	8358 [C] (012) AMT-G Ch 8	8359 [C] (012) AC 43-4A	8360 [C] (012) AMT-G Ch 8
8361 [B] (012) AMT-G Ch 8	8362 [C] (012) AMT-G Ch 8		

8363. Intergranular corrosion in aluminum alloy parts

A—may be detected by surface pitting, and white, powdery deposit formed on the surface of the metal.
B—commonly appears as threadlike filaments of corrosion products under a dense film of paint.
C—cannot always be detected by surface indications.

Intergranular corrosion forms along the grain boundaries within an aluminum alloy.

Since this type of corrosion does not necessarily extend all the way to the surface of the metal in its early stages, it is quite possible for intergranular corrosion to reach an advanced state before it shows up on the surface.

8363-1. Which of the following may not be detectable even by careful visual inspection of the surface of aluminum alloy parts or structures?

A—Filiform corrosion.
B—Intergranular corrosion.
C—Uniform etch corrosion.

Intergranular corrosion is an attack along the grain boundaries of an alloy and commonly results from a lack of uniformity in the alloy structure. Intergranular corrosion is difficult to detect in its early stage, and ultrasonic and eddy current inspection methods must be used.

8364. What may be used to remove corrosion from highly stressed steel surfaces?

A—Steel wire brushes.
B—Fine-grit aluminum oxide.
C—Medium-grit carborundum paper.

Corrosion removal can be done with mild abrasive papers such as rouge or fine grit aluminum oxide, or fine buffing compounds on cloth buffing wheels. Any corrosion on the surface of a highly stressed steel part is potentially dangerous, and all of the corrosion products must be removed.

8365. A primary cause of intergranular corrosion is

A—improper heat treatment.
B—dissimilar metal contact.
C—improper application of primer.

One of the primary causes for intergranular corrosion is improper heat treatment.

If there is a delay in the time between the removal of a metal part from the heat treatment oven and the time the part is quenched, the grains of the metal have an opportunity to grow large enough that an electrical potential exists across the grain boundaries.

This potential within the metal causes the formation of intergranular corrosion.

8366. Corrosion should be removed from magnesium parts with a

A—stiff, nonmetallic brush.
B—silicon carbide brush.
C—carborundum abrasive.

Mechanical removal of corrosion from magnesium parts should be limited to the use of stiff hog-bristle brushes and similar nonmetallic cleaning tools.

8367. Why is it important not to rotate the crankshaft after the corrosion preventive mixture has been put into the cylinders on engines prepared for storage?

A—Fuel may be drawn into one or more cylinders and dilute or wash off the corrosion preventive mixture.
B—The seal of corrosion preventive mixture will be broken.
C—Engine damage can occur from hydraulic lock.

When a reciprocating engine is prepared for storage, the inside of the cylinders are sprayed with a mixture of engine oil and a preservative oil.

The oil mixture forms a seal on the cylinder wall and across the top of the piston. This mixture keeps air and moisture away from the metal surface.

If the propeller is turned, the pistons will move and break the seal so that air and moisture can reach the cylinder walls and cause them to rust.

8368. Which of the following is an acceptable first step procedure to help prevent scratching when cleaning a transparent plastic surface?

A—Gently wipe the surface with a clean, dry, soft cloth.
B—Flush the surface with clean water.
C—Gently wipe the surface with a clean, soft cloth moistened with de-mineralized or distilled water.

When cleaning the transparent plastic windshield of an aircraft, you should first flush it with a stream of clean fresh water to remove all sand and grit from the surface.

After the surface is free of anything that can scratch the soft plastic, it can be washed with soap and water and then rinsed.

Answers

8363 [C] (012) AMT-G Ch 8	8363-1 [B] (009) AMT-G Ch 8	8364 [B] (012) AMT-G Ch 8	8365 [A] (012) AC 43.13-1
8366 [A] (012) AMT-G Ch 8	8367 [B] (012) AMT-G Ch 8	8368 [B] (012) AMT-G Ch 8	

8369. What should be done to prevent rapid deterioration when oil or grease come in contact with a tire?

A—Wipe the tire thoroughly with a dry cloth, and then rinse with clean water.
B—Wipe the tire with a dry cloth followed by a washdown and rinse with soap and water.
C—Wipe the tire with a cloth dampened with aromatic naphtha and then wipe dry with a clean cloth.

When an aircraft tire comes in contact with oil or grease, remove all of the excess material by wiping it with a dry cloth. Then wash the tire with a solution of mild soap and warm water. Rinse the tire with fresh water and dry it with compressed air.

8370. Galvanic corrosion is likely to be most rapid and severe when

A—the surface area of the cathodic metal is smaller than surface area of the anodic metal.
B—the surface areas of the anodic and cathodic metals are approximately the same.
C—the surface area of the anodic metal is smaller than the surface area of the cathodic metal.

Galvanic corrosion occurs when two dissimilar metals make electrical contact in the presence of an electrolyte. The rate at which corrosion occurs depends on the difference in the activities of the two metals. The greater the difference, the faster the corrosion occurs. The rate of galvanic corrosion also depends on the size of the parts in contact. If the surface area of the corroding material, the anode, is smaller than the surface area of the less active metal, the cathode, corrosion will be rapid and severe.

8371. Corrosion caused by galvanic action is the result of

A—excessive anodization.
B—contact between two unlike metals.
C—excessive etching.

Galvanic corrosion is caused by an electrolytic action that takes place when two metals that have a different place in the galvanic scale are in contact with each other and are covered with an electrolyte.

The more anodic of the metals reacts with the electrolyte and some of it changes into salts (it corrodes).

8372. Which of these materials is the most anodic?

A—Cadmium.
B—7075-T6 aluminum alloy.
C—Magnesium.

Magnesium is the most anodic of these materials. Some of the common metals in the order of their electrochemical activity are:

(Most anodic)
Magnesium
Zinc
Cadmium
7075 Aluminum alloy
2024 Aluminum alloy
Mild steel
Copper
Stainless steel
Chromium
Gold
(Most cathodic)

8373. The interior surface of sealed structural steel tubing would be best protected against corrosion by which of the following?

A—Charging the tubing with dry nitrogen prior to sealing.
B—Evacuating moisture from the tubing before sealing.
C—A coating of linseed oil.

The inside of structural steel tubing on an aircraft is protected from rust and corrosion by drilling small holes in the end of each section of the tube and pumping linseed oil through the hole.

After the inside is thoroughly coated, the excess oil is drained out and the hole is sealed with a drive screw or by welding it shut.

Answers
8369 [B] (009) AMT-G Ch 8 8370 [C] (009) AMT-G Ch 8 8371 [B] (009) AMT-G Ch 8 8372 [C] (009) AC 43-4A
8373 [C] (009,012) AMT-G Ch 8

8374. Which of these materials is the most cathodic?

A—Zinc.
B—2024 aluminum alloy.
C—Stainless steel.

Stainless steel is the most cathodic of these materials. Some of the common metals in the order of their electrochemical activity are:

(Most anodic)
Magnesium
Zinc
Cadmium
7075 Aluminum alloy
2024 Aluminum alloy
Mild steel
Copper
Stainless steel
Chromium
Gold
(Most cathodic)

8375. Of the following, when and/or where is galvanic corrosion is most likely to occur?

A—When an electrolyte (water) covers the surface of an aluminum skin, seeps into the cracks between lap joints, and oxygen is excluded from the area.
B—At the interface of a steel fastener and aluminum alloy inspection plate in the presence of an electrolyte.
C—In an area of unprotected metal exposed to an atmosphere containing battery fumes, exhaust gases, or industrial contaminants.

Galvanic corrosion occurs any time two dissimilar metals make electrical contact in the presence of an electrolyte.

8376. One way of obtaining increased resistance to stress corrosion cracking is by

A—relieving compressive stresses (via heat treatment) on the metal surface.
B—creating compressive stresses (via shot peening) on the metal surface.
C—producing nonuniform deformation while cold working during the manufacturing process.

Stress-corrosion cracking is an intergranular cracking of the metal which is caused by a combination of stress and corrosion.

Shot peening a metal surface increases its resistance to stress corrosion cracking by creating compressive stresses on the surface. Any applied tensile stress must first overcome the surface compression before the tensile stress is felt.

8377. (1) In the corrosion process, it is the cathodic area or dissimilar cathodic material that corrodes.

(2) In the Galvanic or Electro-Chemical Series for metals, the most anodic metals are those that will give up electrons most easily.

Regarding the above statements,

A—only 1 is true.
B—only 2 is true.
C—both 1 and 2 are true.

Statement 2 is true. Corrosion occurs in an anodic material when it gives up electrons to a cathodic material. The more easily a material gives up electrons, the more anodic, or corrosive, it is.

Statement 1 is false. It is the anodic, not the cathodic, material that is destroyed in the corrosion process.

8378. Spilled mercury on aluminum

A—greatly increases susceptibility to hydrogen embrittlement.
B—may cause impaired corrosion resistance if left in prolonged contact.
C—causes rapid and severe corrosion that is very difficult to control.

Mercury spilled in an aircraft requires immediate action for its isolation and recovery to prevent it causing corrosion damage and embrittlement of the aluminum structural components. Mercury is highly toxic and spreads very easily from one surface to another.

Answers
8374 [C] (012) AC 43-4A
8375 [B] (009,012) AMT-G Ch 8
8376 [B] (012) AC 43-4A
8377 [B] (009,012) AMT-G Ch 8
8378 [C] (012) AMT-G Ch 8

Mathematics

8379. What power of 10 is equal to 1,000,000,000?

A—10 to the sixth power.
B—10 to the tenth power.
C—10 to the ninth power.

An easy way to tell the power of 10 to which a number has been raised is to count the number of places the decimal would have to be moved to leave a number between 1 and 10.

In this problem, the decimal would have to be moved nine places to the left.

1,000,000,000 is 1×10^9

8379-1. What is defined as a group of bits representing a complete piece of information?

A—Byte.
B—Bit.
C—Word.

A byte is composed of a group of 8 bits and represents a complete piece of information in a binary system.

8379-2. Convert the binary number 00001111 to a whole number.

A—31
B—15
C—8

The binary number 00001111 is converted bit by bit into whole number: 1000 = 8; 0100 = 4; 0010 = 2; and 0001 = 1; thus the entire binary number equals 8 + 4 + 2 + 1 = 15 as a whole number.

8379-3. Convert 7 to binary form.

A—0111
B—0011
C—1110

To convert a decimal number to a binary number, the place values in the binary system are used to create a sum of numbers that equal the value of the decimal number being converted. Start with the largest binary place value and subtract from the decimal number. Continue this process until all of the binary digits are determined. 7 = 0111 in binary.

8380. Find the square root of 1,746.

A—41.7852
B—41.7752
C—40.7742

The square root of a number is the number that, when multiplied by itself, gives the number.

By using an electronic calculator, we find that the square root of 1,746 is 41.785165.

8381. (Refer to Figure 52.) Solve the equation.

A—115
B—4.472
C—5

$$(\sqrt{(-4)^0+6+(\sqrt[4]{1296})(\sqrt{3})^2}=$$

Figure 52. Equation

To solve this equation, follow these steps: clear all of the parentheses, perform the multiplication, then the addition. Finally take the square root of the number you have just obtained.

Any number raised to the zero power is 1.

$(-4)^0 = 1$

The fourth root of 1,296 is the same as 1,296 raised to the 1/4 power.

$1{,}296^{0.25} = 6$

The square of the square root of 3 = 3

$$\sqrt{(-4)^0 + 6 + (\sqrt[4]{1296})(\sqrt{3})^2}$$
$$= \sqrt{1 + 6 + (6)(3)}$$
$$= \sqrt{1 + 6 + 18}$$
$$= \sqrt{25}$$
$$= 5$$

8382. Find the square root of 3722.1835.

A—61.00971
B—61.00
C—61.0097

The square root of a number is the number that, when multiplied by itself, gives the number.

By using an electronic calculator, we find that the square root of 3,722.1835 is 61.00970005.

Answers

8379 [C] (044,053) AMT-G Ch 2
8379-1 [A] (031) AMT-G Ch 4
8379-2 [B] (031) AMT-G Ch 2
8379-3 [A] (031) AMT-G Ch 2
8380 [A] (044,053) AMT-G Ch 2
8381 [C] (044,053) AMT-G Ch 2
8382 [C] (044,053) AMT-G Ch 2

8383. Which of the following is equal to the square root of (-1776) ÷ (-2) – 632?

A—128
B—256
C—16

Solve this problem in three steps:

1. *Divide -1776 by -2: -1776 ÷ -2 = 888*
2. *Subtract 632 from 888: 888 – 632 = 256*
3. *Find the square root of 256:*

8383-1. (Refer to Figure 69.) Solve the equation.

A—12
B—60
C—76

$$(\sqrt{100} + \sqrt{36} - \sqrt{16}) =$$

Figure 69. Equation

The square root of 100 is 10.

The square root of 36 is 6.

The square root of 16 is 4.

10 + 6 – 4 = 12

8384. 64 cubed equals

A—4
B—192
C—262,144

The cube of a number is found by multiplying the number by itself three times.

$64^3 = 64 \times 64 \times 64 = 262{,}144$

8385. Find the value of 10 raised to the negative sixth power.

A—0.000001
B—0.000010
C—0.0001

Ten raised to the negative sixth power (10^{-6}) is equal to 0.000 001.

This negative number is the reciprocal of the positive sixth power of ten. It is found by dividing the number 1 by the sixth power of 10 (1,000,000).

8386. What is the square root of 4 raised to the fifth power?

A—32
B—64
C—20

The square root of four is two.

Two raised to the fifth power is 32.

8387. The number 3.47 × 10 to the negative fourth power is equal to

A—.00347
B—34,700
C—.000347

The value of 3.47×10^{-4} is found by multiplying 3.47 by 1 divided by 10,000 (1×10^4).

$3.47 \times 10^{-4} = 0.000347$

8388. Which alternative answer is equal to 16,300?

A—1.63 × 10 to the fourth power.
B—1.63 × 10 to the negative third power.
C—163 × 10 to the negative second power.

$1.63 \times 10^4 = 16{,}300$

$1.63 \times 10^{-3} = 0.00163$

$163 \times 10^{-2} = 1.63$

8389. Find the square root of 124.9924.

A—111.8 × 10 to the third power.
B—.1118 × 10 to the negative second power.
C—1,118 × 10 to the negative second power.

The square root of 124.9924 is 11.18.

$111.8 \times 10^3 = 111{,}800$

$.1118 \times 10^{-2} = 0.001118$

$1{,}118 \times 10^{-2} = 11.18$

8390. What is the square root of 16 raised to the fourth power?

A—1,024
B—4,096
C—256

The square root of 16 is 4.

4 raised to the fourth power is 256.

Answers
8383 [C] (044,053) AMT-G Ch 2
8383-1 [A] (053) AMT-G Ch 2
8384 [C] (053) AMT-G Ch 2
8385 [A] (044,053) AMT-G Ch 2
8386 [A] (044,053) AMT-G Ch 2
8387 [C] (044,053) AMT-G Ch 2
8388 [A] (044,053) AMT-G Ch 2
8389 [C] (053) AMT-G Ch 2
8390 [C] (044,053) AMT-G Ch 2

8391. (Refer to Figure 53.) Solve the equation.

A—.0297
B—.1680
C—.0419

$$\frac{\sqrt[2]{31} + \sqrt[2]{43}}{(17)^2} =$$

Figure 53. Equation

The square root of 31 is 5.5677.

The square root of 43 is 6.5574.

The square of 17 is 289.

$$\frac{5.5677 + 6.5574}{289} = 0.0419$$

8392. The result of 7 raised to the third power plus the square root of 39 is equal to

A—349.24
B—.34924
C—343.24

7 raised to the third power is 343.

The square root of 39 is 6.245.

The sum of these two numbers is 349.245.

8393. Find the square root of 1,824.

A—42.708 x 10 to the negative second power.
B—.42708.
C—.42708 x 10 to the second power.

The square root of 1,824 is 42.708.

$42.708 \times 10^{-2} = 0.42708$

$.42708 \times 10^{2} = 42.708$

8393-1. (Refer to Figure 65.) Which of the figures is using scientific notation?

A—1.
B—2.
C—both 1 and 2.

1. $3.47 \times 10^{4} = 34{,}700.$
2. $2(4^{10}) = 2{,}097{,}152.$

Figure 65. Scientific notation

Equation 1 uses scientific notation, equation 2 does not. Scientific notation requires 10 to be raised to a power. Four raised to the tenth power does not qualify as scientific notation.

8393-2. (Refer to Figure 70.) Which alternative answer is equal to 5.59?

A—1.
B—2.
C—3.

1. $(\sqrt{31}) + (\sqrt{43}) \div 17^2$
2. $(\sqrt{31}) + \sqrt{43}) \div 17^2$
3. $(\sqrt{31}) + (\sqrt{43}) - 17^2$

Figure 70. Alternative answer

You must follow the order of operations rule:

1. $(\sqrt{31}) + (\sqrt{43}) \div 17^2$
   $(5.56) + (6.56 \div 289)$
   $5.56 + .02 = 5.58$

2. $(\sqrt{31} + \sqrt{43}) \div 17^2$
   $(5.56 + 6.56) \div 289$
   $12.12 \div .04 = 12.16$

3. $(\sqrt{31}) + (\sqrt{43}) - 17^2$
   $5.56 + 6.56 - 289 = -276.88$

Answers
8391 [C] (044,053) AMT-G Ch 2 8392 [A] (044,053) AMT-G Ch 2 8393 [C] (053) AMT-G Ch 2 8393-1 [A] (053) AMT-G Ch 2
8393-2 [A] (053) AMT-G Ch 2

8393-3. (Refer to Figure 67). Solve the equation.

A—5.58.
B—12.16.
C—0.042.

$$\frac{\sqrt{31} + \sqrt{43}}{(17)^2} =$$

Figure 67. Equation

Follow the order of operations rule:

$\sqrt{31} + \sqrt{43} = 5.56 + 6.56 = 12.12$

$12.12 \div 17^2 = 12.12 \div 289 = 0.042$

8393-4. (Refer to Figure 68.) Which results in the largest number?

A—1.
B—2.
C—3.

1. $(4.631)^5$
2. 4.631×10^5
3. 4.631×10^{-5}

Figure 68. Alternative answer

1. *$4.631^5 = 2129.97205201$*
2. *$4.631 \times 10^5 = 4.631 \times 1000 = 463{,}100$*
3. *$4.631 \times 10^{-5} = 4.631 \times 0.00001 = .00004631$*

8394. The total piston displacement in a reciprocating engine is

A—the volume displaced by only one piston during one-half revolution of the crankshaft.
B—the volume displaced by all the pistons during one revolution of the crankshaft.
C—the volume displaced by all the pistons during two revolutions of the crankshaft.

The piston displacement of an engine is the total volume swept by the pistons in one revolution of the crankshaft.

The piston displacement is found by multiplying the area of the piston head by the length of the stroke (this gives the displacement of one cylinder).

Multiply the displacement of one cylinder by the number of cylinders in the engine.

8394-1. What is the surface area of a cube where a side (edge) measures 7.25 inches?

A—381.078 cubic inches.
B—315.375 square inches.
C—52.5625 square inches.

Each surface of the cube is 7.252 = 52.5625 square inches.

A cube has six surfaces so the total surface area is:

$52.5625 \times 6 = 315.375$ square inches.

8395. (Refer to Figure 54.) Compute the area of the trapezoid.

A—52.5 square feet.
B—60 square feet.
C—76.5 square feet.

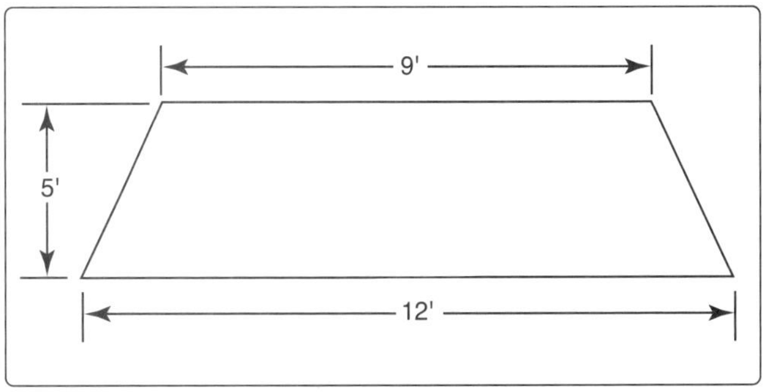

Figure 54. Trapezoid area

The area of a trapezoid is found by multiplying its altitude (5 feet in this problem) by the average length of the two bases (the average of 9 feet and 12 feet is 10.5 feet).

The area of this trapezoid is $5 \times 10.5 = 52.5$ square feet.

Answers
8393-3 [C] (053) AMT-G Ch 2   8393-4 [B] (053) AMT-G Ch 2   8394 [B] (044) AMT-P Ch 2   8394-1 [B] (044,055) AMT-G Ch 2
8395 [A] (044) AMT-G Ch 2

8395-1. (Refer to Figure 71.) What is the volume of a sphere with a radius of 4.5 inches?

A—47.71 cubic inches.
B—381.7 square inches.
C—381.7 cubic inches.

$$V = 1/6\pi D^3$$

Figure 71. Volume of a sphere

$V = (1/6) \times \pi D^3$

$V = (1/6) \times \pi \times 93$

$V = (1/6) \times \pi \times 729$

$V = 381.7$

8396. What size sheet of metal is required to fabricate a cylinder 20 inches long and 8 inches in diameter?

(Note: $C = \pi \times D$)

A—20 inches × 25-5/32 inches.
B—20 inches × 24-9/64 inches.
C—20 inches × 25-9/64 inches.

The sheet metal needed to fabricate a cylinder 20 inches long and 8 inches in diameter is 20 inches long and 25-9/64 inches wide.

$8 \times \pi\ (3.1416) = 25.1328$

25.1328 is slightly less than 9/64.

8397. (Refer to Figure 55.) Find the area of the triangle shown.

A—12 square inches.
B—6 square inches.
C—15 square inches.

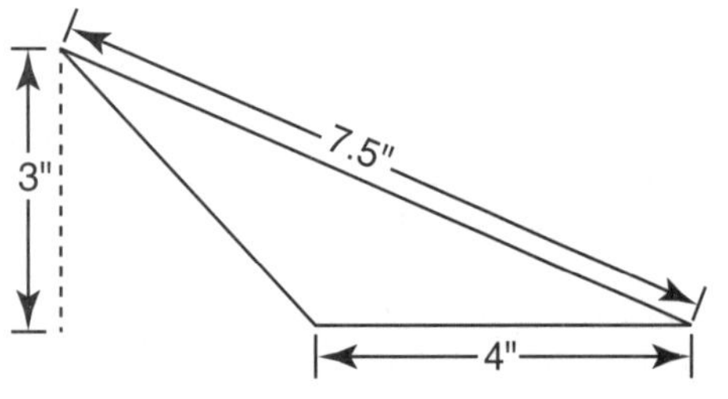

Figure 55. Triangle area

The area of a triangle is one half of the product of its base times its altitude.

The base of this triangle is 4 inches and the altitude is 3 inches. The area is $(4 \times 3) \div 2 = 6$ square inches.

8398. What force is exerted on the piston in a hydraulic cylinder if the area of the piston is 1.2 square inches and the fluid pressure is 850 PSI?

A—1,020 pounds.
B—960 pounds.
C—850 pounds.

The force exerted on a piston by hydraulic fluid is found by multiplying the area of the piston by the amount of pressure acting on each square inch of the piston.

In this problem the area is 1.2 square inches and a pressure of 850 pounds acts on each square inch. The force is 1,020 pounds.

8399. A rectangular-shaped fuel tank measures 60 inches in length, 30 inches in width, and 12 inches in depth. How many cubic feet are within the tank?

A—12.5
B—15.0
C—21.0

The volume of a rectangular solid figure (such as this fuel tank) is found by multiplying its length, width, and depth together.

$$V = L \times W \times D$$
$$= \frac{60}{12} \times \frac{30}{12} \times \frac{12}{12}$$
$$= 5 \times 2.5 \times 1$$
$$= 12.5 \text{ cubic feet}$$

The volume is 12.5 cubic feet.

8400. Select the container size that will be equal in volume to 60 gallons of fuel.

(7.5 gal = 1 cu ft)

A—7.5 cubic feet.
B—8.0 cubic feet.
C—8.5 cubic feet.

Since a one-cubic-foot container will hold 7.5 gallons, an 8-cubic-foot container will hold 60 gallons.

$$\frac{60}{7.5} = 8$$

Answers

8395-1 [C] (044) AMT-G Ch 2	8396 [C] (044) AMT-G Ch 2	8397 [B] (044,055) AMT-G Ch 2	8398 [A] (055) AMT-G Ch 2
8399 [A] (044,055) AMT-G Ch 2	8400 [B] (044,055) AMT-G Ch 2		

8401. (Refer to Figure 56.) Compute the area of the trapezoid.

A—24 square feet.
B—48 square feet.
C—10 square feet.

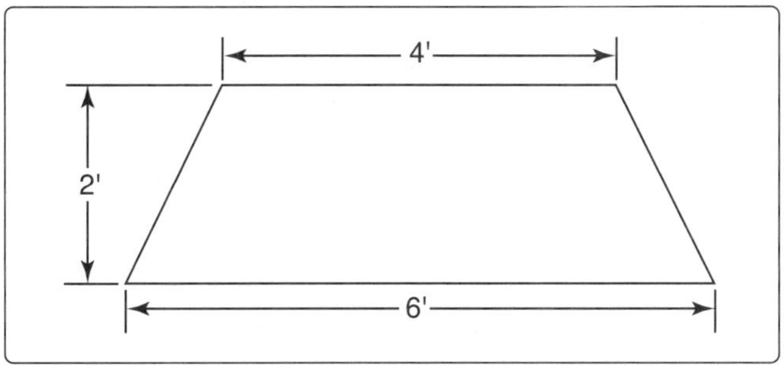

Figure 56. Trapezoid area

The area of a trapezoid is found by multiplying its altitude (2 feet in this problem) by the average length of the two bases (the average of 4 feet and 6 feet is 5 feet).

The area of this trapezoid is 10 square feet.

8402. (Refer to Figure 57.) Determine the area of the triangle formed by points A, B, and C.

A to B = 7.5 inches
A to D = 16.8 inches

A—42 square inches.
B—63 square inches.
C—126 square inches.

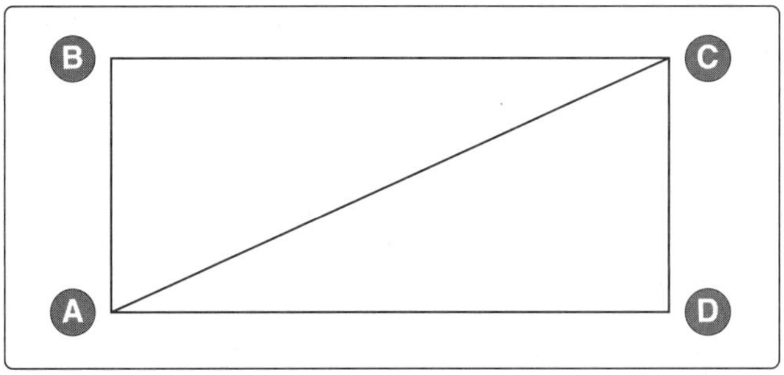

Figure 57. Triangle area

The area of a triangle is equal to one-half the product of its base and its altitude.

In this problem, the base is the distance A to D, which is 16.8 inches (this is the same as the distance B to C).

The altitude is the distance A to B, which is 7.5 inches.

$$\begin{aligned} Area &= \frac{16.8 \times 7.5}{2} \\ &= \frac{126}{2} \\ &= 63 \text{ square inches} \end{aligned}$$

8403. What is the piston displacement of a master cylinder with a 1.5-inch diameter bore and a piston stroke of 4 inches?

A—9.4247 cubic inches.
B—7.0686 cubic inches.
C—6.1541 cubic inches.

The piston displacement of a master cylinder is found by multiplying the area of the piston head by its stroke.

The area of the piston is found by squaring its diameter (1.5 inch in this problem) and multiplying this by the constant 0.7854 (one-fourth of π).

When the area of 1.767 square inches is multiplied by the stroke of 4.0 inches, we find that the displacement of the master cylinder to be 7.0686 cubic inches.

$$\begin{aligned} PD &= 0.7854 \times B^2 \times S \\ &= 0.7854 \times 1.5^2 \times 4 \\ &= 7.0686 \text{ cubic inches} \end{aligned}$$

8404. How many gallons of fuel will be contained in a rectangular-shaped tank which measures 2 feet in width, 3 feet in length, and 1 foot 8 inches in depth?

(7.5 gal = 1 cu ft)

A—66.6
B—75
C—45

The volume of a rectangular solid figure (such as this fuel tank) is found by multiplying its length, width, and depth together.

$$\begin{aligned} V &= L \times W \times D \\ &= 3 \times 2 \times \frac{20}{12} \\ &= 10 \text{ cubic feet} \end{aligned}$$

Since 1 cubic foot of tank space will hold 7.5 gallons, and there are 10 cubic feet of space in the tank, the tank will hold 10 times 7.5 gallons or 75 gallons of fuel.

Answers

8401 [C] (044) AMT-G Ch 2 8402 [B] (044,055) AMT-G Ch 2 8403 [B] (044) AMT-G Ch 2 8404 [B] (044,055) AMT-G Ch 2

8405. A rectangular shaped fuel tank measures 27-1/2 inches in length, 3/4 foot in width, and 8-1/4 inches in depth. How many gallons will the tank contain?

(231 cu in = 1 gal)

A—7.366
B—8.83
C—170.156

The volume of a rectangular solid figure (such as this fuel tank) is found by multiplying its length, width, and depth together. All dimensions must be in the same units. 3/4 foot = 9 inches.

$$V = L \times W \times D$$
$$= 27.5 \times 9 \times 8.25$$
$$= 2{,}041.875 \text{ cubic inches}$$

Since there are 231 cubic inches in each gallon, we must divide the total volume of 2,041.875 by 231 to find the capacity of the tank in gallons.

$$\text{Capacity} = \frac{2041.875}{231}$$
$$= 8.83 \text{ gallons}$$

This tank will hold 8.83 gallons of fuel.

8406. A four-cylinder aircraft engine has a cylinder bore of 3.78 inches and is 8.5 inches deep. With the piston on bottom center, the top of the piston measures 4.0 inches from the bottom of the cylinder. What is the approximate piston displacement of this engine?

A—200 cubic inches.
B—360 cubic inches.
C—235 cubic inches.

The piston displacement of one cylinder of a reciprocating engine is found by multiplying the area of the piston head by the length of the stroke.

The area of the piston is found by squaring the bore (3.78 inches in this problem) and multiplying this by the constant 0.7854 (one-fourth of π).

When the area of 11.22 square inches is multiplied by the stroke of 4.5 inches (the depth of the cylinder minus the distance from the top of the piston at BDC to the bottom of the cylinder), we find that the displacement of one cylinder is 50.49 cubic inches.

This is a four-cylinder engine, so the total displacement is four times that of a single cylinder. The total displacement is 201.96 cubic inches.

$$\text{Area} = \frac{\pi}{4} \times B^2$$
$$= 0.7854 \times 3.78^2$$
$$= 11.22 \text{ square inches}$$
$$\text{Stroke} = 8.5 - 4 = 4.5 \text{ inches}$$
$$PD = \text{Area} \times \text{Stroke} \times \text{Number of cylinders}$$
$$= 11.22 \times 4.5 \times 4$$
$$= 201.96 \text{ cubic inches}$$

8407. A rectangular-shaped fuel tank measures 37-1/2 inches in length, 14 inches in width, and 8-1/4 inches in depth. How many cubic inches are within the tank?

A—59.75
B—433.125
C—4,331.25

The volume of a rectangular solid figure (such as this fuel tank) is found by multiplying its length, width, and depth together.

$$V = L \times W \times D$$
$$= 37.5 \times 14 \times 8.25$$
$$= 4{,}331.25 \text{ cubic inches}$$

8408. A six-cylinder engine with a bore of 3.5 inches, a cylinder height of 7 inches and a stroke of 4.5 inches will have a total piston displacement of

A—256.88 cubic inches.
B—259.77 cubic inches.
C—43.3 cubic inches.

The piston displacement of one cylinder of a reciprocating engine is found by multiplying the area of the piston head by the length of the stroke.

The area of the piston is found by squaring the bore (3.5 inches in this problem) and multiplying this by the constant 0.7854 (one fourth of π).

When the area of 9.621 square inches is multiplied by the stroke of 4.5 inches, we find that the displacement of one cylinder is 43.295 cubic inches.

This is a six-cylinder engine, so the total displacement is six times that of a single cylinder. The total displacement is 259.77 cubic inches.

$$\text{Area} = \frac{\pi}{4} \times B^2$$
$$= 0.7854 \times 3.5^2$$
$$= 9.621 \text{ square inches}$$
$$\text{Stroke} = 4.5 \text{ inches}$$
$$PD = \text{Area} \times \text{Stroke} \times \text{Number of cylinders}$$
$$= 9.621 \times 4.5 \times 6$$
$$= 259.77 \text{ cubic inches}$$

Answers
8405 [B] (044) AMT-G Ch 2
8406 [A] (044) AMT-G Ch 2
8407 [C] (044) AMT-G Ch 2
8408 [B] (044,055) AMT-G Ch 2

8409. Select the fraction which is equal to 0.0250.

A—1/4
B—1/40
C—1/400

1/40 is equal to 0.025.

1/4 is equal to 0.25.

1/400 is equal to 0.0025.

8410. 1.21875 is equal to

A—83/64
B—19/16
C—39/32

Divide the decimal fractional part of this mixed number by the decimal equivalent of 1/64.

$.21875 \div 0.015625 = 14$

The common fraction equivalent to 1.21875 is 1-14/64. This is the same as 78/64 or 39/32.

8411. If the volume of a cylinder with the piston at bottom center is 84 cubic inches and the piston displacement is 70 cubic inches, then the compression ratio is

A—7:1
B—1.2:1
C—6:1

The volume of a cylinder with the piston at the top of its stroke is found by subtracting the piston displacement of the cylinder from the volume of the cylinder with the piston at the bottom of its stroke.

$$\begin{aligned} \text{Volume at top} &= \text{Volume at bottom} - \text{displacement} \\ &= 84 - 70 \\ &= 14 \text{ cubic inches} \end{aligned}$$

The compression ratio of the cylinder is the ratio of the volume of the cylinder with the piston at the bottom of its stroke to the volume of the cylinder with the piston at the top of its stroke.

$$\begin{aligned} C.R. &= \text{Volume at bottom} \div \text{volume at top} \\ &= 84 \div 14 \\ &= 6 \end{aligned}$$

This engine has a compression ratio of 6:1.

8412. Express 7/8 as a percent.

A—8.75 percent.
B—.875 percent.
C—87.5 percent.

To convert 7/8 into a percentage, divide seven by eight and multiply this by 100.

$7 \div 8 = 0.875$

$0.875 \times 100 = 87.5$ *percent*

8413. What is the speed of a spur gear with 42 teeth driven by a pinion gear with 14 teeth turning 420 RPM?

A—588 RPM.
B—160 RPM.
C—140 RPM.

The speed ratio is the reciprocal of gear ratio.

The spur gear with 42 teeth is driven by a pinion gear with 14 teeth. This is a gear ratio of 3:1. The spur gear will turn at 1/3 the speed of the pinion gear.

If the pinion gear turns at a speed of 420 RPM, the spur gear will turn at a speed of

$420 \div 3 = 140$ *RPM.*

8414. An engine develops 108 horsepower at 87 percent power. What horsepower would be developed at 65 percent power?

A—81
B—70
C—61

If an engine develops 108 horsepower at 87 percent power, its 100 percent power is 108 ÷ 0.87 = 124.13 horsepower.

Its horsepower at 65 percent power is found by multiplying 124.13 by 0.65, or 80.68 horsepower.

8415. A certain aircraft bolt has an overall length of 1-1/2 inches, with a shank length of 1-3/16 inches, and a threaded portion length of 5/8 inch. What is the grip length?

A—.5625 inch.
B—.8750 inch.
C—.3125 inch.

The grip length of a bolt is the length of the unthreaded portion of the shank. If the shank is 1-3/16 (1.1875) inches long, and the threaded portion is 5/8 (0.625) inch, the grip length is 1.1875 – 0.625 = 0.5625 inch.

Answers

8409 [B] (053) AMT-G Ch 2	8410 [C] (053) AMT-G Ch 2	8411 [C] (053) AMT-P Ch 2	8412 [C] (053) AMT-G Ch 2
8413 [C] (053) AMT-G Ch 3	8414 [A] (053) AMT-G Ch 2	8415 [A] (053) AMT-G Ch 7	

8416. Select the fractional equivalent for a 0.0625 inch thick sheet of aluminum.

A—1/16
B—3/64
C—1/32

In order to change this decimal fraction into a common fraction, divide the number by the decimal equivalent of 1/64 (0.015625).

0.0625 ÷ 0.015625 = 4/64

This is the same as 1/16 inch.

8416-1. Examples of units used in the conventional (U.S. or English) measurement include

A—inch, meter, and gram.
B—inch, kilo, and liter.
C—inch, ounce, and pound.

Some of the conventional U.S. or English units of measure are: inches, feet, yards, miles, ounces, pints, gallons, and pounds.

8417. Express 5/8 as a percent.

A—.625 percent.
B—6.25 percent.
C—62.5 percent.

To convert 5/8 into a percentage, divide five by eight and multiply this by 100.

5 ÷ 8 = 0.625

0.625 × 100 = 62.5 percent

8418. Select the decimal which is most nearly equal to 77/64.

A—0.08311
B—0.8311
C—1.2031

To convert a common fraction into a decimal fraction, divide the numerator by the denominator.

77 ÷ 64 = 1.203125

8419. An airplane flying a distance of 750 miles used 60 gallons of gasoline. How many gallons will it need to travel 2,500 miles?

A—31,250
B—9,375
C—200

If the airplane uses 60 gallons of gasoline while flying 750 miles, it is getting 750 ÷ 60 or 12.5 miles per gallon of fuel burned.

At this rate of fuel consumption, it will require 2,500 ÷ 12.5 = 200 gallons of fuel to fly 2,500 miles.

8420. What is the speed ratio of an input gear with 36 teeth meshed to a gear with 20 teeth?

A—9:5
B—1:0.56
C—1:1.8

The speed ratio is the reciprocal of the gear ratio.

The large gear has 36 teeth and the small gear has 20 teeth. This is a gear ratio of 1.8:1, or a speed ratio of 1:1.8.

8421. A pinion gear with 14 teeth is driving a spur gear with 42 teeth at 140 RPM. Determine the speed of the pinion gear.

A—588 RPM.
B—420 RPM.
C—126 RPM.

The speed ratio is the reciprocal of the gear ratio.

The spur gear with 42 teeth is driven by a pinion gear of 14 teeth. This is a gear ratio of 3:1. The spur gear will turn at 1/3 the speed of the pinion gear.

If the spur gear turns at a speed of 140 RPM, the pinion gear will have to turn at a speed of 420 RPM.

8422. The parts department's profit is 12 percent on a new part. How much does the part cost if the selling price is $145.60?

A—$128.13
B—$125.60
C—$130.00

In this problem, the cost of the magneto is equal to 100 percent. Since a 12 percent profit is specified, the selling price must be 112 percent.

If the selling price (112%) is equal to $145.60, the cost (100%) can be found by dividing the selling price by 1.12.

$145.60 ÷ 1.12 = $130.00

Answers

8416 [A] (053) AMT-G Ch 2	8416-1 [C] (057) AMT-G Ch 2	8417 [C] (053) AMT-G Ch 2	8418 [C] (053) AMT-G Ch 2
8419 [C] (053) AMT-G Ch 2	8420 [C] (053) AMT-G Ch 3	8421 [B] (053) AMT-G Ch 3	8422 [C] (053) AMT-G Ch 2

8423. If an engine is turning 1,965 rpm at 65 percent power, what is its maximum rpm?

A—2,653
B—3,023
C—3,242

1,965 RPM is 65% of 3,023 RPM.

1,965 ÷ 0.65 = 3,023

8424. An engine of 98 horsepower maximum is running at 75 percent power. What is the horsepower being developed?

A—87.00
B—33.30
C—73.50

Seventy-five percent of 98 horsepower is equal to

98 x 0.75 = 73.50 horsepower.

8425. A blueprint shows a hole of 0.17187 to be drilled. Which fraction size drill bit is most nearly equal?

A—11/64
B—9/32
C—11/32

The hole specified on the blueprint has a diameter of 0.17187 inch. It could be drilled with a 11/64 drill.

11/64 is equal to 0.171875.

9/32 is equal to 0.28125.

11/32 is equal to 0.34375.

8426. Which decimal is most nearly equal to a bend radius of 31/64?

A—0.2065
B—0.4844
C—0.3164

To convert the common fraction 31/64 into a decimal fraction, divide the numerator, 31, by the denominator, 64.

31 ÷ 64 = 0.484375

8427. Sixty-five engines are what percent of 80 engines?

A—81 percent.
B—65 percent.
C—52 percent.

To find the percentage of engines represented by 65 out of 80, we find the ratio of 65 to 80 by dividing 65 by 80.

65 ÷ 80 = 0.8125

Then we change this decimal fraction into a percentage by multiplying it by 100. Sixty-five engines is 81.25 percent of 80 engines.

8428. The radius of a piece of round stock is 7/32. Select the decimal which is most nearly equal to the diameter.

A—0.2187
B—0.4375
C—0.3531

The diameter of the stock is two times the radius.

We need to find the decimal equivalent of 2 x 7/32, or 7/16 inch.

By dividing the numerator by the denominator, we find that we will need a piece of round stock with a diameter of 0.4375 inch.

8429. Maximum life for a certain part is 1100 hours. Recently, 15 of these parts were removed from different aircraft with an average life of 835.3 hours. What percent of the maximum part life has been achieved?

A—75.9 percent.
B—76.9 percent.
C—75.0 percent.

In this problem, 1100 hours represents 100 percent of the life of the part. The percentage represented by 835.3 hours can be found by dividing 835.3 by 1100, and multiplying this answer by 100.

835.3 ÷ 1100 = 0.759

0.759 x 100 = 75.9 percent

8430. What is the ratio of 10 feet to 30 inches?

A—4:1
B—1:3
C—3:1

Ten feet is equal to 120 inches. The ratio of 120 ÷ 30 is 4:1.

Answers

8423 [B] (053) AMT-G Ch 2	8424 [C] (053) AMT-G Ch 2	8425 [A] (053) AMT-G Ch 2	8426 [B] (053) AMT-G Ch 2
8427 [A] (053) AMT-G Ch 2	8428 [B] (053) AMT-G Ch 2	8429 [A] (053) AMT-G Ch 2	8430 [A] (053) AMT-G Ch 2

8431. How much current does a 30-volt, 1/2 horsepower motor that is 85 percent efficient draw from the bus?

(Note: 1 horsepower = 746 watts)

A—14.6 amperes.
B—12.4 amperes.
C—14.3 amperes.

The motor produces one-half horsepower (373 watts) at 100 percent efficiency, but it is only 85 percent efficient. 373 ÷ 0.85 = 438.8 watts of power used by the motor.

Current drawn by the motor is found by dividing the power by the voltage:

$I = P \div E$

$I = 438.8 \div 30$

$I = 14.62$ *amps*

8432. Solve the equation.

[(4 × -3)+(-9 × 2)] ÷ 2 =

A—-30
B—-15
C—-5

In a problem of this type, work from the inside outward:

1. *First solve the parts of the problem inside the parentheses.*

   $4 \times -3 = -12$

   $-9 \times 2 = -18$

2. *Now combine the two values just found.*

   $-12 + -18 = -30$

3. *Divide this answer by 2.*

   $-30 \div 2 = -15$

8433. Solve the equation.

(64 × 3/8) ÷ 3/4 =

A—18
B—24
C—32

First work the part of the problem inside the parenthesis, and then do the division.

$64 \times 3/8 = 24$

$24 \div 3/4 = 32$

8434. Solve the equation.

(32 × 3/8) ÷ 1/6 =

A—12
B—2
C—72

1. *First, work the part of the problem inside the parenthesis:*

   $(32 \times 3/8) = 12$

2. *Now divide 12 by 1/6. To divide by a fraction, invert the divisor (1/6) and multiply.*

   $12 \div 1/6 = 12 \times 6 = 72$

8435. What is the ratio of a gasoline fuel load of 200 gallons to one of 1,680 pounds?

A—5:7
B—2:3
C—5:42

Gasoline has a nominal weight of 6 pounds per gallon. So, 200 gallons of gasoline will weigh 1,200 pounds. The ratio of a load of 1,200-pound load to one of 1,680 pounds is the ratio of:

1,200 ÷ 1,680 = 0.7142.

The ratio 5:7 is 0.7142.

The ratio of 2:3 is 0.6667.

The ratio of 5:42 is 0.1190.

8436. Solve the equation.

1/2 (-30 + 34) 5 =

A—10
B—95
C—160

First, solve the part of the problem inside the parenthesis, then multiply by 1/2 (divide by 2) and finally multiply by five.

$(-30 + 34) = 4$
$4 \div 2 = 2$
$2 \times 5 = 10$

Answers

8431 [A] (053) AMT-G Ch 4
8432 [B] (053) AMT-G Ch 2
8433 [C] (053) AMT-G Ch 2
8434 [C] (053) AMT-G Ch 2
8435 [A] (053) AMT-G Ch 2
8436 [A] (053) AMT-G Ch 2

8437. (Refer to Figure 58.) Solve the equation.

A—174.85
B—68.037
C—14.002

$$\frac{(-35 + 25)\,(-7) + (\pi)\,(16^{-2})}{\sqrt{25}} =$$

Figure 58. Equation

1. *First, solve the parts of the problem inside parentheses:*

   (-35 + 25) = (-10)

2. *Combine the factors (the parts) of the first term (the part of the problem to the left of the plus sign).*

   (-10) × (-7) = 70

3. *Clear the parenthesis on the right of the plus sign by raising 16 to its $^{-2}$ power.*

   $16^{-2} = 1/16^{2} = 1/256 = 0.003906$

4. *Multiply the two factors of the second term.*

   (3.1416) × (0.003906) = 0.01227

5. *Add the two terms above the line.*

   70 + 0.0122 = 70.0122

6. *Divide this by the square root of 25, which is 5.*

   70.0122 ÷ 5 = 14.002

8438. (Refer to Figure 59.) Solve the equation.

A—+31.25
B—-5.20
C—-31.25

$$\frac{-4\overline{)125}}{-6\overline{)-36}} =$$

Figure 59. Equation

This problem can be rewritten as 125 ÷ -4, divided by -36 ÷ -6.

125 ÷ -4 = -31.25

-36 ÷ -6 = 6

-31.25 ÷ 6 = -5.208

8439. Solve the equation.

4 – 3[-6(2 + 3) + 4] =

A—82
B—-25
C—-71

1. *Begin this problem by working the inside parentheses, and then work outward.*

   (2 + 3) = 5

   (-6 × 5) = -30

   (-30 + 4) = -26

2. *Next, the multiplication is done.*

   3 × -26 = -78

3. *Now, perform the subtraction.*

   4 – (-78) = 82

8440. Solve the equation.

-6[-9(-8 + 4) – 2(7 + 3)] =

A—-332
B—216
C—-96

1. *Begin the problem by working the inside parentheses in the first term.*

   (-8 + 4) = -4

2. *Combine the factors in the first term.*

   -9 × -4 = 36

3. *Clear the parenthesis in the second term.*

   (7 + 3) = 10

4. *Multiply this value by 2.*

   10 × 2 = 20

5. *Combine the two terms in the brackets.*

   36 – 20 = 16

6. *Multiply this by -6.*

   -6 × 16 = -96

Answers

8437 [C] (053) AMT-G Ch 2 8438 [B] (053) AMT-G Ch 2 8439 [A] (053) AMT-G Ch 2 8440 [C] (053) AMT-G Ch 2

8441. Solve the equation.

$(-3 + 2)(-12 - 4) + (-4 + 6) \times 3$

A—20
B—22
C—28

1. *Begin this problem by clearing the parentheses.*
   $(-3 + 2) = -1$
   $(-12 - 4) = -16$
   $(-4 + 6) = 2$
2. *Then perform the multiplication.*
   $-1 \times -16 = 16$
   $2 \times 3 = 6$
3. *And finally the addition.*
   $16 + 6 = 22$

8442. (Refer to Figure 60.) Solve the equation.

A—11.9
B—11.7
C—11.09

$$\frac{(-5+23)(-2)+(3^{-3})(\sqrt{64})}{-27 \div 9} =$$

Figure 60. Equation

1. *Begin this problem by clearing the parentheses.*
   $(-5 + 23) = 18$
   $(3^{-3}) = 0.037$
   $\sqrt{64} = 8$
2. *Perform the multiplication in the numerator.*
   $18 \times -2 = -36$
   $0.037 \times 8 = 0.296$
3. *Perform the addition in the numerator.*
   $-36 + 0.296 = -35.704$
4. *Perform the division in the denominator.*
   $-27 \div 9 = -3$
5. *Divide the numerator by the denominator.*
   $-35.704 \div -3 = 11.90$

8442-1. (Refer to the Figure 66.) Solve the equation.

A—35,998
B—36,002
C—62,208

$$-4 + 6 + 10^3 (\sqrt{1296}) =$$

Figure 66. Equation

$-4 + 6 + 10^3(\sqrt{1296})$ simplifies to: $2 + 1{,}000(36)$, which equals 36,002.

Answers
8441 [B] (053) AMT-G Ch 2 8442 [A] (053) AMT-G Ch 2 8442-1 [B] (053) AMT-G Ch 2

Maintenance Forms and Records

8443. Where is the record of compliance with Airworthiness Directives or manufacturers' service bulletins normally indicated?

A—FAA Form 337.
B—Aircraft maintenance records.
C—Flight manual.

The aircraft maintenance records (generally in the form of logbooks) are the correct place to record compliance with FAA Airworthiness Directives or manufacturer's service bulletins.

8444. If work performed on an aircraft has been done satisfactorily, the signature of an authorized person on the maintenance records for maintenance or alterations performed constitutes

A—approval of the aircraft for return to service.
B—approval for return to service only for the work performed.
C—verification that the maintenance or alterations were performed referencing approved maintenance data.

The signature constitutes the approval for return to service only for the work performed.

8445. During an annual inspection, if a defect is found which makes the aircraft unairworthy, the person disapproving must

A—void the aircraft's Airworthiness Certificate.
B—submit a Malfunction or Defect Report.
C—provide a written notice of the defect to the owner.

If, during an annual inspection, a defect is found which makes the aircraft unairworthy, the person disapproving the aircraft must give the owner a signed and dated written list of the discrepancies that caused the unairworthy condition.

8446. What is the means by which the FAA notifies aircraft owners and other interested persons of unsafe conditions and prescribes the condition under which the product may continue to be operated?

A—Airworthiness Directives.
B—Aviation Maintenance Alerts.
C—Aviation Safety Data.

If a condition is found that causes a particular design of aircraft to fail to meet its certification for airworthiness, the FAA can issue an AD.

An AD describes the conditions that must be met to allow the aircraft to continue to be operated.

8447. Which is an appliance major repair?

A—Overhaul of a hydraulic pressure pump.
B—Repairs to a propeller governor or its control.
C—Troubleshooting and repairing broken circuits in landing light circuits.

Overhaul of pressure-type carburetors and pressure-type fuel, oil, and hydraulic pumps are examples of appliance major repairs.

8448. Where should you find this entry?

"Removed right wing from aircraft and removed skin from outer 6 feet. Repaired buckled spar 49 inches from tip in accordance with figure 8 in the manufacturer's structural repair manual No. 28-1."

A—Aircraft engine maintenance record.
B—Aircraft minor repair and alteration record.
C—FAA Form 337.

The description of the repair, as is shown here, would be made on FAA Form 337 (Major Repair and Alteration Form).

This form must be completed when an airframe, engine, propeller, or appliance has been subjected to a major repair or major alteration.

8449. Which maintenance action is an airframe major repair?

A—Changes to the wing or to fixed or movable control surfaces which affect flutter and vibration characteristics.
B—Rewinding the field coil of an electrical accessory.
C—The repair of portions of skin sheets by making additional seams.

According to the list of major alterations, major repairs and preventive maintenance listed in 14 CFR Part 43, Appendix A, the repair of portions of skin sheets by making additional seams is considered to be an airframe major repair.

Neither of the other alternatives listed here is an airframe major repair.

Answers

8443 [B] (076) AMT-G Ch 13	8444 [B] (086) §43.9	8445 [C] (086) §43.11	8446 [A] (048) AMT-G Ch 11
8447 [A] (023) 14 CFR 43 App A	8448 [C] (076) FAA-G-8082-11	8449 [C] (023) 14 CFR 43	

8450. Which aircraft record entry is the best description of the replacement of several damaged heli-coils in a casting?

A—Eight 1/4—20 inch standard heli-coils were replaced. The damaged inserts were extracted, the tapped holes gaged, then new inserts installed, and tangs removed.
B—Eight 1/4—20 inch standard heli-coils were installed in place of damaged ones.
C—Eight 1/4—20 inch standard heli-coil inserts were repaired by replacing the damaged inserts with a lock-type insert, after the tapped holes were checked for corrosion.

Heli-coils are patented, precision-formed screw-thread coils of 18-8 stainless steel wire having a diamond-shaped cross section.

Heli-coil inserts are replaced by extracting the damaged insert with a special extracting tool, gaging the holes with a Heli-coil thread gage, installing the new insert using the proper inserting tool and finally, breaking off the tang with the proper break-off tool.

8451. Which maintenance record entry best describes the action taken for a control cable showing approximately 20 percent wear on several of the individual outer wires at a fairlead?

A—Wear within acceptable limits, repair not necessary.
B—Removed and replaced the control cable and rerigged the system.
C—Cable repositioned, worn area moved away from fairlead.

Flexible and extra-flexible control cable should be replaced when the individual wires in each strand appear to blend together (outer wires worn 40 to 50 percent).

Since these wires are only worn 20 percent, the wear is within acceptable limits and repair is not necessary.

8452. Which maintenance record entry best describes the action taken for a .125-inch deep dent in a straight section of 1/2-inch aluminum alloy tubing?

A—Dented section removed and replaced with identical new tubing flared to 45°.
B—Dent within acceptable limits, repair not necessary.
C—Dented section removed and replaced with identical new tubing flared to 37°.

The dent is in a straight portion of the tube and is deep enough to warrant its removal. A dent of up to 0.1 inch (20 percent of the tube diameter) deep would be acceptable and would not have to be removed.

The dented section would have to be removed and replaced with identical new tubing flared to 37°.

8452-1. Which statement is true regarding the requirements for maintenance record format?

A—Any format that provides record continuity and includes the required information may be used.
B—The format provided by the manufacturer of the aircraft must be retained.
C—Any desired change from manufacturer provided format requires approval from the Federal Aviation Administration.

AC 43-9 paragraph 5.b. states that maintenance records may be kept in any format that provides record continuity, includes required contents, lends itself to the addition of new entries, provides for signature entry, and is intelligible.

8452-2. When a 100-hour inspection is completed, if separate maintenance records for the airframe, powerplant(s), and propeller(s) are maintained, where is the entry for the inspection recorded?

A—In each record.
B—In the airframe record only.
C—In any one of the records.

AC 43-9 paragraph 10.d. states that if the owner maintains separate records for the airframe, powerplants, and propellers, the entry for the 100-hour inspection is entered in each, while the annual inspection is only required to be entered into the airframe record.

8452-3. For aircraft operated under Part 91, when is aircraft total time required to be recorded in aircraft maintenance records?

A—After satisfactorily completing maintenance, preventive maintenance, rebuilding, and alteration (excluding inspections).
B—After satisfactorily completing inspections.
C—After satisfactorily completing airframe, component, or propeller maintenance.

14 CFR §43.11 states that the person approving for return to service an aircraft, airframe, aircraft engine, propeller, appliance, or component part after any inspection performed in accordance with Part 91...shall make an entry in the maintenance record of that equipment containing the following information...(2) The date of the inspection and aircraft total time in service.

Answers

8450 [A] (076) AMT-G Ch 13	8451 [A] (076) AC 43.13-1	8452 [C] (019) AMT-G Ch 13	8452-1 [A] (022) AC 43-9
8452-2 [A] (022) AC 43-9	8452-3 [B] (076) §43.11(a)(2)		

8452-4. For aircraft operated under Part 91, what difference is there, if any, between the record entry requirements for maintenance (e.g., repair or alteration) and the record entry requirements for inspections (beyond the description of the work performed and the type and extent of inspection)?

A—There is no difference.
B—Aircraft total time is required to be included only in the maintenance entry.
C—Aircraft total time is required to be included only in the inspection entry.

14 CFR §43.11 states that the person approving for return to service an aircraft, airframe, aircraft engine, propeller, appliance, or component part after any inspection performed in accordance with Part 91...shall make an entry in the maintenance record of that equipment containing the following information...(2) The date of the inspection and aircraft total time in service.

Records specified in 14 CFR §43.9 do not require the recording of the aircraft total time.

8452-5. If more space is needed for a work description entered on FAA Form 337, what information should be included on the attached sheet(s), in addition to the rest of the work description?

A—Make, model, and serial number of the aircraft.
B—Aircraft nationality and registration mark, and the date the work was accomplished.
C—Name, date, and office designator of the FAA inspector from the supervising office.

AC 43.9-1F paragraph 6.h.(3) states that if additional space is needed to describe the repair or alteration, attach sheets bearing the aircraft nationality and registration mark and the date the work was completed.

8452-6. A person installing a product, part, or appliance on a type certificated product must make certain that the item's records document the

A—product, part, or material meets FAA airworthiness standards.
B—source from which the part came.
C—product or material was not produced under an FAA production approval.

Any product, part, or material installed on a type certificate product must meet FAA airworthiness standards.

8453. Which aircraft record entry best describes a repair of a dent in a tubular steel structure dented at a cluster?

A—Removed and replaced the damaged member.
B—Welded a reinforcing plate over the dented area.
C—Filled the damaged area with a molten metal and dressed to the original contour.

If an aircraft welded-steel tubular structure is dented at a cluster, a patch plate of the same material and as thick as the thickest member of the cluster is cut and welded over the dented area.

8454. Who is responsible for making the entry in the maintenance records after an annual, 100-hour, or progressive inspection?

A—The owner or operator of the aircraft.
B—The person approving or disapproving for return to service.
C—The designee or inspector representing the FAA Administrator.

According to 14 CFR §43.11(a): "The person approving or disapproving for return to service an aircraft, airframe, aircraft engine, propeller, or appliance after any annual, 100-hour, or progressive inspection required by Part 91 shall make an entry in the maintenance record of that equipment..."

8454-1. For aircraft operated under Part 91, which of the following records must be retained for at least one year, or until the work is repeated or superseded?

A—Records of time since overhaul of items requiring overhaul on a time specified basis.
B—Records of maintenance, alterations, preventive maintenance, 100-hour, annual, and progressive inspections.
C—Records of the current inspection status of the aircraft, including time since last required inspection.

14 CFR §91.417 states that records of the maintenance, preventive maintenance, and alteration and records of the 100-hour, annual, progressive, and other required or approved inspections, as appropriate for each aircraft (including the airframe) and each engine, propeller, rotor, and appliance of an aircraft must include the total time in service of the airframe, each engine, each propeller, and each rotor, and shall be retained until the work is repeated or superseded by other work or for 1 year after the work is performed.

Answers
8452-4 [C] (022,076) §43.9, 43.11
8452-5 [B] (022,023) AC 43.9-1F
8452-6 [A] (063) AMT-G Ch 11
8453 [B] (076) AC 43.13-1
8454 [B] (076) §43.11
8454-1 [B] (076) §91.417

8454-2. A certificated mechanic without an inspection authorization who signs the appropriate block on FAA Form 337 is doing what?

A—Certifying that the work was done in accordance with the requirements of 14 CFR Part 43.
B—Approving the work for return to service.
C—Certifying the maintenance information used as FAA-approved data.

When a certificated mechanic without an inspection authorization signs the conformity statement in item 6 of the FAA Form 337, he or she is certifying that the repair and/or alteration made to the unit(s) identified in item 4 and described on the reverse or attachments hereto have been made in accordance with the requirements of 14 CFR Part 43 and that the information furnished herein is true and correct to the best of his or her knowledge.

8454-3. For aircraft operated under Part 91, which of the following records must be retained and transferred with the aircraft when it is sold?

A—Records of maintenance, alterations, preventive maintenance, 100-hour, annual, and progressive inspections.
B—Records of inspections performed in accordance with 14 CFR Part 43, Appendix D.
C—Records of the current status of applicable ADs, and date and time when recurring ADs are next due.

14 CFR §91.417 (a) and (b) state that among the records that must be retained and transferred with the aircraft when it is sold is the current status of the applicable ADs including for each the method of compliance, the AD number, and revision date; also, if the AD involves recurring action, the time and date when the next action is required.

8455. An aircraft owner was provided a list of discrepancies on an aircraft that was not approved for return to service after an annual inspection. Which of the following statements is/are true concerning who may correct the discrepancies?

1. Only a mechanic with an inspection authorization.
2. An appropriately rated mechanic.
3. Any certificated repair station.

A—2 and 3.
B—2.
C—1.

If an aircraft was not approved for return to service after an annual inspection, a list of discrepancies that prevented the aircraft from being airworthy is given to the aircraft owner or operator. These discrepancies may be corrected by an appropriately rated mechanic and the aircraft approved for return to service.

8455-1. When a discrepancy list is provided to an aircraft owner or operator after an inspection, it says in effect that

A—the item inspected is unairworthy.
B—except for these discrepancies, the item inspected is airworthy.
C—the item inspected may or may not be airworthy depending on the discrepancies found.

AC 43-9C paragraph 11.b. states that when a discrepancy list is provided to an owner or operator, it says in effect, that except for these discrepancies, the item inspected is airworthy.

8455-2. In order to reconstruct lost or destroyed aircraft maintenance records, what is it necessary to establish?

A—Dates of all maintenance, preventive maintenance and alterations.
B—Dates and/or times of all 100-hour, annual, or progressive inspections.
C—Total time-in-service of the airframe.

AC 43-9C paragraph 12 states that in order to reconstruct lost or destroyed maintenance records, it is necessary to establish the total time-in-service of the airframe.

Answers

8454-2 [A] (082) AMT-G Ch 13
8454-3 [C] (022) AMT-G Ch 13
8455 [B] (022) §43.3(b)
8455-1 [B] (022) AC 43-9C
8455-2 [C] (022) AC 43-9C

8456. When approving for return to service after maintenance or alteration, the approving person must enter in the maintenance record of the aircraft

A—the date the maintenance or alteration was begun, a description (or reference to acceptable data) of work performed, the name of the person performing the work (if someone else), signature, and certificate number.
B—a description (or reference to acceptable data) of work performed, date of completion, the name of the person performing the work (if someone else), signature, and certificate number.
C—a description (or reference to acceptable data) of work performed, date of completion, the name of the person performing the work (if someone else), signature, certificate number, and kind of certificate held.

A maintenance record entry that is made after maintenance or alteration must contain the following:

1. *A description (or reference to data acceptable to the Administrator) of the work performed;*
2. *The date of completion of the work performed;*
3. *The name of the person performing the work if other than the person approving the work for return to service; and*
4. *The signature, certificate number, and kind of certificate held by the person approving the work for return to service.*

8457. What is/are the appropriate action(s) concerning minor repairs performed on a certificated aircraft?

1. FAA Form 337 must be completed.
2. Entries must be made in the aircraft's maintenance record.
3. The owner of the aircraft must submit a record of all minor repairs to the FAA at least annually.

A—2.
B—2 and 3.
C—1 and 2.

When a minor repair is performed on a certificated aircraft, an entry must be made in the aircraft permanent records.

8457-1. When work is performed on an aircraft that necessitates the use of FAA Form 337, who should prepare the form?

A—The person who performs or supervises the work.
B—The person who approves for return to service.
C—Either the person who approves for return to service, or the aircraft owner or operator.

AC 43.9-1F paragraph 6 states that the person who performs or supervises a major repair or major alteration should prepare the FAA Form 337.

8457-2. What is the status of data used as a basis for approving major repairs or alterations for return to service?

A—Data must be least FAA-acceptable when it is used for that purpose.
B—Data must be FAA-approved prior to its use for that purpose.
C—Data may be FAA-approved after its use for that purpose.

AC 43.9-1F paragraph 6.h.(2) states that data used as a basis for approving major repairs or alterations for return to service must be FAA-approved prior to its use for that purpose.

8457-3. Which statement is true regarding the use of FAA Form 337?

A—FAA Form 337 is authorized for use with both U.S. and foreign registered aircraft.
B—FAA Form 337 is authorized for use with U.S. registered aircraft, and foreign registered aircraft when located in the United States.
C—FAA Form 337 is not authorized for use with other than U.S. registered aircraft.

AC 43.9-1F paragraph 7.d. states that FAA Form 337 is not authorized for use on other than U.S.-registered aircraft.

Answers
8456 [C] (086) §43.9
8457 [A] (076) AMT-G Ch 13
8457-1 [A] (028) AC 43.9-1F
8457-2 [B] (028) AC 43.9-1F
8457-3 [C] (028) AC 43.9-1F

8458. After making a certain repair to an aircraft engine that is to be returned to service, an FAA Form 337 is prepared. How many copies are required and what is the disposition of the completed forms?

A—Two; one copy for the aircraft owner and one copy for the FAA.
B—Two; one copy for the FAA and one copy for the permanent records of the repairing agency or individual.
C—Three; one copy for the aircraft owner, one copy for the FAA, and one copy for the permanent records of the repairing agency or individual.

When a major repair or a major alteration has been made to any equipment that requires an FAA Form 337, the form must be prepared in duplicate.

The original goes to the aircraft owner to be kept with the aircraft records. The copy is forwarded to the local FAA office within 48 hours after the aircraft is approved for return to service.

8459. Who is responsible for upkeep of the required maintenance records for an aircraft?

A—The maintaining repair station or authorized inspector.
B—The maintaining certificated mechanic.
C—The aircraft owner.

According to 14 CFR §91.417, the aircraft owner or operator is responsible for "ensuring that maintenance personnel make appropriate entries in the aircraft and maintenance records indicating the aircraft has been approved for return to service."

8460. An aircraft was not approved for return to service after an annual inspection and the owner wanted to fly the aircraft to another maintenance base. Which statement is correct?

A—The owner must obtain a special flight permit.
B—The owner may fly without restriction up to 10 hours.
C—The owner may fly in the restricted category up to 10 hours.

If an aircraft fails to pass an annual inspection but is considered by the technician conducting the inspection to be safe for flight, it may be issued a special flight authorization under the provision of 14 CFR §21.197(a)(1), to allow the aircraft to be flown to another maintenance base where the required maintenance can be performed.

8461. Each person performing an annual or 100-hour inspection shall use a checklist that contains at least those items in the appendix of

A—14 CFR Part 43.
B—14 CFR Part 65.
C—AC 43.13-3.

All 100-hour and annual inspections must be conducted with the use of a checklist.

14 CFR Part 43, Appendix D, lists the basic areas that must be included on the inspection checklist.

8462. An FAA Form 337 is used to record and document

A—preventive and unscheduled maintenance, and special inspections.
B—major and minor repairs, and major and minor alterations.
C—major repairs and major alterations.

FAA Form 337 is used to describe any major repairs or major alterations that have been made to an airframe, powerplant, propeller, or appliance.

8463. After a mechanic holding an airframe and powerplant rating completes a 100-hour inspection, what action is required before the aircraft is returned to service?

A—Make the proper entries in the aircraft's maintenance record.
B—An operational check of all systems.
C—A mechanic with an inspection authorization must approve the inspection.

After a mechanic holding the appropriate ratings completes a 100-hour inspection of an aircraft, the appropriate entries must be made in the aircraft maintenance records before the aircraft can be returned to service.

8464. Which of the following may a certificated airframe and powerplant mechanic perform on aircraft and approve for return to service?

1. A 100-hour inspection.
2. An annual inspection, under specified circumstances.
3. A progressive inspection, under specified circumstances.

A—1, 2.
B—1, 3.
C—1, 2, and 3.

Answers

8458 [A] (022,023) 14 CFR 43
8459 [C] (022) §91.417
8460 [A] (077) §21.197
8461 [A] (059) §43.15(c)
8462 [C] (023) 14 CFR 43
8463 [A] (086) §43.9
8464 [B] (086) §65.85, 65.87 & 43.15(d)(2)

According to 14 CFR §§65.85 and 65.87, a certificated mechanic with airframe and powerplant ratings may perform a 100-hour inspection on an airframe and powerplant and approve the aircraft for return for service.

An inspection authorization is required to conduct an annual and a progressive inspection and approve the aircraft for return to service. The exception to this is found in 14 CFR §43.15(d)(2) which states, regarding a progressive inspection, "If the aircraft is away from the station where inspections are normally conducted, an appropriately rated mechanic, a certificated repair station, or the manufacturer of the aircraft may perform inspections in accordance with the procedures and using the forms of the person who would otherwise perform the inspection."

8464-1. What is ATA iSpec 2200?

A—Standardized electronic documentation for aircraft models.
B—Fuel specifications for transport-category airplanes.
C—Airline transport catalog for aircraft parts.

ATA iSpec 2200 is a compilation of what used to be ATA Spec 100 and ATA Spec 2100. This ATA iSpec 2200 standardizes the format in which maintenance information is presented in aircraft maintenance manuals, and makes it available in electronic format.

Basic Physics

8465. If a double-acting actuating cylinder in a 3,000 psi system has a piston with a surface area of three square inches on the extension side, and a rod with a cross-section area of one square inch attached to the piston on the other side, approximately how much force will the actuator be able to produce when retracting?

A—9,000 pounds.
B—6,000 pounds.
C—3,000 pounds.

The force a hydraulic actuator can exert is determined by the area of the piston and the pressure of the fluid acting on the piston.

The effective area on the retracting side of the piston is two square inches.

2 sq. in. × 3,000 psi = 6,000 pounds of force

8466. The boiling point of a given liquid varies

A—directly with pressure.
B—inversely with pressure.
C—directly with density.

The boiling point of a liquid varies directly with the pressure above the liquid. The greater the pressure, the higher the boiling point.

8467. Which of the following is NOT considered a method of heat transfer?

A—Convection.
B—Conduction.
C—Diffusion.

Heat can be transferred from a body having a high level of heat energy to a body having a lower level of heat energy by three methods: conduction (actual physical contact), convection (transfer through vertical currents), and radiation (transfer by electromagnetic waves).

Diffusion is not a method of heat transfer.

8468. An engine that weighs 350 pounds is removed from an aircraft by means of a mobile hoist. The engine is raised 3 feet above its attachment mount, and the entire assembly is then moved forward 12 feet. A constant force of 70 pounds is required to move the loaded hoist. What is the total work input required to move the hoist?

A—840 foot-pounds.
B—1,890 foot-pounds.
C—1,050 foot-pounds.

More information is given with this problem than is needed; therefore, it can cause confusion. The only work asked for is the amount needed to move the hoist.

The hoist is moved for a distance of 12 feet and a constant force of 70 pounds is needed to move it.

The work done to move the hoist is 12 × 70 = 840 foot-pounds.

8469. Which condition is the actual amount of water vapor in a mixture of air and water?

A—Relative humidity.
B—Dewpoint.
C—Absolute humidity.

Absolute humidity is the actual amount of water in a volume of air, and it is measured in such units as grams per cubic meter.

Answers

8464-1 [A] (086) FAA-H-8083-30
8465 [B] (027) AMT-G Ch 3
8466 [A] (027) AMT-G Ch 3
8467 [C] (027) AMT-G Ch 3
8468 [A] (027) AMT-G Ch 3
8469 [C] (027) AMT-G

8470. Under which conditions will the rate of flow of a liquid through a metering orifice (or jet) be the greatest (all other factors being equal)?

A—Unmetered pressure, 18 psi; metered pressure, 17.5 psi; atmospheric pressure, 14.5 psi.
B—Unmetered pressure, 23 psi; metered pressure, 12 psi; atmospheric pressure, 14.3 psi.
C—Unmetered pressure, 17 PSI; metered pressure, 5 psi; atmospheric pressure, 14.7 psi.

In answering this question, we must recognize that the atmospheric pressure acts equally on both sides of the metering jet and therefore does not enter into the problem. The metering jet with the greatest pressure differential across it will have the greatest rate of flow through it.

Jet A has a pressure differential of 0.5 psi differential.

Jet B has a pressure differential of 11 psi differential.

Jet C has a pressure differential of 12 psi differential.

8471. (Refer to Figure 61.) The amount of force applied to rope A to lift the weight is

A—12 pounds.
B—15 pounds.
C—20 pounds.

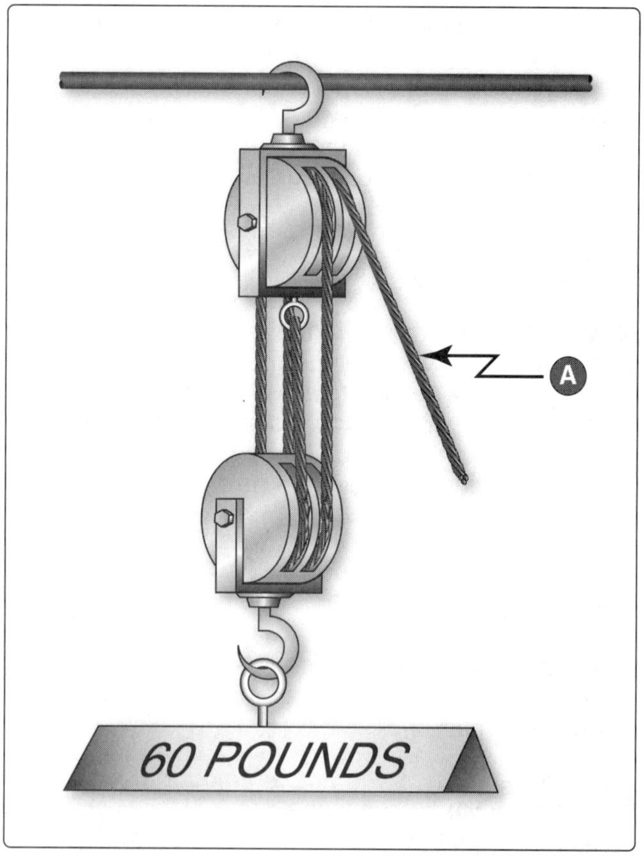

Figure 61. Physics

This block and tackle supports the weight with four ropes, and this gives it a mechanical advantage of four.

To lift a 60-pound weight, a force of 15 pounds must be exerted on rope A.

Rope A will have to be pulled four times the distance the weight is lifted.

8472. Which will weigh the least?

A—98 parts of dry air and 2 parts of water vapor.
B—35 parts of dry air and 65 parts of water vapor.
C—50 parts of dry air and 50 parts of water vapor.

Water vapor is only about 5/8 as heavy as an equal volume of dry air. The more water vapor in the air, the less the air weighs.

In choice A there is 2 percent water vapor.

In choice B there is 65 percent water vapor.

In choice C there is 50 percent water vapor.

8473. Which is the ratio of the water vapor actually present in the atmosphere to the amount that would be present if the air were saturated at the prevailing temperature and pressure?

A—Absolute humidity.
B—Relative humidity.
C—Dewpoint.

Relative humidity is the ratio of the amount of water vapor actually present in the atmosphere to the amount that would be present if the air were saturated at the prevailing temperature and pressure.

8474. The speed of sound in the atmosphere

A—varies according to the frequency of the sound.
B—changes with a change in temperature.
C—changes with a change in pressure.

The speed of sound in the atmosphere varies with the temperature of the atmosphere.

8474-1. The speed of sound in the atmosphere is most affected by variations in which of the following?

A—Sound frequency.
B—Ambient temperature.
C—Barometric pressure.

The speed of sound in the atmosphere varies with the ambient temperature of the atmosphere.

Answers

8470 [C] (027) AMT-G Ch 3
8471 [B] (027) AMT-G Ch 3
8472 [B] (008) AMT-G Ch 3
8473 [B] (008) AMT-G
8474 [B] (008) AMT-G Ch 3
8474-1 [B] (007) AMT-G Ch 3

8475. If the volume of a confined gas is doubled (without the addition of more gas), the pressure will (assume the temperature remains constant)

A—increase in direct proportion to the volume increase.
B—remain the same.
C—be reduced to one-half its original value.

The pressure of a gas in an enclosed container varies inversely as the volume of the container, if the absolute temperature of the gas remains constant.

Doubling the volume of the container will decrease the pressure of the enclosed gas to a value of one-half its original pressure.

8476. If the temperature of a confined liquid is held constant and its pressure is tripled, the volume will

A—triple.
B—be reduced to one-third its original volume.
C—remain the same.

A liquid is considered to be a noncompressible fluid. Its volume changes with a change in its temperature but it remains relatively constant as its pressure changes.

If the pressure on a confined liquid is tripled, the volume of the liquid will remain virtually the same.

8477. How much work input is required to lower (not drop) a 120-pound weight from the top of a 3-foot table to the floor?

A—120 pounds of force.
B—360 foot-pounds.
C—40 foot-pounds.

Work is the product of the amount of force applied to an object times the distance through which the force causes the object to move.

As much force is needed to hold back an object when it is being lowered as it does to raise the object.

If 120 pounds of force is needed to hold back a weight as it is lowered for 3 feet, 360 foot-pounds of work has been done.

8478. Which atmospheric conditions will cause the true landing speed of an aircraft to be the greatest?

A—Low temperature with low humidity.
B—High temperature with low humidity.
C—High temperature with high humidity.

The true landing speed of an aircraft is determined by the density of the air.

The amount of aerodynamic lift produced by the wing of an airplane or the rotor of a helicopter is determined by several things. Among these are the shape of the airfoil, the speed of the airfoil through the air, and the density of the air. The denser the air, the lower the speed that will produce the same amount of lift.

Density of the air depends upon both its temperature and its humidity. The hotter the air, the less dense. The more water vapor in the air (the higher its humidity), the less dense the air.

An airplane will have to fly the fastest to produce the required lift under conditions of high temperature and high humidity.

8479. If the fluid pressure is 800 PSI in a 1/2-inch line supplying an actuating cylinder with a piston area of 10 square inches, the force exerted on the piston will be

A—4,000 pounds.
B—8,000 pounds.
C—800 pounds.

The size of the line that supplies fluid to an actuating cylinder has nothing to do with the amount of force the piston in the cylinder can exert.

When a pressure of 800 psi acts on a piston with an area of 10 square inches, a force of 800 × 10 = 8,000 pounds is produced.

8480. In physics, which of the following factors are necessary to determine power?

A—Force exerted, distance moved, and work.
B—Distance moved and time required.
C—Force exerted, distance moved, and time required.

Power is the time rate of doing work.

In order to determine the amount of work done, we must know the amount of force used and the distance through which this force acted. Force times distance is equal to work.

The amount of power needed is found by dividing the amount of work done by the time used in doing the work.

To find the amount of power needed to do a job, we must know the force, the distance, and the time.

Answers

8475 [C] (027) AMT-G Ch 3	8476 [C] (027) AMT-G Ch 3	8477 [B] (099) AMT-G Ch 3	8478 [C] (099) AMT-G
8479 [B] (099) AMT-G Ch 3	8480 [C] (099) AMT-G Ch 3		

8481. What force must be applied to roll a 120-pound barrel up an inclined plane 9 feet long to a height of 3 feet (disregard friction)?

L ÷ I = R ÷ E

L = Length of ramp, measured along the slope.

I = Height of ramp.

R = Weight of object to be raised or lowered.

E = Force required to raise or lower object.

A—40 pounds.
B—120 pounds.
C—360 pounds.

This is a simple mechanical advantage problem.

We roll the barrel three times as far as we lift it, so the force we must exert to roll the barrel up the inclined plane is only one third of the weight of the barrel.

We must exert a force of 40 pounds to roll a 120-pound barrel up the 9-foot inclined plane to lift it 3 feet.

8482. Which statement concerning heat and/or temperature is true?

A—There is an inverse relationship between temperature and heat.
B—Temperature is a measure of the kinetic energy of the molecules of any substance.
C—Temperature is a measure of the potential energy of the molecules of any substance.

Heat is a form of energy, and temperature is a measure of the intensity of the kinetic energy of the molecules in a substance.

Heat energy, in the form of latent heat, can be added to an object or taken from it without changing its temperature. But, the temperature of an object changes directly with the amount of sensible heat put into it or taken from it.

8483. What is absolute humidity?

A—The temperature to which humid air must be cooled at constant pressure to become saturated.
B—The actual amount of the water vapor in a mixture of air and water.
C—The ratio of the water vapor actually present in the atmosphere to the amount that would be present if the air were saturated at the prevailing temperature and pressure.

Absolute humidity is the actual amount of water in a volume of air. It is measured in such units as grams per cubic meter.

8484. The temperature to which humid air must be cooled at constant pressure to become saturated is called

A—dewpoint.
B—absolute humidity.
C—relative humidity.

The temperature to which a body of air must be lowered before the water vapor in the air condenses out as visible, liquid water is called the dew point of the air.

8485. If both the volume and the absolute temperature of a confined gas are doubled, the pressure will

A—not change.
B—be halved.
C—become four times as great.

The pressure exerted by a confined gas is directly proportional to its absolute temperature. If the absolute temperature is doubled, the pressure will also double.

The pressure exerted by a confined gas is inversely proportional to its volume. If its volume is doubled, the pressure will decrease to a value that is one half of the original.

If both the volume and the absolute temperature of a confined gas are doubled, the two changes will cancel each other, so the pressure of the gas will not change.

8486. If all, or a significant part of a stall strip is missing on an airplane wing, a likely result will be

A—asymmetrical lateral control at or near stall angles of attack.
B—decreased lift in the area of installation at high angles of attack.
C—asymmetrical lateral control at low angles of attack.

Stall strips are small triangular spoilers, or wedges, attached to the leading edge in the root area of a wing that has a tendency to stall at the tip before the root. Stalls beginning at the tip cause a loss of aileron effectiveness, and therefore lateral control, when it is most needed.

At high angles of attack, stall strips disrupt the airflow over the wing root and force it to stall before the portion of the wing ahead of the aileron.

If all or a significant part of a stall strip is missing, the stall on the affected wing will begin near the tip and decrease the effectiveness of the aileron, requiring asymmetrical lateral control at or near the stall angle of attack. More aileron deflection will be needed to raise the wing with the missing stall strip than the wing with the intact strip.

Answers

8481 [A] (099) AMT-G Ch 3
8482 [B] (027) AMT-G Ch 3
8483 [B] (027) AMT-G
8484 [A] (027) AMT-G
8485 [A] (008) AMT-G Ch 3
8486 [A] (007) FAA-H-8083-3

8486-1. The purpose of stall strips on airplane wings is to

A—increase lift in the areas of installation.
B—prevent stall in the areas of installation.
C—ensure that the wing root areas stall first.

Stall strips are small triangular spoilers, or wedges, attached to the leading edge at the root area of a wing that has a tendency to stall at the tip before the root. Stalls beginning at the tip cause a loss of aileron effectiveness, and therefore lateral control, when it is most needed.

At high angles of attack, stall strips disrupt the airflow over the wing root and force it to stall before the portion of the wing ahead of the aileron.

8487. An airplane wing is designed to produce lift resulting from

A—positive air pressure below and above the wing's surface along with the downward deflection of air.
B—positive air pressure below the wing's surface and negative air pressure above the wing's surface along with the downward deflection of air.
C—negative air pressure below the wing's surface and positive air pressure above the wing's surface along with the downward deflection of air.

Aerodynamic lift is produced on an airfoil by the pressure difference across the airfoil along with the downward deflection of air. The pressure below the wing surface is greater than that above the wing. The pressure below the wing may be considered positive and that above the wing negative.

8487-1. Which of the following is Newton's first law of motion, generally termed the law of inertia?

A—To every action there is an equal and opposite reaction. If a force is applied to an object, the object will supply a resistive force exactly equal to and in the opposite direction of the force applied.
B—Force is proportional to the product of mass and acceleration. When a force acts upon a body, the momentum of that body is changed.
C—Objects at rest tend to remain at rest and objects in motion tend to remain in motion at the same speed and in the same direction, unless acted on by an external force.

Newton's first law explains that when an object is at rest, it tries to remain at rest. But when it is moving, it tries to keep moving in a straight line and will not speed up, slow down, or turn unless it is acted upon by an outside force. This tendency of the object to remain in its original condition of motion is called inertia.

8488. The purpose of aircraft wing dihedral is to

A—increase lateral stability.
B—increase longitudinal stability.
C—increase lift coefficient of the wing.

Dihedral or the upward slant of the wing from the fuselage is used to increase the lateral stability. Lateral stability is roll stability and is stability about the longitudinal axis.

8489. Aspect ratio of a wing is defined as the ratio of the

A—wingspan to the wing root.
B—square of the chord to the wingspan.
C—wingspan to the mean chord.

The aspect ratio of a wing is the ratio of the wing span to the mean, or average, chord. For a nonrectangular wing, aspect ratio is found by dividing the square of the wing span by the wing area.

8490. A wing with a very high aspect ratio (in comparison with a low aspect ratio wing) will have

A—increased drag at high angles of attack.
B—a low stall speed.
C—poor control qualities at low airspeeds.

Wings with a high aspect ratio have low drag at high angles of attack, low stalling speed, and good control at low airspeeds. Sailplanes have very high aspect ratios and fly slowly.

8491. The desired effect of using winglets on an aircraft's wingtips is to

A—increase the lift to drag ratio.
B—reduce the aspect ratio.
C—optimize wing dihedral and improve lateral stability

Winglets, small upturned vertical surfaces mounted on the wing tips, reduce drag by reducing the spanwise flow of air, therefore reducing vortices. The desired effect of using winglets on an aircraft's wingtips is to increase the lift to drag (L/D) ratio of the wing.

8491-1. The main rotor system on a helicopter is classified in three groups. Which of those listed is NOT one of these groups?

A—The fully articulated rotor system.
B—The flexible-beam rotor system.
C—The semi-rigid rotor system.

The classification of main rotor systems is based on how the blades move relative to the main rotor hub. The principal classifications are known as fully articulated, semi-rigid, and rigid.

Answers

8486-1 [C] (007) FAA-H-8083-3	8487 [B] (055) FAA-H-8083-3	8487-1 [C] (099) AMT-G Ch 4	8488 [A] (007) FAA-H-8083-3
8489 [C] (007) FAA-H-8083-3	8490 [B] (007) FAA-H-8083-3	8491 [A] (007) AMT-STRUC 1	8491-1 [B] (007) AMT-G Ch 3

8491-2. Which of the following statements is correct?

A—When the cyclic pitch control lever is raised, the blade angle of all the rotor blades increases uniformly and they create the lift that allows the helicopter to take off vertically.
B—When the collective pitch control lever is raised, the blade angle of all the rotor blades increases uniformly and they create the lift that allows the helicopter to take off vertically.
C—When the collective pitch control lever is raised, the blade angle of the aft rotor blades decreases uniformly and they create the lift that allows the helicopter to take off vertically.

The primary flight controls on a helicopter are the collective and cyclic control levers and anti-torque pedals. When the collective pitch control lever is raised, the blade angle of all the rotor blades increases uniformly and they create the lift that allows the helicopter to take off vertically. The cyclic pitch control lever, like the yoke of an airplane, can be pulled back or pushed forward (for backward or forward motion), and can be moved left and right (to bank left or right).

Maintenance Publications

8492. Airworthiness Directives are issued primarily to

A—provide information about malfunction or defect trends.
B—present recommended maintenance procedures for correcting potentially hazardous defects.
C—correct an unsafe condition.

The FAA issues ADs to correct unsafe conditions that have been discovered on certificated aircraft, engines, propellers, or appliances.

An unsafe condition causes the device to fail to meet the conditions for its certification. An AD specifies the corrective action that must be taken to return the device to the conditions specified for its certification.

8493. (1) A Supplemental Type Certificate (STC) may be issued to more than one applicant for the same design change, providing each applicant shows compliance with the applicable airworthiness requirement.

(2) An installation of an item manufactured in accordance with the Technical Standard Order (TSO) system requires no further approval for installation in a particular aircraft.

Regarding the above statements,

A—both 1 and 2 are true.
B—neither 1 nor 2 is true.
C—only 1 is true.

Statement 1 is true. More than one person may apply for a STC that covers the same change to an aircraft.

An STC is not a patent and it is not protected. Each applicant must furnish proof that their alteration meets all of the applicable airworthiness requirements.

Statement 2 is not true. A part produced according to a TSO requires specific approval for installation on a particular aircraft. Even though the part is built according to a TSO, it may be neither suitable nor approved for the particular aircraft.

8493-1. What does the acronym TSO mean regarding a type certificated aircraft part, material, component and/or process?

A—Training Specific Organization.
B—Type Supplement Original.
C—Technical Standard Order.

A Technical Standard Order (TSO) is an approval for the manufacture of a component for use on certificated aircraft.

8494. Primary responsibility for compliance with Airworthiness Directives lies with the

A—aircraft owner or operator.
B—certificated mechanic holding an Inspection Authorization who conducts appropriate inspections.
C—certificated mechanic who maintains the aircraft.

The aircraft owner or operator is responsible for determining that the aircraft continues to meet the requirements for its certification. This includes the compliance with all ADs.

8495. An aircraft Type Certificate Data Sheet contains

A—maximum fuel grade to be used.
B—control surface adjustment points.
C—location of the datum.

Since the location of all items in an aircraft are measured from the datum and this datum can be at any location the aircraft manufacturer chooses, the technician must know exactly where this reference is located.

The location of the datum is included in the information furnished on a Type Certificate Data Sheet.

Answers

8491-2 [B] (007) FAA-H-8083-30
8494 [A] (063) 14 CFR 39
8492 [C] (048) 14 CFR 39
8495 [C] (097) AMT-G
8493 [C] (028) 14 CFR 21
8493-1 [C] (066) AMT-G Ch 11

8496. Suitability for use of a specific propeller with a particular engine-airplane combination can be determined by reference to what informational source?

A—Propeller Specifications or Propeller Type Certificate Data Sheet.
B—Aircraft Specifications or Aircraft Type Certificate Data Sheet.
C—Alphabetical Index of Current Propeller Type Certificate Data Sheets, Specifications, and Listings.

The Aircraft Specifications or Type Certificate Data Sheets list all of the allowable engine-propeller combinations approved for a specific aircraft.

8497. When an aircraft is sold domestically, the Airworthiness Certificate

A—must be surrendered to the local Flight Standards District Office.
B—becomes invalid until the new owner makes application for a new Airworthiness Certificate.
C—is transferred with the aircraft at the time of sale.

The Airworthiness Certificate issued to an aircraft is transferred with the aircraft to the new owner when the aircraft is sold.

8498. The issuance of an Airworthiness Certificate is governed by

A—14 CFR Part 23.
B—14 CFR Part 21.
C—14 CFR Part 39.

14 CFR Part 21 entitled "Certification Procedures for Products and Parts" governs the issuance of an Airworthiness Certificate.

8499. Specifications pertaining to an aircraft model manufactured under a type certificate of which less than 50 are shown on the FAA Aircraft Registry, can be found in the

A—Aircraft Listing.
B—Summary of Discontinued Aircraft Specifications.
C—FAA Statistical Handbook of Civil Aircraft Specifications.

The certification specifications for aircraft of which there are fewer than 50 currently in service or of which there were fewer than 50 certificated are found in the Aircraft Listing.

8500. Where are technical descriptions of certificated propellers found?

A—Applicable Airworthiness Directives.
B—Aircraft Specifications.
C—Propeller Type Certificate Data Sheets.

Technical specifications for certificated aircraft propellers are found in the Propeller Type Certificate Data Sheets.

8501. What information is generally contained in Aircraft Specifications or Type Certificate Data Sheets?

A—Empty weight of the aircraft.
B—Useful load of aircraft.
C—Control surface movements.

The amount of control surface movement determines the structural loads that can be put on an aircraft and also the flight characteristics of the aircraft.

Because this information is so critical, it is included on the Type Certificate Data Sheets of an aircraft.

8502. Placards required on an aircraft are specified in

A—AC 43.13-1B.
B—The Federal Aviation Regulations under which the aircraft was type certificated.
C—Aircraft Specifications or Type Certificate Data Sheets.

Placards that furnish information vital to the safety of flight and that must be installed in a certificated aircraft are specified in the Type Certificate Data Sheets for the aircraft.

8503. Technical information about older aircraft models, of which no more than 50 remain in service, can be found in the

A—Aircraft Listing.
B—Summary of Deleted and Discontinued Aircraft Specifications.
C—Index of Antique Aircraft.

The certification specifications for aircraft of which there are fewer than 50 currently in service, or of which there were fewer than 50 certificated, are found in the Aircraft Listing.

Answers

8496 [B]	(004)	AMT-G	8497 [C]	(025)	§21.179	8498 [B]	(066)	14 CFR 21	8499 [A]	(021)	14 CFR 21
8500 [C]	(097)	AMT-G Ch 13	8501 [C]	(097)	AMT-G Ch 13	8502 [C]	(097)	§43.11(b)	8503 [A]	(021)	AMT-G Ch 11

8503-1. Which of the following are sometimes used as authorization to deviate from an aircraft's original type design?

A—FAA Form 337, Supplemental Type Certificate, and Technical Standard Order.
B—Supplemental Type Certificate, Airworthiness Directive, and Technical Standard Order.
C—FAA Form 337, Supplemental Type Certificate, and Airworthiness Directive.

The FAA Form 337 is the form the FAA uses to authorize a major alteration that may deviate from the aircraft's original type design.

An STC is an authorization for a major change in the type design that is not great enough to require a new application for a type certificate.

An AD identifies an unsafe condition that exists in a product and that is likely to exist or develop in other products of the same type design. ADs may require alterations that deviate from the aircraft's original type design.

A TSO is a minimum performance standard used to evaluate an article. An article can be a material, part, component, process, or appliance (see 14 CFR §21.1(b)(2)). Each TSO covers a certain type of article. When authorized to manufacture an article to a TSO standard, this is referred to as a TSO authorization. Receiving a TSO authorization is both a design and production approval but is not used as an authorization to deviate from an aircraft's original type design.

8504. (1) The Federal Aviation Regulations require approval after compliance with the data of a Supplemental Type Certificate.

(2) An installation of an item manufactured in accordance with the Technical Standard Order system requires no further approval for installation in a particular aircraft.

Regarding the above statements,

A—only 2 is true.
B—neither 1 nor 2 is true.
C—only 1 is true.

Statement 1 is true. After an aircraft has been altered in accordance with a Supplemental Type Certificate, it must be inspected for conformity with the information included in the STC before it can be approved for return to service.

Statement 2 is not true. Even though a part has been manufactured according to a Technical Standard Order, it is not necessarily approved for installation on a particular civil aircraft.

8505. Which regulation provides information regarding instrument range markings for an airplane certificated in the normal category?

A—14 CFR Part 21.
B—14 CFR Part 25.
C—14 CFR Part 23.

Information regarding instrument range markings that must be used on aircraft certificated in the normal category is found in 14 CFR Part 23, "Airworthiness Standards: Normal, Utility, Acrobatic and Commuter Category Airplanes."

8505-1. Which regulation provides the airworthiness standards for an airplane certificated in the normal category?

A—14 CFR Part 27.
B—14 CFR Part 25.
C—14 CFR Part 23.

14 CFR Part 27 provides the airworthiness standards for normal category rotorcraft. Part 25 provides airworthiness standards for transport category airplanes. Part 23 provides airworthiness standards for normal, utility, acrobatic, and commuter category airplanes.

8505-2. What regulations are covered by 14 CFR Part 1?

A—Certification of airmen other than crewmembers.
B—General operating and flight rules.
C—Definitions and abbreviations.

14 CFR Part 1 covers definitions and abbreviations. This regulation is helpful for learning the legal terms and their associated meanings as well as the many acronyms used in aviation.

8506. (1) Propellers are NOT included in the Airworthiness Directive system.

(2) A certificated powerplant mechanic may make a minor repair on an aluminum propeller and approve for return to service.

Regarding the above statements,

A—only 2 is true.
B—both 1 and 2 are true.
C—neither 1 nor 2 is true.

Statement 1 is false. Propellers are included in the Airworthiness Directive system.

Statement 2 is true. A certificated powerplant mechanic can make a minor repair to an aluminum propeller and can approve it for return to service.

Answers

8503-1 [C] (021) AMT-G Ch 13	8504 [C] (028) §43.13	8505 [C] (066) §23.1543	8505-1 [C] (066) 14 CFR 23
8505-2 [C] (066) 14 CFR 1	8506 [A] (048) §39.1		

8507. An aircraft mechanic is privileged to perform major alterations on U.S. certificated aircraft; however, the work must be done in accordance with FAA-approved technical data before the aircraft can be returned to service. Which is NOT approved data?

A—Airworthiness Directives.
B—AC 43.13-2A.
C—Supplemental Type Certificates.

The FAA issues or approves two types of data for aircraft:

1. *Regulatory data is approved data that specifies the way something will be done. It is specific and it must be complied with as it applies.*
2. *Data in Advisory Circulars, such as that in AC 43.13-2A, is advisory in nature and is "acceptable data." While it shows a way that things can be done, it is neither specific nor mandatory. It is not considered to be "approved data."*

8508. What is the maintenance recording responsibility of the person who complies with an Airworthiness Directive?

A—Advise the aircraft owner/operator of the work performed.
B—Make an entry in the maintenance record of that equipment.
C—Advise the FAA office of the work performed, by submitting an FAA Form 337.

When a technician complies with an Airworthiness Directive, it is his or her responsibility to make an entry in the maintenance record of the affected equipment. This entry must include the method of compliance and the date of compliance.

8509. (1) Manufacturer's data and FAA publications such as Airworthiness Directives, Type Certificate Data Sheets, and advisory circulars are all approved data.

(2) FAA publications such as Technical Standard Orders, Airworthiness Directives, Type Certificate Data Sheets, and Aircraft Specifications and Supplemental Type Certificates are all approved data.

Regarding the above statements,

A—both 1 and 2 are true.
B—only 1 is true.
C—only 2 is true.

Statement 1 is not true. Not all manufacturer's data is FAA approved and Advisory Circulars are not considered to be approved data.

Statement 2 is true. All of the items listed in this statement are considered to be approved data.

8509-1. A Technical Standard Order (TSO) is issued by whom?

A—The Aircraft industry.
B—Part manufacturers.
C—The Administrator.

TSOs are issued by the Administrator under 14 CFR Part 21.

8510. The Air Transport Association of America (ATA) Specification No. 100

(1) establishes a standard for the presentation of technical data in maintenance manuals.

(2) divides the aircraft into numbered systems and subsystems in order to simplify locating maintenance instructions.

Regarding the above statements,

A—both 1 and 2 are true.
B—neither 1 nor 2 is true.
C—only 1 is true.

Statement 1 is true. The ATA Specification 100 is a standard for arranging and presenting technical data in maintenance manuals.

Statement 2 is also true. The ATA Specification 100 divides the aircraft into numbered systems and subsystems to simplify locating maintenance instructions.

8511. Aviation Maintenance Alerts (formerly General Aviation Airworthiness Alerts)

A—provide mandatory procedures to prevent or correct serious aircraft problems.
B—provide information about aircraft problems and suggested corrective actions.
C—provide temporary emergency procedures until Airworthiness Directives can be issued.

Aviation Maintenance Alerts, formerly General Aviation Airworthiness Alerts, provide a common communication channel through which the aviation community can economically interchange service experience and thereby cooperate in the improvement of aeronautical product durability, reliability, and safety. The contents include items that have been reported to be significant but have not been evaluated fully by the time the material went to press.

Answers

8507 [B] (028) FAA-G-8082-11
8508 [B] (048) FAA-G-8082-11
8509 [C] (028) FAA-G-8082-11
8509-1 [C] (066) AMT-G Ch 11
8510 [A] (026) AMT-G Ch 11
8511 [B] (021) AMT-G Ch 11

8512. (Refer to Figure 62, 62A, & 62B as necessary.) Which doubler(s) require(s) heat treatment before installation?

A—-101.
B—-102.
C—Both.

Doubler -102 is made of .040 7075-O Alclad. This material is in its annealed (-O) condition, and it must be heat-treated to its -T6 condition before it is installed.

Doubler -101 is made of 2024-T3 Alclad which is already heat-treated.

According to General Notes-200 in Figure 62A, the -102 doubler should be heat-treated to -T6 condition in accordance with Process Specification 5602.

8512-1. (Refer to Figures 62, 62A, and 62B as necessary.) How many parts will need to be fabricated by the mechanic in the construction and installation of one doubler?

A—2.
B—3.
C—4.

The mechanic must fabricate three parts to install the doubler. For the -100 installation, one doubler -101 and two clips -103 are needed. For the -200 installation, one doubler -102 and two clips -103 are needed.

8513. (Refer to Figure 62, 62A, & 62B as necessary.) Using only the information given (when bend allowance, set back, etc. have been calculated) which doubler is it possible to construct and install?

A—-101.
B—-102.
C—Both.

There is enough information given here to construct and install the -101 doubler. There is not enough information to construct the stronger -102 doubler in the -200 installation. The -102 doubler requires certain Process Specifications that are not furnished.

8514. (Refer to Figure 62.) The -100 in the title block (Area 1) is applicable to which doubler part number(s)?

A—-101.
B—-102.
C—Both.

In Figure 62, follow the column for the -100 assembly upward to see the components it requires.

The -101 doubler is in this column.

8515. (Refer to Figure 63.) An aircraft has a total time in service of 468 hours. The Airworthiness Directive given was initially complied with at 454 hours in service. How many additional hours in service may be accumulated before the Airworthiness Directive must again be complied with?

A—46.
B—200.
C—186.

The aircraft has less than 500 hours total time in service, so compliance with the AD falls in category I.

The AD has been complied with and the aircraft has operated for 14 hours since the compliance.

The AD must be complied with each 200 hours of time in service, so the aircraft can operate for another 186 hours before the AD note must be complied with again.

8515-1. The following words are an example of what kind of statement in an AD? "Required within the next 25 hours time-in-service after the effective date of this AD, unless already accomplished."

A—Amendment.
B—Compliance.
C—Applicability.

"Within the next 25 hours time-in-service after the effective date of this AD," is a statement of compliance time or date.

8515-2. The action required by an AD may take what form?

1. Inspection.
2. Part(s) replacement.
3. Design modification.
4. Change in operating procedure(s).
5. Overall change in the content, form and disposition of aircraft maintenance records.

A—1, 2, 3, and/or 4.
B—1, 2, 3, and/or 5.
C—1, 2, 3, 4, and/or 5.

The action required by an AD is described in the Compliance statement which specifies the action that is required by the AD, and specifies the method of compliance.

*An AD does **not** specify an overall change in maintenance records.*

Answers

8512 [B] (004) AMT-G	8512-1 [B] (013) AMT-G	8513 [A] (048) AMT-G	8514 [A] (014) Part 43 App A
8515 [C] (048) 14 CFR 39	8515-1 [B] (048) AMT-G Ch 11	8515-2 [A] (048) AMT-G Ch 11	

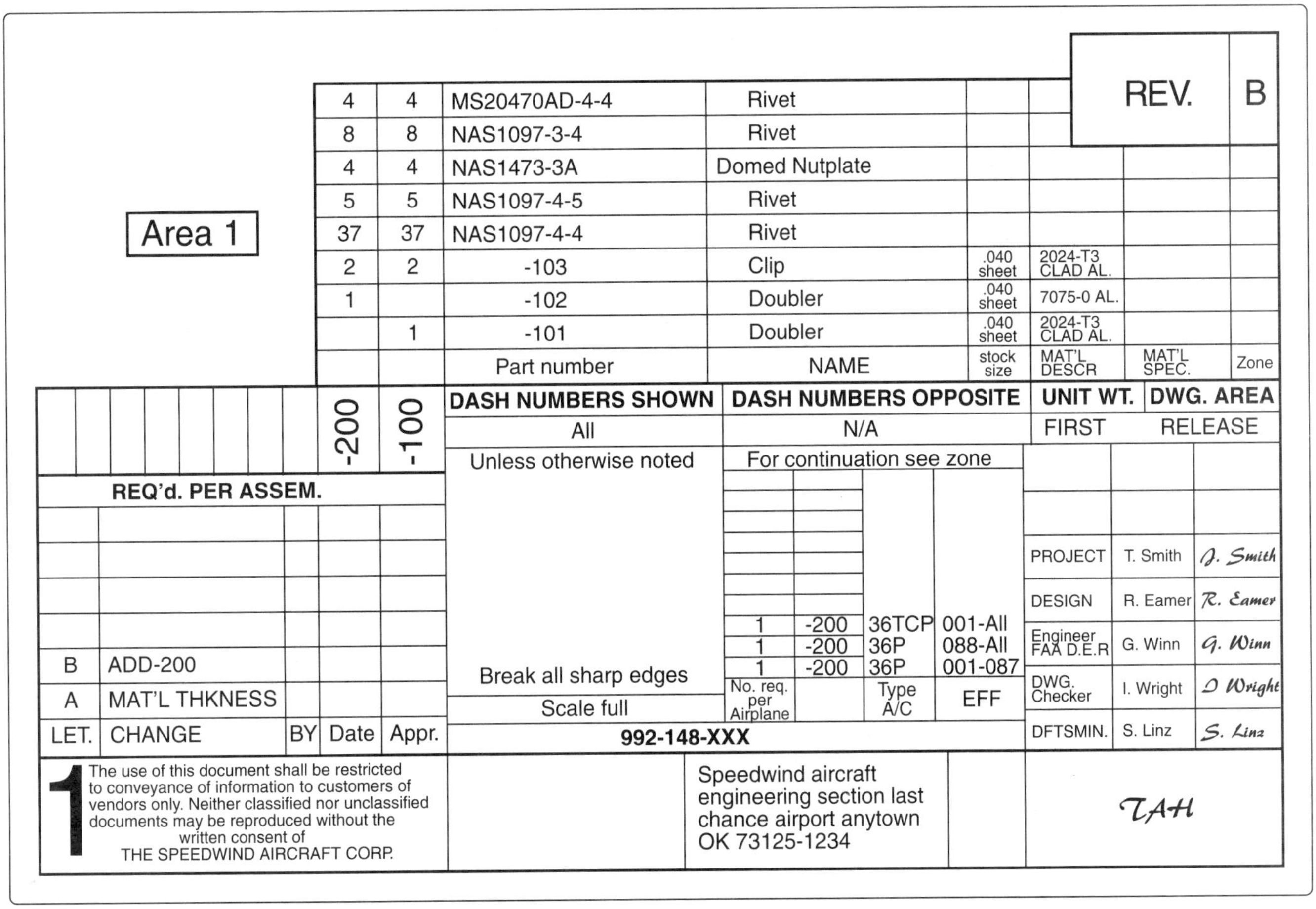

Figure 62. Maintenance data – part 1 of 3

Editor's Note:
Figure 62 is a three-part illustration that is used to answer questions 8512, 8513, and 8514. Figure 62 contains Area 1, Figure 62A contains Areas 2 and 3, and Figure 62B contains Area 4. All of the areas must be considered when answering these questions. Figures 62A and B are found on the following pages.

8515-3. Type Certificate Data Sheets are issued for which of the following products?

A—Aircraft, engines, and propellers.
B—Aircraft, engines, and appliances.
C—Aircraft, engines, propellers, and appliances.

Type Certificate Data Sheets and Specifications set forth essential factors and other conditions which are necessary for U.S. airworthiness certification of aircraft, engines and propellers.

8516. The following is a table of airspeed limits as given in an FAA-issued aircraft specification:

Normal operating speed .... 260 knots
Never-exceed speed .... 293 knots
Maximum landing gear operation speed .... 174 knots
Maximum flap extended speed .... 139 knots

The high end of the white arc on the airspeed instrument would be at

A—260 knots.
B—293 knots.
C—139 knots.

The maximum flap extended speed is marked on an aircraft airspeed indicator by the top of the white arc.
The white arc would extend to 139 knots.

Answers
8515-3 [A] (097) AMT-G Ch 11   8516 [C] (051) §23.1545

AREA 2

GENERAL NOTES - 100

1. ALL BENDS +/– .5 deg.
2. All holes +/– .003.
3. Apply Alodine 1,000.
4. Prime with MIL-P-23377 or equivalent.
5. Trim S-1 C just aft of the clip at STA. 355.750 and forward of the front face of the STA. 370.25 frame and remove from the airplane.
6. Position the –101 doubler as shown. Install wet with NAS1097AD-4-4 and -4-5 rivets and a faying surface seal of PR 1,422. Pick up the rivet row that was in S-1 C and the aft rivets in sta. 370.25. Tie doubler into front frame with clips as shown using MS20470AD-4-4 rivets through the clips and the frame.
7. Install 4 NAS1473-3A nutplates with NAS1097-3-4 rivets through the skin and doubler to retain the antenna.
8. Strip paint and primer from under the antenna footprint.
9. Treat skin with Alodine 1,000.
10. Install antenna and apply weather seal fillet around antenna base.

AREA 3

GENERAL NOTES - 200

Note: P.S. = Process Specification
IAW = in accordance with

1. ALL BENDS IAW P.S. 1,000.
2. All holes IAW P.S. 1,015.
3. Heat treat –102 to –T6 IAW P.S. 5,602.
4. Alodine IAW P.S. 10,000.
5. Prime IAW P.S. 10,125.
6. Trim S-1 C just aft of the clip at STA. 355.750 and forward of the front face of the STA. 370.25 frame and remove from airplane.
7. Position the –102 doubler as shown. Install wet with NAS1097AD-4-4 and -4-5 rivets, and a faying surface seal IAW P.S. 41,255. Pick up the rivet row that was S-1 C and the aft rivets in STA. 370.25. Add two edge rows as shown. Tie doubler into front frame with clips as shown using MS20470AD-4-4 rivets through the clips and the frame.
8. Install 4 NAS1473-3A nutplates with NAS 1097-3-4 rivets through the skin and doubler to retain the antenna.
9. Strip paint and primer from under the antenna footprint.
10. Treat skin IAW P.S. 10,000.
11. Install antenna and apply weather seal fillet around antenna base.

Figure 62A. Maintenance data – part 2 of 3

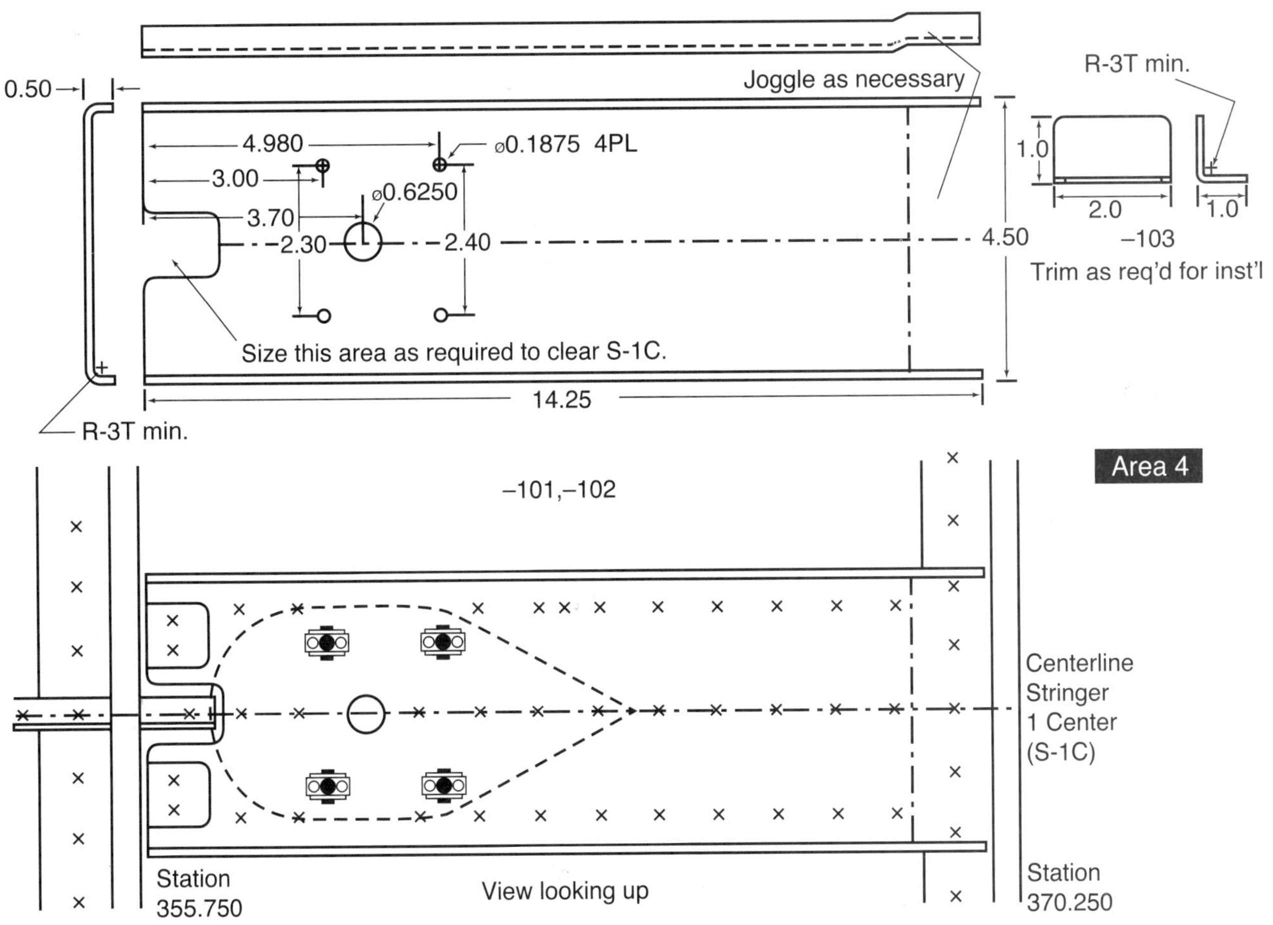

Figure 62B. Maintenance data – part 3 of 3

The following is the compliance portion of an Airworthiness Directive.

"Compliance required as indicated, unless already accomplished:

I. Aircraft with less than 500 hours total time in service: Inspect in accordance with instructions below at 500 hours total time, or within the next 50 hours time in service after the effective date of this AD, and repeat after each subsequent 200 hours in service.

II. Aircraft with 500 hours through 1,000 hours total time in service: Inspect in accordance with instructions below within the next 50 hours time in service after the effective date of this AD, and repeat after each subsequent 200 hours in service.

III. Aircraft with more than 1,000 hours time in service: Inspect in accordance with instructions below within the next 25 hours time in service after the effective date of this AD, and repeat after each subsequent 200 hours in service."

Figure 63. Airworthiness directive excerpt

8516-1. When is a mechanic responsible for checking AD compliance?

A—Never, the owner or operator is solely responsible.
B—When performing an inspection required under part 91, 125, or 135.
C—Anytime an aircraft or portion thereof is returned to service.

It is the responsibility of the mechanic performing an inspection required under Part 91, 125, or 135 to determine the status of any AD affecting the airframe, engine, propeller, rotor, and any installed appliances.

8516-2. How long are AD compliance records required to be kept?

A—Until the work is repeated or superseded by other work.
B—For one year after the work is performed, or until the work is repeated or superseded by other work.
C—They shall be retained, and then transferred with the aircraft when it is sold.

14 CFR §91.417(b)(2) states that the record of the current status of applicable AD including, for each, the method of compliance, the AD number, and revision date be retained and transferred with the aircraft at the time the aircraft is sold.

8516-3. What does the Type Certificate Data Sheet designation code "2 PCSM" mean? (K01)

A—Two place (number of seats), closed, sea, monoplane.
B—Two wing (biplane), primary category, semimonocoque (airframe).
C—Neither of the other two choices.

The FAA uses coded information for the configuration of aircraft and engines in the Type Certificate Data Sheets. The code 2 PCSM identifies the aircraft as a two-place, closed, sea, monoplane.

8516-4. Which of the following includes all the regulatory definitions of "maintenance"?

A—Overhaul, repair, parts replacement, and preservation, and preventive maintenance.
B—Overhaul, repair, parts replacement, preservation, inspection, and preventive maintenance.
C—Overhaul, repair, parts replacement, inspection, and preservation.

14 CFR Part 1 defines maintenance as inspection, overhaul, repair, preservation, and the replacement of parts, but ***excludes*** *preventive maintenance.*

8516-5. What is the maximum penalty for cheating or other unauthorized conduct when taking an FAA mechanic test?

A—Ineligibility to receive any certificate or rating for one year.
B—Ineligibility to receive any certificate or rating for one year, and suspension or revocation of any certificate held.
C—Ineligibility to receive any certificate or rating for one year, and suspension of any certificate held.

14 CFR §65.18(b) states that no person who cheats, gives or receives help from another, takes a part of the test for another, uses unauthorized material during the test is eligible for any airman or ground instructor certificate or rating for a period of one year after the date of that act. In addition, the commission of that act is a basis for suspending or revoking any airman or ground instructor certificate held by that person.

8517. A complete detailed inspection and adjustment of the valve mechanism will be made at the first 25 hours after the engine has been placed in service. Subsequent inspections of the valve mechanism will be made each second 50-hour period.

From the above statement, at what intervals will valve mechanism inspections be performed?

A—100 hours.
B—50 hours.
C—125 hours.

Since the valve mechanism is required to be inspected only every second 50-hour period, the engine can operate for 100 hours between valve mechanism inspections.

8518. Check thrust bearing nuts for tightness on new or newly overhauled engines at the first 50-hour inspection following installation. Subsequent inspections on thrust bearing nuts will be made at each third 50-hour inspection.

From the above statement, at what intervals should you check the thrust bearing nut for tightness?

A—150 hours.
B—200 hours.
C—250 hours.

Since the thrust bearing nuts must be checked for tightness after the first 50 hours in service and then on every third 50-hour inspection, the engine can operate for 150 hours between inspections of tightness of the thrust bearing nuts.

Answers

8516-1 [B] (048) AMT-G Ch 11
8516-2 [C] (048) §91.417
8516-3 [A] (097) AMT-G
8516-4 [C] (052) 14 CFR Part 1
8516-5 [B] (054) §65.18
8517 [A] (004) §43.13
8518 [A] (004) §43.13

Aviation Mechanic Privileges and Limitations

8519. Certificated mechanics with a powerplant rating may perform

A—any inspection required by the Federal Aviation Regulations on a powerplant or propeller or any component thereof, and may release the same to service.
B—100-hour and/or annual inspections required by the Federal Aviation Regulations on powerplants, propellers, or any components thereof, and may release the same to service.
C—100-hour inspections required by the Federal Aviation Regulations on a powerplant, propeller, or any component thereof, and may release the same to service.

A certificated mechanic holding a powerplant rating is authorized to perform a 100-hour inspection on a powerplant or propeller or any component thereof and may release the same for service.

8520. A repair, as performed on an airframe, shall mean

A—the upkeep and preservation of the airframe including the component parts thereof.
B—the restoration of the airframe to a condition for safe operation after damage or deterioration.
C—simple or minor preservation operations and the replacement of small standard parts not involving complex assembly operations.

A repair to an aircraft structure is an operation that restores the structure to a condition for safe operation after it has become deteriorated or has been damaged.

8520-1. Under the Federal Aviation Regulations, an aviation maintenance technician is required to perform maintenance on an aircraft so that it

A—always meets its original type design.
B—is at least equal to its original or properly altered condition.
C—exceeds minimum standards with regard to aerodynamic function, structural strength, resistance to vibration, and other qualities affecting airworthiness.

14 CFR §43.13(b) states: Each person maintaining or altering, or performing preventive maintenance, shall do that work in such a manner and use materials of such a quality, that the condition of the aircraft, airframe, aircraft engine, propeller or appliance worked on will be at least equal to its original or properly altered condition (with regard to aerodynamic function, structural strength, resistance to vibration and deterioration, and other qualities affecting airworthiness).

8521. The replacement of fabric on fabric-covered parts such as wings, fuselages, stabilizers, or control surfaces is considered to be a

A—minor repair unless the new cover is different in any way from the original cover.
B—minor repair unless the underlying structure is altered or repaired.
C—major repair even though no other alteration or repair is performed.

Replacing the fabric on fabric-covered parts such as wings, fuselages, stabilizers, or control surfaces is considered to be a major repair even though no other alteration or repair is performed.

8522. Which is classified as a major repair?

A—The splicing of skin sheets.
B—Installation of new engine mounts obtained from the aircraft manufacturer.
C—Any repair of damaged stressed metal skin.

14 CFR Part 43, Appendix A (b)(1)(xxiv) lists the splicing of skin sheets as an airframe major repair.

8523. The 100-hour inspection required by Federal Aviation Regulations for certain aircraft being operated for hire may be performed by

A—persons working under the supervision of an appropriately rated mechanic, but the aircraft must be approved by the mechanic for return to service.
B—appropriately rated mechanics only if they have an inspection authorization.
C—appropriately rated mechanics and approved by them for return to service.

A 100-hour inspection of an aircraft that is operated for hire may be performed by an appropriately rated mechanic and approved by him or her for return to service.

8524. A person working under the supervision of a certificated mechanic with an airframe and powerplant rating is not authorized to perform

A—repair of a wing brace strut by welding.
B—a 100-hour inspection.
C—repair of an engine mount by riveting.

A 100-hour inspection is the only procedure listed in these alternatives that a person working under the supervision of an appropriately rated mechanic is not allowed to perform. Only a mechanic holding the appropriate ratings can perform the inspection.

Answers

8519 [C] (082) §65.87	8520 [B] (023) 14 CFR 43	8520-1 [B] (063) §43.13(b)	8521 [C] (023) 14 CFR 43
8522 [A] (079) 14 CFR 43	8523 [C] (082) §65.87	8524 [B] (082) §65.81	

8525. Certificated mechanics, under their general certificate privileges, may

A—perform minor repairs to instruments.
B—perform 100-hour inspection of instruments.
C—perform minor alterations to instruments.

A properly certificated mechanic may perform a 100-hour inspection of instruments, but he or she may not make any repair or alteration to an instrument.

8526. An Airworthiness Directive requires that a propeller be altered. Certificated mechanics could

A—perform and approve the work for return to service if it is a minor alteration.
B—not perform the work because it is an alteration.
C—not perform the work because they are not allowed to perform and approve for return to service, repairs or alterations to propellers.

A certificated mechanic with a powerplant rating is authorized to perform the work called for in an AD on a propeller that requires a minor alteration to the propeller.

After complying with the AD, the mechanic can approve the propeller for return to service.

8527. The replacement of a damaged vertical stabilizer with a new identical stabilizer purchased from the aircraft manufacturer is considered a

A—minor alteration.
B—major repair.
C—minor repair.

The replacement of a damaged vertical stabilizer with a new identical stabilizer purchased from the aircraft manufacturer is a minor repair.

A rule of thumb for determining whether a repair is minor or major is that if the part can be bolted on and not require any riveting or welding, the repair is minor. This rule of thumb might well have exceptions.

8528. FAA certificated mechanics may

A—approve for return to service a major repair for which they are rated.
B—supervise and approve a 100-hour inspection.
C—approve for return to service a minor alteration they have performed appropriate to the rating(s) they hold.

FAA-certificated mechanics may approve for return to service a minor alteration they have performed appropriate to the rating(s) they hold.

This privilege, of course, assumes that the mechanic understands the current instructions of the manufacturer and has the maintenance manuals for the specific operation concerned.

A certificated mechanic is not authorized to supervise a 100-hour inspection.

8529. A certificated mechanic with a powerplant rating may perform the

A—annual inspection required by the Federal Aviation Regulations on a powerplant or any component thereof and approve and return the same to service.
B—100-hour inspection required by the Federal Aviation Regulations on a powerplant or any component thereof and approve and return the same to service.
C—100-hour inspection required by the Federal Aviation Regulations on an airframe, powerplant or any otter component thereof and approve and return the same to service.

A certificated mechanic with a powerplant rating is authorized to conduct a 100-hour inspection on a powerplant or any component thereof and approve the return to service of the same.

8530. What part of the Federal Aviation Regulations prescribes the requirements for issuing mechanic certificates and associated ratings and the general operating rules for the holders of these certificates and ratings?

A—14 CFR Part 43.
B—14 CFR Part 91.
C—14 CFR Part 65.

14 CFR Part 65, "Certification: Airmen Other Than Flight Crewmembers" prescribes the requirements for the issuance of mechanic certificates and associated ratings and the general operating rules for the holders of these certificates and ratings.

Answers

8525 [B] (082) §65.81
8526 [A] (082) §65.81(a)
8527 [C] (079) Part 43 App A
8528 [C] (082) §65.81
8529 [B] (082) §65.87
8530 [C] (082) 14 CFR 65

8530-1. 14 CFR Part 65 contains regulations regarding the certification of

A—pilots, flight Instructors, and ground instructors.
B—airmen other than flight crewmembers.
C—flight crewmembers other than pilots.

14 CFR Part 65, "Certification: Airmen Other Than Flight Crewmembers," prescribes the requirements for the issuance of mechanic certificates and associated ratings, air traffic control operators, aircraft dispatchers, repairmen, and parachute riggers and the general operating rules for the holders of these certificates and ratings.

8530-2. 14 CFR Part 65 Subpart D contains regulations regarding the certification of

A—repairmen.
B—pilots.
C—mechanics.

14 CFR Part 65, "Certification: Airmen Other Than Flight Crewmembers," prescribes the requirements for the issuance of mechanic certificates and associated ratings, air traffic control operators, aircraft dispatchers, repairmen, and parachute riggers and the general operating rules for the holders of these certificates and ratings. Subpart D specifically covers mechanics. Subpart E specifically covers repairman. Pilot certification is covered in 14 CFR Part 61.

8531. A certificated mechanic shall not exercise the privileges of the certificate and rating unless, within the preceding 24 months, the Administrator has found that the certificate holder is able to do the work or the certificate holder has

A—served as a mechanic under the certificate and rating for at least 18 months.
B—served as a mechanic under the certificate and rating for at least 12 months.
C—served as a mechanic under the certificate and rating for at least 6 months.

A certificated mechanic shall not exercise the privileges of the certificate and rating unless, within the preceding 24 months, the Administrator has found that the certificate holder is able to do the work or the certificate holder has served as a mechanic of the certificate and rating for at least six months.

8531-1. Under Title 14 of the Code of Federal Regulations, what is the maximum penalty for falsification, alteration, or fraudulent reproduction of certificates, logbooks, reports, and records?

A—Ineligibility to receive any certificate or rating for one year.
B—Imprisonment for one year and a $5,000 fine.
C—Suspension or revocation of any certificate held.

14 CFR §65.20 states that any person who falsifies or makes a fraudulent entry in a logbook, report, or record is subject to the suspension or revocation of any airman or ground instructor certificate or rating held by that person.

8531-2. How long does the holder of a certificate issued under Part 65 have to notify the FAA after any change in permanent mailing address?

A—30 days.
B—120 days.
C—90 days.

14 CFR §65.21 states that within 30 days after any change in their permanent mailing address, the holder of a certificate issued under this part shall notify the Department of Transportation, Federal Aviation Administration, Airman Certification Branch, Post Office Box 25082, Oklahoma City, OK 73125 in writing, of their new address.

8531-3. How long is a mechanic certificate with airframe and/or powerplant rating(s) valid?

A—Until the holder is relieved of duties for which the holder was employed and certificated.
B—Until voluntarily surrendered, permanently revoked, or temporarily suspended.
C—24 months after the holder has last exercised the privileges of the certificate.

14 CFR §65.15 states that a mechanic certificate with airframe and/or powerplant rating is effective until it is surrendered, suspended, or revoked.

8531-4. Why is a mechanic applicant issued a temporary certificate after successful completion of the required tests?

A—To allow for review of their application and supplementary documents.
B—So that a background check/investigation may be completed.
C—Both of the other two choices.

14 CFR §65.13 provides for a temporary certificate and rating effective for a period of 120 days to be issued to a qualified applicant, pending review of their application and supplementary documents and the issue of the certificate and ratings for which they applied.

Answers

8530-1 [B] (082) 14 CFR 65	8530-2 [C] 14 CFR 65	8531 [C] (082) §65.83	8531-1 [C] (054) §65.20
8531-2 [A] (067) §65.21	8531-3 [B] (082) §65.15	8531-4 [A] (082) §65.13	

8531-5. What is the maximum duration of a temporary airman certificate?

A—60 days.
B—90 days.
C—120 days.

14 CFR §65.13 provides for a temporary certificate and rating effective for a period of 120 days to be issued to a qualified applicant.

8531-6. When may an otherwise qualified mechanic who does not read, write, speak, and understand the English language be eligible to apply for a mechanic certificate?

A—When a special authorization has been issued by the supervising FAA Flight Standards Office.
B—When employed outside the United States by a U.S. air carrier.
C—When employed outside the United States.

14 CFR §65.71(a)(2) requires that the applicant for a mechanic certificate be able to read, write, speak, and understand the English language, or in the case of an applicant who is employed outside of the United States by a U.S. air carrier, have their certificate endorsed "Valid only outside the United States."

8531-7. Which of the following statements is true for a certificated and appropriately rated mechanic regarding repairs and alterations?

A—He or she may perform an airframe major repair or major alteration, but cannot approve the work for return to service.
B—He or she may perform airframe minor repairs and minor alterations and approve the work for return to service, but cannot perform an airframe major repair or major alteration.
C—He or she may perform an airframe major repair or major alteration and approve the work, but not the entire aircraft, for return to service.

14 CFR §65.81(a) states that a certificated mechanic may perform or supervise the maintenance, preventive maintenance or alteration of an aircraft or appliance, or a part thereof for which he or she is rated (but excluding major repairs to or major alterations of propellers, and any repair to, or alteration of instruments).

The mechanic must complete the FAA Form 337, filling in the compliance statement, but the person approving the work for return to service must hold an Inspection Authorization.

8531-8. Which of the following is an instance when a special flight permit may not be issued?

A—Flying passengers on a scheduled operation.
B—Flying the aircraft to a location where repairs or maintenance can be performed.
C—Flying a customer demonstration flight.

A special flight permit may be issued for an aircraft that may not currently meet applicable airworthiness requirements but is capable of safe flight, for the following purposes:

1. *Flying the aircraft to a base where repairs, alterations, or maintenance are to be performed, or to a point of storage.*
2. *Delivering or exporting the aircraft.*
3. *Production flight testing new production aircraft.*
4. *Evacuating aircraft from areas of impending danger.*
5. *Conducting customer demonstration flights in new production aircraft that have satisfactorily completed production flight tests.*
6. *Operating an aircraft at a weight in excess of its maximum certificated takeoff weight under specific circumstances.*

To request a special flight permit, the applicant must submit to the FAA: the purpose of the flight, the proposed itinerary, the crew required to operate the aircraft and its equipment, the ways in which the aircraft does not comply with the applicable airworthiness requirements, any restrictions the FAA deems necessary for the purpose of prescribing operating limitations. Flying passengers on a scheduled operation is not one of the allowed reasons for a special flight permit.

8532. (1) Certificated mechanics with an airframe rating may perform a minor repair to an airspeed indicator providing they have the necessary equipment available.

(2) Certificated mechanics with a powerplant rating may perform a major repair to a propeller providing they have the necessary equipment available.

Regarding the above statements,

A—only 1 is true.
B—neither 1 nor 2 is true.
C—only 2 is true.

Statement 1 is not true. No certificated mechanic, regardless of his or her ratings, is allowed to perform minor or major repairs, or minor or major alterations to instruments.

Statement 2 is not true. A mechanic holding a powerplant rating cannot perform major repairs or major alterations to propellers.

Answers

8531-5 [C] (082) §65.13
8531-6 [B] (082) §65.71
8531-7 [A] (082) §65.81
8531-8 [A] (082) §21.197,21.199
8532 [B] (082) §65.81

8533. Who is responsible for determining that materials used in aircraft maintenance and repair are of the proper type and conform to the appropriate standards?

A—The installing person or agency.
B—The owner or operator of the aircraft.
C—The manufacturer of the aircraft.

It is the responsibility of the person or agency (the certificated mechanic or the approved repair station) performing aircraft maintenance or making repairs to an aircraft, to make sure that all of the materials used in the maintenance or repair conform to the appropriate standards.

8534. Which of these publications contains standards for protrusion of bolts, studs, and screws through self-locking nuts?

A—AC 43.13-1B.
B—AC 43.13-2.
C—Aircraft Specifications or Type Certificate Data Sheets.

AC 43.13-1B states that "After the nut has been tightened, make sure that the bolt or stud has at least one thread showing past the nut."

8535. The replacement of a damaged engine mount with a new identical engine mount purchased from the aircraft manufacturer is considered a

A—major or minor repair, depending upon the complexity of the installation.
B—major repair.
C—minor repair.

The replacement of a part such as an engine mount with a new, identical part obtained from the aircraft manufacturer is considered to be an airframe minor repair.

8536. Who has the authority to approve for return to service a propeller after a 100-hour inspection?

1. A mechanic with a powerplant rating.
2. Any certificated repairman.
3. A non-certificated mechanic working under the supervision of a certificated mechanic with airframe and powerplant ratings.

A—1.
B—2.
C—1 and 3.

A certificated mechanic holding a powerplant rating is authorized to perform a 100-hour inspection on a propeller and may approve the same for return to service.

8537. Instrument repairs may be performed

A—by the instrument manufacturer only.
B—by an FAA-approved instrument repair station.
C—on airframe instruments by mechanics with an airframe rating.

Repairs to an instrument, either major or minor repairs, may be performed only by an FAA-approved instrument repair station. The manufacturer of the instrument has this type of rating.

8538. How is a quality system assured?

A—By an independent organization.
B—By a dependent organization.
C—By an internal reporting and auditing system.

A quality system must include procedures for planning, conducting, and documenting internal audits to ensure compliance with the approved quality system. The procedures must include reporting results of internal audits to the manager responsible for implementing corrective and preventive actions.

8539. According to Dr. James Reason, there are two types of human failure which can occur. They are:

A—active and latent.
B—mental and physical.
C—proper and improper.

There are two types of failure which can occur—active and latent. An active failure is one in which the effects are immediate. A latent failure occurs as a result of a decision made or action taken long before the incident or accident actually occurs.

8540. Many areas of aviation have shifted their focus from eliminating error to

A—preventing and managing error.
B—identifying and mitigating error.
C—reducing and containing error.

The goal of the Maintenance Error Decision Aid (MEDA) is to investigate errors, understand root causes, prevent and manage accidents (most of the factors that contribute to an error can be managed).

Answers

8533 [A]	(063)	§43.13(6)	8534 [A]	(051)	AC 43.13-1	8535 [C]	(079)	14 CFR 43	8536 [A]	(086)	§65.87
8537 [B]	(082)	§43.3	8538 [C]	(111)	§21.137	8539 [A]	(107)	FAA-H-8083-30	8540 [A]	(107)	FAA-H-8083-30

8541. When we think of aviation safety in a contemporary way, human error is

A—the starting point.
B—the ending point.
C—the intervention point.

The "SHEL" model is another concept for investigating and evaluating maintenance errors. The acronym SHEL represents software, hardware, environment, and liveware—with the human as the starting point for all.

8542. All of the following are consequences of human error, except

A—mental stressor.
B—catastrophic.
C—personal injury.

Human error is defined as a human action with unintended consequences. There are four consequences of human error: little or no effect, damage to equipment/hardware, personal injury, or catastrophic damage.

8543. The positive aspects of human factor issues are referred to as the

A—Magnificent Seven.
B—Dirty Dozen.
C—MEDA.

Subsequent to the development of the "Dirty Dozen," the "Magnificent Seven" list of human factors issues was developed and focused on positive aspects. These seven issues are:

1. *We work to accentuate the positive and eliminate the negative.*
2. *Safety is not a game because the price of losing is too high.*
3. *Just for today—zero error.*
4. *We all do our part to prevent Murphy from hitting the jackpot.*
5. *Our signature is our word and more precious than gold.*
6. *We are all part of the team.*
7. *We always work with a safety net.*

8544. The SHEL model is another human factors tool. The goal is to determine not only what the problem is, but also

A—where and why it exists.
B—how we prevent the problem.
C—how many factors contribute to the error.

The goal of the SHEL model is to determine not only what the problem is, but where and why it exists.

8545. The three types of human error are

A—omission, commission, and extraneous.
B—active, latent, and stressor.
C—mental, situational, and physiological.

Human error is the unintentional act of performing a task incorrectly that can potentially degrade the system. There are three types of human error:

1. *Omission: not performing an act or task.*
2. *Commission: accomplishing a task incorrectly.*
3. *Extraneous: performing a task not authorized.*

Answers
8541 [A] (107) FAA-H-8083-30   8542 [A] (032) FAA-H-8083-30   8543 [A] (116) FAA-H-8083-30   8544 [A] (107) FAA-H-8083-30
8545 [A] (107) FAA-H-8083-30

General Oral & Practical Study Guide

The Oral and Practical Tests

Prerequisites

All applicants must have met the prescribed experience requirements as stated in 14 CFR §65.77. In addition, all applicants must provide:

1. Proof of having unexpired passing credit for the Aviation Mechanic General (AMG) Knowledge Test by presenting an Airman Knowledge Test Report (except when properly authorized under the provisions of 14 CFR §65.80 to take the practical tests before the airman knowledge tests).
2. Identification with a photograph and signature.

Test Standards

The examiner will download an oral and practical examination that is generated at random for each applicant that reflects all the knowledge and skill "Areas of Operation."

Areas of Operation are subject areas in which aviation mechanic applicants must have knowledge or demonstrate skill.

"Tasks" are the items that should be performed according to standards acceptable to the examiner.

"Reference" identifies the publication(s) that describe the task. Information contained in manufacturer and/or FAA approved data always takes precedence over textbook referenced data.

The objective of each Task lists the elements that must be satisfactorily performed to demon-strate competency in the Task.

The objective includes:
1. Specifically what the applicant will be able to do.
2. Conditions under which the Task is to be performed.
3. Acceptable standards of performance.

These terms apply to each Task:
- "Inspect" means to examine by sight and touch.
- "Check" means to verify proper operation.
- "Troubleshoot" means to analyze and identify malfunctions.
- "Service" means to perform functions that ensure continued operation.
- "Repair" means to correct a defective condition.
- "Overhaul" means to disassemble, inspect, repair as necessary, and check.

The applicant should be well prepared in all knowledge and skill areas included in the standards.

Satisfactory performance to meet the requirements for certification is based on the applicant's ability to:
1. Show basic knowledge.
2. Demonstrate basic mechanic skills.
3. Perform the Tasks within the standards of the reference materials.

The practical test is passed if, in the judgment of the examiner, the applicant demonstrates the prescribed level of proficiency on the assigned Tasks in each Area of Operation. Each practical examination item must be performed, at a minimum, to the performance level in the practical test standards. For mechanic testing, there are three practical performance levels:
- Level 1: You must know basic facts and principles and be able to locate information and reference materials. You do not have to interpret information or demonstrate a physical skill.
- Level 2: Know and understand principles, theories, operations, and concepts. You must be able to find, interpret, and apply maintenance data and information. You must be able to select and utilize the appropriate tools and equipment. While you need to demonstrate adequate performance skills, you do not need to demonstrate skill at a high or return-to-service quality level.
- Level 3: Know and understand principles, theories, operations, and concepts. You must be able to find, interpret, and apply maintenance data and information, select and utilize the appropriate tools and equipment to the overall operation and maintenance of an aircraft. You must be able to demonstrate the ability to work independently and make accurate judgments of airworthiness. You must demonstrate skills at a high level which includes the ability to perform return-to-service levels of work.

If, in the judgment of the examiner, the applicant does not meet the standards of any Task performed, the associated Area of Operation is failed and therefore, the practical test is failed.

Typical areas of unsatisfactory performance and grounds for disqualification are:

1. Any action or lack of action by the applicant that requires corrective intervention by the examiner for reasons of safety.
2. Failure to follow recommended maintenance practices and/or reference material while performing projects.
3. Exceeding tolerances stated in the reference material.
4. Failure to recognize improper procedures.
5. The inability to perform to a return-to-service standard, where applicable.
6. Inadequate knowledge in any of the subject areas.

When an applicant fails a test the examiner will record the applicant's unsatisfactory performance and Tasks not completed in terms of Areas of Operation appropriate to the practical test conducted.

Basic Electricity

Study Materials

Aviation Mechanic Series: General textbook .... ASA .... Chapter 4
Aviation Maintenance Technician Handbook—General FAA-H-8083-30A .... FAA .... Chapter 12

Typical Oral Questions

1. What is the basic unit of voltage?
   The volt.

2. What is the basic unit of current?
   The amp.

3. What is the basic unit of resistance?
   The ohm.

4. Which law of electricity is the most important for an aircraft mechanic to know?
   Ohm's law.

5. What are the three elements in Ohm's law?
   Voltage, current, and resistance (volts, amps, and ohms).

6. What are five sources of electrical energy?
   Magnetism, chemical energy, light, heat and pressure.

7. What four things affect the resistance of an electrical conductor?
   The material, the cross-sectional area, the length and the temperature.

8. How can you tell the resistance of a composition resistor?
   By a series of colored bands around one end of the resistor.

9. What three things must all electrical circuits contain?
   A source of electrical energy, a load to use the energy, and conductors to join the source and the load.

10. What is the purpose of a capacitor?
    To store electrical energy in electrostatic fields.

11. What is the basic unit of capacitance?
    The farad.

12. Why should electrolytic capacitors not be used in an AC circuit?
    They are polarized. An electrolytic capacitor will pass current of one polarity, but will block current of the opposite polarity.

13. What is meant by inductance?
    The ability to store electrical energy in electromagnetic fields.

14. What is the basic unit of inductance?
    The henry.

15. What is meant by impedance?
    The total opposition to the flow of alternating current. It is the vector sum of resistance, capacitive reactance and inductive reactance.

16. How can you find the polarity of an electromagnet?
    Hold the electromagnet in your left hand with your fingers encircling the coil in the direction the electrons flow. Your thumb will point to the north end of the electromagnet.

17. In what units is impedance measured?
    In ohms.

18. What is the basic unit of electrical power in a DC circuit?
    The watt.

19. What is meant by a kilowatt?
    1,000 watts.

20. What happens to the current in a DC circuit if the voltage is increased but the resistance remains the same?
    The current increases.

21. What are three types of DC circuits, with regard to the placement of the various circuit components?
    Series, parallel and series-parallel.

22. How many cells are there in a 24-volt lead-acid battery?
    12.

23. What is the specific gravity of the electrolyte in a fully charged lead-acid battery?

    Between 1.275 and 1.300.

24. What is the range of temperatures of the electrolyte in a lead-acid battery that does not require that you apply a correction when measuring its specific gravity?

    Between 70 degrees and 90 degrees Fahrenheit.

25. What instrument is used to measure the specific gravity of the electrolyte in a lead-acid battery?

    A hydrometer.

26. How is a lead-acid battery compartment treated to protect it from corrosion?

    Paint it with an asphaltic (tar base) paint or with polyurethane enamel.

27. What is used to neutralize spilled electrolyte from a lead-acid battery?

    A solution of bicarbonate of soda and water.

28. How high should the electrolyte level be in a properly serviced lead-acid battery?

    Only up to the level of the indicator in the cell.

29. What precautions should be taken in a maintenance shop where both lead-acid and nickel-cadmium batteries are serviced?

    The two types of batteries should be kept separate, and the tools used on one type should not be used on the other.

30. Why is a hydrometer not used to measure the state of charge of a nickel-cadmium battery?

    The electrolyte of a nickel-cadmium battery does not enter into the chemical changes that occur when the battery is charged or discharged. Its specific gravity does not change appreciably.

31. What is used to neutralize spilled electrolyte from a nickel-cadmium battery?

    A solution of boric acid and water.

32. What is meant by electromagnetic induction?

    The transfer of electrical energy from one conductor to another that is not electrically connected

33. How many ohms are in a megohm?

    One million (1,000,000).

34. What part of an amp is a milliamp?

    One thousandth (0.001).

Typical Practical Projects

1. Compute the voltage and current in an electrical circuit specified by the examiner.
2. Find the total resistance of a combination of resistors that are connected in series.
3. Find the total resistance of a combination of resistors that are connected in parallel.
4. Find the power used by an electric motor when the voltage and the current are known.
5. Identify for the examiner electrical symbols used in an aircraft service manual.
6. Measure the voltage drop across each of the components in a series circuit specified by the examiner.
7. Check an electrical circuit for opens or shorts, using an ohmmeter.
8. Measure the current in an electrical circuit, using a multimeter.
9. Measure the resistance of several components, using an ohmmeter.
10. Use an electrical schematic diagram to locate the source of a malfunction described by the examiner.
11. Measure the state of charge of a lead-acid battery.
12. Correctly connect a lead-acid battery to a constant-current battery charger.
13. Correctly remove electrolyte that has been spilled from a lead-acid battery, and protect the surface around the battery from corrosion.
14. Select the proper size terminal and correctly swage it to an electrical wire.
15. Given a group of composition resistors, identify the resistance and tolerance of each one by the color code.
16. Demonstrate to the examiner the correct way to remove and install an aircraft lead-acid battery.
17. Demonstrate to the examiner the correct way to check a solid-state diode to determine whether or not it is good, or if it is open or shorted.

Aircraft Drawings

Study Materials

Aviation Mechanic Series: General textbook .... ASA .... Chapter 5

Aviation Maintenance Technician Handbook—General FAA-H-8083-30A .... FAA .... Chapter 4

Typical Oral Questions

1. What is meant by tolerance on an aircraft drawing?

   The allowable plus or minus variation from the dimension given on the drawing.

2. What is meant by clearance on an aircraft drawing?

   The amount of space, or separation, that is allowed between two components or parts.

3. What information is given in the title block of an aircraft drawing?

   The name and address of the company who made the part, the name of the part, the scale of the drawing, the name of the draftsman, the name of the engineer approving the part and the number of the part (the drawing number).

4. How are dimensions shown on an aircraft drawing?

   By numbers shown in the break of a dimension line.

5. How can you know that the aircraft drawing you are using is the most current version of the drawing?

   By the number in the revision block and by the log of the most recent drawings.

6. How many views can there be in an orthographic projection?

   Six.

7. How many views are used to show most objects in an aircraft drawing?

   Three.

8. What is the purpose of a center line on an aircraft drawing?

   This is the line that shows the center of the object in the drawing.

9. What is a fuselage station number?

   The distance in inches from the datum, measured along the longitudinal axis of the fuselage.

10. Where is the title block normally located on an aircraft drawing?

    In the lower right-hand corner of the drawing.

11. What is the purpose of a cutting plane on an aircraft drawing?

    It shows where an object has been cut to allow an auxiliary drawing to be made. The arrows on a cutting plane show the direction the auxiliary drawing is viewed.

12. How is the alternate position of a part shown on an aircraft drawing?

    By a thin line made up of a series of long dashes separated by two short dashes.

Typical Practical Projects

1. Identify the following lines on an aircraft drawing specified by the examiner:
   a. Center line
   b. Hidden line
   c. Alternate-position line
   d. Cutting plane

2. Using a performance chart for a specific aircraft engine, find the brake horsepower developed when the RPM and BMEP are known.

3. Using the electrical wire chart from AC 43.13-1B, find the correct size wire to use when the current, allowable voltage drop, and length of wire are known.

4. Using a brake specific fuel consumption curve for a specific aircraft engine, find the fuel flow in gallons per hour for a given RPM.

5. Find the dimensions that are specified by the examiner of an object on an aircraft drawing.

6. Make a sketch of an aircraft repair specified by the examiner, giving all of the information that is needed to make the repair.

7. Locate a part on an aircraft drawing specified by the examiner by using the zone numbers.

8. Identify the change number of an aircraft drawing specified by the examiner.

9. Make a sketch of an aircraft part, using the scale the examiner designates.

10. Using an electrical schematic diagram specified by the examiner, identify the components shown by the schematic symbols.

Weight and Balance

Study Materials

Aviation Mechanic Series: General textbook	ASA	Chapter 6
Aviation Maintenance Technician Handbook—General FAA-H-8083-30A	FAA	Chapter 6
Advisory Circular 43.13-1B	FAA	Pages 10-1–10-22

Typical Oral Questions

1. Where must a record be kept of the current empty weight and the current center of gravity of an aircraft?

   In the aircraft flight manual or weight and balance records required by 14 CFR §23.1583.

2. What is meant by the datum that is used for weight and balance computations?

   A readily identified reference chosen by the aircraft manufacturer from which all longitudinal locations on the aircraft are referenced.

3. Why are the distances of all of the items installed in an aircraft measured from the datum when computing weight and balance?

   This makes it possible to find the point about which the aircraft would balance (the center of gravity).

4. What are two reasons weight and balance control are important in an aircraft?

   For safety of flight and for most efficient performance of the aircraft.

5. What is meant by moment in the computation of weight and balance?

   A force that tends to cause rotation. It is the product of the weight of an object in pounds and the distance of the object from the datum in inches.

6. How do you find the moment of an item that is installed in an aircraft?

   Multiply the weight of the item in pounds by its distance from the datum in inches.

7. What is meant by the arm of an item that is installed in an aircraft?

   The distance, in inches, between the center of gravity of the item and the datum.

8. Why must we consider the category under which an aircraft is licensed when we compute its weight and balance?

   The different categories under which an aircraft can be licensed have different maximum gross weights and different center of gravity ranges.

9. Where can you find the leveling means that are specified for a particular aircraft?

   In the Type Certificate Data Sheets for the aircraft.

10. Where is the arm of an item installed in an aircraft recorded?

    In the Type Certificate Data Sheets for the aircraft.

11. What must be done to find the empty weight of an aircraft if it has been weighed with fuel in its tanks?

    The weight of the fuel and its moment must be subtracted from the weight and moment of the aircraft as it was weighed.

12. What is meant by the tare weight that is used in a weight and balance computation?

    The weight of the chocks and other items that are used to hold the aircraft on the scales.

13. What must be done to the tare weight when an aircraft is weighed?

    It must be subtracted from the scale reading to find the weight of the aircraft.

14. What is meant by minimum fuel as is used in the computation of aircraft weight and balance?

    No more fuel than the quantity necessary for one-half hour of operation at rated maximum continuous power. It is the maximum amount of fuel used in weight and balance computations when low fuel may adversely affect the most critical balance conditions.

15. What is meant by the maximum zero fuel weight of an aircraft?

    The maximum permissible weight of a loaded aircraft (passengers, crew, cargo, etc.), less its fuel.

16. What is meant by undrainable fuel?

    The fuel that is left in the tank, lines and components when the aircraft is placed in level flight position and the fuel drained at the main fuel strainer. This is also called residual fuel.

17. Describe the way you would find the empty weight and empty weight center of gravity of an airplane if there are no weight and balance records available.

    The aircraft is weighed, and the empty weight center of gravity is computed. These values are recorded in new weight and balance records that are started for the aircraft.

18. What is meant by permanent ballast for an aircraft?

    Weight that is permanently installed in an aircraft to bring the empty weight center of gravity into allowable limits.

19. Which has the more critical center of gravity range, an airplane or a helicopter?

    A helicopter.

20. What equipment must be installed in an aircraft when it is weighed to find its empty weight center of gravity?

    All of the equipment that is listed in the Aircraft Equipment List as "required equipment" or as equipment that is permanently installed.

21. What is the significance of the empty weight center of gravity range of an aircraft?

    If the empty weight center of gravity falls within the EWCG range, the aircraft cannot be legally loaded in such a way that its loaded center of gravity will fall outside of the allowable loaded CG range. Not all aircraft have an EWCG range.

22. Why is empty weight center of gravity range not given in the Type Certificate Data Sheets for some aircraft?

    The empty weight center of gravity range is given only for aircraft that cannot be legally loaded in such a way that their loaded center of gravity will fall outside of the allowable limits.

Typical Practical Projects

1. Find the new empty weight and empty weight center of gravity for this aircraft after it has been altered by removing two seats and replacing them with a cabinet, one seat, and some radio gear.

    Aircraft empty weight = 2,886 pounds
    Empty weight total moment = 107,865.78
    Each removed seat weighs 15 pounds, located at station 73.
    Installed cabinet weighs 97 pounds, installed at station 73.
    New seat weighs 20 pounds, installed at station 73.
    Radio gear weighs 30 pounds, installed at station 97.

2. Find the amount of ballast that is needed to bring this aircraft into its proper center of gravity range:

    Aircraft as loaded weighs 4,954 pounds.
    Aircraft loaded center of gravity is +30.5 inches aft of the datum.
    Loaded center of gravity range is +32.0 to +42.1 inches aft of the datum.
    The ballast arm is +162 inches.

3. Find the distance in inches to the left of the fulcrum that a box, weighing 20 pounds, would have to be placed in order to balance a board that contains a box weighing 10 pounds located four feet to the right of the fulcrum, and one weighing five pounds that is located two feet to the right of the fulcrum.

4. Find the empty weight and the empty weight center of gravity of an airplane that has the following scale weights:

    Left main wheel = 1,765 pounds, arm = +195.5 inches
    Right main wheel = 1,775 pounds, arm = +195.5 inches
    Nosewheel = 2,322 pounds, arm = +83.5 inches

5. Find the empty weight and empty weight center of gravity of an aircraft that is specified by the examiner.

6. Find the center of gravity of a fully loaded aircraft specified by the examiner.

7. Find the amount of fuel that is needed by an aircraft specified by the examiner as the minimum fuel for an adverse loaded center of gravity condition.

8. Prepare an aircraft specified by the examiner for weighing.

9. Find the loaded weight and the loaded weight center of gravity of a helicopter specified by the examiner. Determine whether or not it falls within its weight and center of gravity limits.

10. Use the center of gravity envelope in a weight and balance report to find the forward and aft center of gravity limits for a specified weight of the aircraft.

11. Locate the datum of an aircraft specified by the examiner, using the appropriate Type Certificate Data Sheets.

Fluid Lines and Fittings

Study Materials

Aviation Mechanic Series: General textbook .... ASA .... Chapter 9
Aviation Maintenance Technician Handbook—General FAA-H-8083-30A .... FAA .... Chapter 9
Advisory Circular 43.13-1B .... FAA .... Pages 9-18–9-26

Typical Oral Questions

1. Of what material are most low-pressure rigid fluid lines made?
   1100-1/2 hard or 3003-1/2 hard aluminum alloy tubing.

2. Is the size of a rigid fluid line determined by its inside or its outside diameter?
   By its outside diameter.

3. When routing a fluid line parallel to an electrical wire bundle, which should be on top?
   The electrical wire bundle should be on top.

4. What is the function of the lay line (the identification stripe) that runs the length of a flexible hose?
   This line shows the mechanic whether or not the line has been twisted when it was installed. The line should be straight, not spiraled.

5. How can you distinguish an AN fluid line fitting from an AC fitting?
   The AN fitting has a shoulder between the end of the flare cone and the first thread. The threads of an AC fitting extend all of the way to the flare cone.

6. Where are quick-disconnect fluid line couplings normally used in an aircraft hydraulic system?
   Quick disconnect couplings are normally used where the engine-driven pump connects into the hydraulic system.

7. Is the size of a flexible hose determined by its inside or its outside diameter?
   By its inside diameter.

8. What is the minimum amount of slack that must be left when a flexible hose is installed in an aircraft hydraulic system?
   The hose should be at least 5% longer than the distance between the fittings. This extra length provides the needed slack.

9. How tight should an MS flareless fitting be tightened?
   Tighten the fitting by hand until it is snug, and then turn it with a wrench for 1/6-turn to 1/3-turn. Never turn it more than 1/3-turn with a wrench.

10. What damage can be caused by overtightening an MS flareless fitting?
    Overtightening drives the cutting edge of the sleeve deeply into the tube and weakens it.

11. What kind of rigid tubing can be flared with a double flare?
    5052-O and 6061-T aluminum alloy tubing in sizes from 1/8-inch to 3/8-inch OD.

12. What is the principal advantage of Teflon hose for use in an aircraft hydraulic system?
    Teflon hose retains its high strength under conditions of high temperature.

13. What precautions should be taken when flaring a piece of aluminum alloy tubing?
    The end of the tubing must be polished so it will not crack when it is stretched with the flaring tool.

14. How much pressure is used to proof test a flexible hose assembly?
    This varies with the hose, but it is generally about two times the recommended operating pressure for the hose.

Typical Practical Projects

1. Make up a piece of rigid tubing that includes cutting it to the correct length, making a bend of the correct angle and radius, and correctly installing the type of fitting specified by the examiner.

2. Make a proper single flare in a piece of aluminum alloy tubing.

3. Make a proper double flare in a piece of aluminum alloy tubing.

4. Install a fitting on a piece of flexible hose and proof test it.

5. Install a piece of rigid tubing in an aircraft, using the correct routing and approved mounting methods.

6. Identify, by the color code, the type of fluid that is carried in various fluid lines in an aircraft.

7. Install and properly preset an MS flareless fitting on a piece of rigid tubing.

8. Repair a piece of damaged rigid tubing by installing a union and the proper connecting fittings.

Materials and Processes

Study Materials

Aviation Mechanic Series: General textbook	ASA	Chapter 7
Aviation Maintenance Technician Handbook—General FAA-H-8083-30A	FAA	Chapter 7
Advisory Circular 43.13-1B	FAA	Pages 5-1–5-56 and 7-1–7-74

Typical Oral Questions

1. What is the proper type of nondestructive inspection to use for locating surface cracks in an aluminum alloy casting or forging?

   Zyglo or dye penetrant.

2. Explain the procedure to use when making a dye penetrant inspection of a part.

   Clean the part thoroughly and apply the penetrant and allow it to soak for the recommended time. Remove all of the penetrant from the surface and apply the developer.

3. Explain the procedure to use when making a magnetic particle inspection of a part.

   Thoroughly clean the part, magnetize it as directed by the appropriate service manual, flow the indicating medium over the surface and inspect it under a "black" light. When the inspection is complete, thoroughly demagnetize the part.

4. What inspection method would be most appropriate for checking a nonferrous metal part for intergranular corrosion?

   Eddy current inspection.

5. What inspection method would be most appropriate for checking the internal structure of an airplane wing for corrosion?

   X-ray inspection.

6. Why is it important that all engine parts which have been inspected by the magnetic particle method be completely demagnetized?

   If the parts are not completely demagnetized, they will attract steel particles that are produced by engine wear and will cause damage to bearing surfaces.

7. Why is it important that all parts be thoroughly cleaned before they are inspected by the dye penetrant method?

   Any grease or dirt in a fault will keep the penetrant from seeping into the fault.

8. Why is it important that a piece of aluminum alloy be quenched immediately after it is removed from the heat-treating oven?

   Any delay in quenching aluminum alloy after it is removed from the oven will allow the grain structure to grow enough that intergranular corrosion is likely to form in the metal.

9. Explain the way a steel structure is normalized after it has been welded.

   Heat the steel structure to a temperature above its critical temperature and allow it to cool in still air.

10. Why is a piece of steel tempered after it has been hardened?

    When steel is hardened, it becomes brittle and tempering removes some of this brittleness.

11. What is meant by an icebox rivet?

    A rivet made of 2017 or 2024 aluminum alloy. These rivets are heat-treated and quenched, then stored in a subfreezing ice box until they are ready to be used. The cold storage delays the hardening of the rivet.

12. What type of loading should be avoided when using a self-locking nut on an aircraft bolt?

    A self-locking nut should not be used for any application where there are any rotational forces applied to the nut or to the bolt.

13. What determines the correct grip length of a bolt used in an aircraft structure?

    The grip length of the bolt should be the same as the combined thicknesses of the materials being held by the bolt.

14. How tight should the nut be installed on a clevis bolt that is used to attach a cable fitting to a control surface horn?

    The nut on a clevis bolt should not be tight enough to prevent the clevis bolt turning in the cable fitting and the horn.

15. Why is it very important that the surface of a piece of clad aluminum alloy not be scratched?

    The pure aluminum used for the cladding is noncorrosive, but the aluminum alloy below the cladding is susceptible to corrosion. If the cladding is scratched through, corrosion could form.

16. What determines the size of tip that is to be used when gas welding steel?

    The thickness of the material being welded. The size of the tip orifice determines the amount of flame produced, and thus the amount of heat that is put into the metal.

17. How is the welding flux removed from a piece of aluminum that has been gas welded?

    It should be removed by scrubbing it with hot water and a bristle brush.

18. What must be done to a welded joint if it must be rewelded?

    All traces of the old weld must be removed so the new weld will penetrate the base metal.

19. What kind of measuring instrument is used to measure the runout of an aircraft engine crankshaft?

    A dial indicator.

20. What measuring instruments are used to measure the fit between a rocker arm shaft and its bushing?

    The outside diameter of the shaft is measured with a micrometer caliper. The inside of the bushing is measured with a telescoping gauge and the same micrometer caliper.

21. What is the smallest size cable that is allowed to be used in the primary control system of an aircraft?

    1/8-inch diameter.

22. What type of control cable must be used when pulleys are used to change the direction of cable travel?

    Extra-flexible cable (7 × 19).

23. Explain the way a piece of aluminum alloy is solution heat-treated.

    The aluminum is heated in an oven to the proper temperature for a specified time; then it is removed and quenched in water.

24. What is meant by precipitation heat treatment of a piece of aluminum alloy?

    After a piece of aluminum has been solution heat-treated, it is held at a specified elevated temperature for a period of time. Precipitation heat-treating is also called artificial aging.

25. How does filiform corrosion usually appear on an aircraft structure?

    As thread-like lines of puffiness under a film of polyurethane or other dense finish system topcoats.

Typical Practical Projects

1. Using dye penetrant, inspect a part furnished by the examiner.
2. Inspect a part by the magnetic particle inspection method. Correctly magnetize the part, inspect it and properly demagnetize it.
3. Use a dial indicator to measure the runout of the crankshaft of an aircraft engine.
4. Use a telescoping gauge and a micrometer caliper to measure the fit between a shaft and its bushing.
5. Measure the diameter of a shaft to the nearest ten-thousandth of an inch, using a vernier micrometer caliper.
6. Properly safety wire two turnbuckles in an aircraft control system. Use the single-wrap method for one turnbuckle and the double-wrap method for the other.
7. Given an assortment of aircraft bolts, identify a close tolerance bolt, a corrosion-resistant steel bolt and an aluminum alloy bolt.
8. Given an assortment of aircraft rivets, identify an AD rivet, a DD rivet, a D rivet and an A rivet.
9. Install a swaged fitting on a piece of aircraft control cable.
10. Correctly install a Heli-coil insert in an aluminum casting.
11. Given a piece of metal with a bad weld, identify the reason the weld is not airworthy.
12. Identify, by the number of strands of wire, a piece of extra-flexible control cable, and measure its diameter.
13. Properly safety a series of bolts that are specified by the examiner.
14. Properly install a cotter pin in a bolt that is fitted with a castellated nut.

Ground Operation and Servicing

Study Materials

Aviation Mechanic Series: General textbook .... ASA .... Chapter 10

Aviation Maintenance Technician Handbook—General FAA-H-8083-30A .... FAA .... Chapter 1

Typical Oral Questions

1. What is the proper way to extinguish an induction system fire that occurs when starting a reciprocating engine?

   Keep the engine running and blow the fire out. If this does not work, use a CO_2 fire extinguisher directed into the carburetor air inlet.

2. What type of fire extinguisher is best suited for extinguishing an induction fire in a reciprocating engine?

   Carbon dioxide.

3. What must be done if a hung start occurs when starting a turbojet engine?

   Terminate the starting operation and find the reason the engine would not accelerate as it should.

4. What is meant by a liquid lock in the cylinder of an aircraft engine, and how is one cleared?

   Oil accumulates in the cylinders below the center line of the engine and prevents the piston moving to the top of its stroke. To clear a liquid lock, remove one of the spark plugs and turn the engine crankshaft until all of the oil is forced out of the cylinder.

5. What special precautions should be taken when towing an aircraft that is equipped with a steerable nosewheel?

   Be sure that the nosewheel does not try to turn past its stops. Some aircraft must have the torsion links on the nosewheel strut disconnected when they are being towed.

6. When starting an aircraft engine that is equipped with a float carburetor, in what position should the carburetor heat control be placed?

   In the "Cold" position.

7. How far ahead of an idling turbojet engine does the danger area extend?

   25 feet.

8. Why is it important that turbine fuel not be mixed with aviation gasoline that is used in an aircraft reciprocating engine?

   The turbine engine fuel will cause the engine to detonate.

9. What grade of aviation gasoline is dyed blue?

   Low-lead 100-octane.

10. What damage is likely to occur if an aircraft reciprocating engine that is designed to use 100-octane fuel is operated with 80-octane fuel?

    Detonation will occur, which will cause such things as bent connecting rods, burned pistons and cracked cylinder heads.

11. What is meant by detonation in an aircraft reciprocating engine?

    Detonation is an uncontrolled burning of the fuel in the cylinder of an engine. It is an explosion, rather than a smooth burning.

12. What is the danger of using a fuel that vaporizes too readily?

    Vapor lock can occur in the fuel lines. This will shut off the flow of fuel to the engine.

13. What type of fuel is Jet-A fuel?

    A fuel with a heavy kerosine base, a flash point of 110–150°F, a freezing point of -40°F, and a heat energy content of 18,600 Btu/pound.

14. What is the significance of the two numbers, 100/130, in the dual rating of aviation gasoline?

    The first number is the octane rating or performance number of the fuel when operating with a lean mixture, and the last number is the octane rating or performance number when operating with a rich mixture.

15. What are two functions of tetraethyl lead that is added to aviation gasoline?

    It increases the critical pressure and temperature of the fuel, and it acts as a lubricant for the valves.

16. What information must be located near the fuel tank filler opening in an aircraft powered by a reciprocating engine?

    The word "Avgas," and the minimum fuel grade.

17. What information must be located near the fuel tank filler opening in an aircraft powered by a turbine engine?

    The words "Jet Fuel," the permissible fuel designations, or references to the AFM for permissible fuel designations. For pressure fueling systems, the maximum permissible fueling supply pressure and the maximum permissible defueling pressure.

18. What action should a mechanic take while taxiing an aircraft on a runway if the tower shines a flashing red light at him?

    Taxi the aircraft clear of the runway in use.

19. What publication lists the standard hand signals that are used for directing a taxiing aircraft?

    Aeronautical Information Manual.

20. What should be done to a reciprocating engine fuel system if turbine fuel is inadvertently put into the tanks and the engine is run?

    The entire fuel system must be drained and flushed with gasoline, the engine given a compression check and all of the cylinders given a borescope inspection. The oil must be drained and all of the filters and strainers checked. After the aircraft is properly fueled, the engine must be given a proper run-up and check.

Typical Practical Projects

1. Properly start, run up and shut down an aircraft reciprocating engine.

2. Properly start, run up and shut down an aircraft turbine engine.

3. Drain a sample of fuel from an aircraft fuel system. Check the fuel for the presence of water and identify the grade of the fuel.

4. Demonstrate to the examiner the correct hand signals to use when directing the operator of an aircraft to:
    a. Start engine number one
    b. Move the aircraft ahead
    c. Stop the aircraft
    d. Emergency stop the aircraft
    e. Shut the engine down

5. Demonstrate to the examiner the correct way to clear the cylinders of an aircraft reciprocating engine of a hydraulic lock.

6. Demonstrate the correct method of securing an aircraft to the flight line tie-downs.

7. Demonstrate the correct way to hand prop an aircraft engine.

8. Properly secure an airplane for overnight storage on an outside tie-down area.

9. Jack one wheel of an airplane so the wheel can be removed. Explain to the examiner the safety precautions that must be taken.

10. Connect a tow bar to an aircraft nosewheel for moving the aircraft. Explain to the examiner the precautions that must be taken when moving the aircraft.

11. Fuel an aircraft using the proper grade and amount of fuel. Explain to the examiner the safety procedures that must be used for this operation.

12. Properly connect auxiliary power to an aircraft for the purpose of starting the engine. Explain to the examiner the safety precautions that should be taken.

13. Taxi an aircraft, using the proper safety procedures.

14. Properly secure a helicopter for overnight storage in an outside parking area accounting for high wind conditions.

Cleaning and Corrosion Control

Study Materials

Aviation Mechanic Series: General textbook .... ASA .... Chapter 8

Aviation Maintenance Technician Handbook—General FAA-H-8083-30A .... FAA .... Chapter 8

Typical Oral Questions

1. Identify the areas of an aircraft that are most prone to corrosion.

   Battery compartment, exhaust system and exhaust trails, wheel wells, lower area of the belly (bilge), piano hinges, areas of dissimilar metal contact, welded areas, inside of fuel tanks especially integral tanks, metal fittings and under high stress, lavatories and foodservice areas.

2. Where is filiform corrosion most likely to occur on an aircraft?

   Under a dense coating of topcoat enamel such as polyurethane. Filiform corrosion is caused by improperly cured primer.

3. Where is fretting corrosion most likely to occur on an aircraft?

   In a location where there is a slight amount of relative movement between two components, and no way for the corrosive residue to be removed as it forms.

4. Where is intergranular corrosion most likely to occur on an aircraft?

   Along the grain boundaries of aluminum alloys that have been improperly heat-treated. Extruded aluminum alloy is susceptible to intergranular corrosion.

5. Where is dissimilar metal corrosion most likely to occur on an aircraft?

   Anywhere different types of metal come in contact with each other, especially where moisture is present.

6. Where is stress corrosion most likely to occur on an aircraft?

   In any metal component that is continually under a tensile stress. The metal around holes in castings that are fitted with pressed-in bushings are susceptible to stress corrosion.

7. What must be done to a piece of aluminum alloy to remove surface corrosion and to treat the metal to prevent further corrosion?

   Remove the corrosion residue with a bristle brush or a nylon scrubber. Neutralize the surface with chromic acid or with some type of conversion coating. Protect the surface from further corrosion with a coat of paint.

8. What is used to keep corrosion from forming on structural aluminum alloy?

   An oxide coating or aluminum cladding.

9. How may rust be removed from a highly stressed metal part?

   By glass bead blasting, by careful polishing with mild abrasive paper or by using fine buffing compound on a cloth buffing wheel.

10. How should corrosion be minimized at piano hinges?

    They should be kept as clean and dry as practicable and lubricated with a low viscosity moisture dispersing agent.

11. What tools are proper for removing corrosion from aluminum alloy?

    Aluminum wool or aluminum wire brushes. Severe corrosion can be removed with a rotary file.

12. What is used to clean transparent plastic windshields and windows of an aircraft?

    Mild soap and plenty of clean water.

13. What is used to neutralize the electrolyte from a lead-acid battery that has been spilled on an aircraft structure?

    A solution of bicarbonate of soda and water.

14. What is used to neutralize the electrolyte from a nickel-cadmium battery that has been spilled on an aircraft structure?

    A solution of boric acid and water, or vinegar.

15. What solvent is recommended for removing grease from aircraft fabric prior to doping it?
    Methyl Ethyl Ketone (MEK) or lacquer thinner.

16. What can be used to repair the anodized surface of an aluminum alloy part?
    A chemical conversion coating such as Alodine.

17. What type of device is used to remove surface corrosion from a piece of magnesium alloy?
    A stiff hog-bristle brush.

18. How is the inside of structural steel tubing protected from corrosion?
    The tubing is filled with hot linseed oil and then drained.

Typical Practical Projects

1. Given samples of corroded aircraft structural materials, identify the type of corrosion and describe the correct procedure for removing the corrosion and treating the damaged area to prevent further corrosion.

2. Remove the corrosion from a piece of aluminum alloy furnished by the examiner and treat the metal to prevent further corrosion.

3. Treat a piece of aircraft structure so moisture cannot reach the metal and cause corrosion.

4. Select the proper cleaning materials and remove grease and exhaust deposits from an aircraft structure.

5. Select the proper cleaning materials and remove oil that has been spilled on an aircraft tire.

6. Demonstrate to the examiner the correct way to remove rust from a highly stressed engine component.

7. Properly remove the finish from a piece of painted aluminum alloy.

8. Properly remove the finish from a piece of painted fiberglass reinforced plastic material.

9. Demonstrate the correct way to clean a transparent plastic cockpit enclosure or windshield.

10. Remove corrosion from a lead-acid battery box and treat the box to prevent further corrosion.

11. Treat the cylinders of a reciprocating engine to prevent rust and corrosion when the engine is being prepared for long-term storage.

12. Treat a piece of welded steel tubular structure to prevent rust and corrosion inside the tubing.

Mathematics

Study Materials

Aviation Mechanic Series: General textbook .... ASA .... Chapter 2
Aviation Maintenance Technician Handbook—General FAA-H-8083-30A .... FAA .... Chapter 3

Typical Oral Questions

1. What formula is used to find the area of a circle?

   $A = 0.7854 \times D^2$

   or

   $A = \pi \times R^2$

2. What formula is used to find the volume of a cylinder?

   $V = 0.7854 \times D^2 \times H$.

3. What formula is used to find the area of a rectangle?

   $A = L \times W$

4. What formula is used to find the volume of a rectangular solid?

   $V = L \times W \times H$

5. What formula is used to find the area of a triangle?

   $A = (B \times H) \div 2$

6. What is the significance of the constant π?

   Pi (π) is the ratio of the circumference to the diameter of any circle.

7. What is the value of the constant π?

   $\pi = 3.1416$

8. What is meant by the root of a number?

   The root of a number is one of two or more equal numbers that, when multiplied together, will produce the number.

9. What is the eighth power of 2?

   256.

10. What is the square root of 4,096?

    64.

11. What is meant by a negative number?

    A number less than 0, or a number that is preceded by a minus sign.

12. What is meant by a ratio and how is a ratio expressed?

    A fraction that compares one number to another; for example, 6:2 is a ratio.

Typical Practical Projects

1. Given a list of common fractions, convert them to decimal fractions.

2. Given a list of decimal fractions, convert them to common fractions with the smallest whole denominator.

3. Given the bore and stroke of an aircraft engine cylinder compute the piston displacement of one cylinder.

4. Given the bore, stroke and clearance volume of an aircraft engine cylinder, compute the compression ratio of the cylinder.

5. Given the span and chord of a rectangular wing, compute the area of the wing.

6. Given the length, width and depth of a fuel tank, find the number of U.S. gallons of fuel the tank will hold.

7. Find the square and cube of a list of numbers.

8. Find the square root of a list of numbers.

9. Add, subtract, multiply, and divide a list of positive and negative numbers.

10. Add, subtract, multiply, and divide a list of common fractions.

11. Find the number that is a given percentage of another number.

12. Change a list of mixed numbers into improper fractions.

13. Given the diameter of a circle, find its area.

14. Find the number of square inches of metal needed to make an open-end cylinder having a given diameter and length.

15. Solve a problem that involves square roots in the numerator and the square of a number in the denominator.

16. Find the area of a trapezoid when the altitude and the length of both of the bases are given.

17. Convert a list of common fractions into percentages.

18. Find the speed of rotation of the shaft of a driven gear when the gear ratio and the rotational speed of the drive gear are given.

Maintenance Forms and Records

Study Materials

Aviation Mechanic Series: General textbook .... ASA .... Chapter 13
Aviation Maintenance Technician Handbook—General FAA-H-8083-30A .... FAA .... Chapter 2
Title 14 of the Code of Federal Regulations, Part 43.. FAA
Title 14 of the Code of Federal Regulations, Part 91.. FAA

Typical Oral Questions

1. What records must be made of a 100-hour inspection before the aircraft is approved for return to service?

   An entry must be made in the aircraft maintenance records that describes the type of inspection, the extent of the inspection, the date of the inspection, the aircraft total time in service, and the signature and certificate number of the person approving or disapproving the aircraft for return to service.

2. What record must be made of the compliance of an Airworthiness Directive?

   An entry must be made in the aircraft maintenance records stating that the AD has been complied with. This entry must include the AD number and revision date, the date of compliance, the aircraft total time in service, the method of compliance and whether or not this is a recurring AD. If it is a recurring AD, the time of next compliance must be noted.

3. What record must be made of a major repair to an aircraft structure?

   An FAA Form 337 must be completed for the repair, and a record must be made in the aircraft maintenance records referencing the Form 337 by its date.

4. How many copies must be made of a Form 337 after a major airframe repair? What is the disposition of each of the copies?

   At least two copies must be made. The original signed form goes to the aircraft owner, and a copy goes to the FAA office.

5. Who is authorized to perform a 100-hour inspection on an aircraft?

   A certificated mechanic who holds an Airframe and a Powerplant rating.

6. Who is authorized to perform an annual inspection on an aircraft?

   A certificated A&P mechanic who holds an Inspection Authorization.

7. For how long must the record of a 100-hour inspection be kept?

   For one year, or until the next 100-hour inspection is completed.

8. Can a certificated A&P mechanic supervise an unlicensed person as the unlicensed person performs a 100-hour inspection on an aircraft?

   No, a certificated mechanic must personally perform the inspection.

9. Where can you find a list of the basic items that must be inspected on a 100-hour inspection?

   In 14 CFR Part 43, Appendix D.

10. Where can you find an example of the correct type of write-up to use for recording a 100-hour inspection in the aircraft maintenance records?

    In 14 CFR §43.11.

11. What is done with the aircraft maintenance records that include the current status of the applicable Airworthiness Directives when the aircraft is sold?

    These maintenance records must be transferred with the aircraft when it is sold.

12. What is meant by a progressive inspection?

    An inspection that is approved by the FAA Flight Standards Office in which an aircraft is inspected according to an approved schedule. This allows the complete inspection to be conducted over a period of time without having to keep the aircraft out of service as long as would be necessary to perform the entire inspection at one time.

13. Who is authorized to rebuild an aircraft engine and issue a zero time maintenance record?

    Only the manufacturer of the engine or a repair station approved by the manufacturer.

14. What action must a mechanic take if the aircraft being inspecting on a 100-hour inspection fails because of an unairworthy component?

    The aircraft maintenance records must indicate that the aircraft has been inspected and found to be in an unairworthy condition because of certain discrepancies. A signed and dated list of these discrepancies must be given to the owner or lessee of the aircraft.

Typical Practical Projects

1. Prepare a Form 337 describing a major repair or major alteration that is specified by the examiner.

2. Prepare a maintenance record entry that approves an aircraft for return to service after a 100-hour inspection.

3. Prepare a maintenance record entry that records the proper compliance with an Airworthiness Directive specified by the examiner.

4. Prepare a maintenance record entry that records the required tests and inspection for an altimeter system that is installed on an aircraft that is flown under Instrument Flight Rules.

5. Given a list of repairs and alterations to an aircraft and engine, identify the operations that require a Form 337 to be filled out.

6. Locate in the Federal Aviation Regulations the description of the tests and inspections that must be performed on altimeter systems, and on ATC transponders.

Basic Physics

Study Materials

Aviation Mechanic Series: General textbook .... ASA .... Chapter 3

Aviation Maintenance Technician Handbook—General FAA-H-8083-30A .... FAA .... Chapter 5

Typical Oral Questions

1. What is meant by matter?

   Anything that occupies space and has weight.

2. What are the three basic physical states in which matter can exist?

   Solid, liquid and gas.

3. What is meant by pressure?

   Force that acts on a unit of area.

4. What is the standard sea level atmospheric pressure expressed in inches of mercury, and in pounds per square inches?

   29.92 inches of mercury and 14.69 pounds per square inch.

5. What characteristic of the atmosphere determines the speed of sound?

   Its temperature.

6. What is meant by the density of air?

   The weight of a given volume of air.

7. How much force is produced by 1,000 psi of hydraulic pressure acting on a piston whose area is 20 square inches?

   20,000 pounds.

8. What is meant by the fulcrum of a lever?

   The point about which the lever rotates.

9. Give an example of a first-class lever, a second-class lever and a third-class lever.

   First-class: A screwdriver being used to pry the lid from a can of paint

   Second-class: A wheelbarrow

   Third-class: A hydraulically retracted landing gear

10. How many cubic inches of fluid is forced out of a cylinder by a piston whose area is 20 square inches when the piston moves five inches?

    100 cubic inches.

11. What is meant by a temperature of absolute zero?

    The temperature at which all molecular movement stops.

12. What is the Celsius equivalent of a temperature of 50°F?

    10°C.

13. What formula is used to find the amount of work done when an object is moved across a floor?

    Work = Force × Distance.

14. What determines the mechanical advantage of an arrangement of ropes and pulleys?

    The number of ropes that support the weight.

15. What determines the mechanical advantage of a gear train?

    The ratio between the number of teeth on the drive gear and the number of teeth on the driven gear.

16. What will happen to the pressure of a confined gas if the temperature of the gas is increased?

    The pressure will increase.

17. What are three methods of heat transfer?

    Conduction, convection and radiation.

18. What is meant by the absolute humidity of the atmosphere?

    The actual amount of water that is in a given volume of air.

Typical Practical Projects

1. Identify from a drawing of a lever furnished by the examiner, the class of lever and its mechanical advantage.

2. Using a dimensioned diagram of a hydraulic cylinder furnished by the examiner, find the amount of force exerted by a specified amount of hydraulic pressure.

3. Find the amount of force needed to roll a barrel of oil up an inclined plane when the length of the plane, the weight of the barrel, and the height the barrel is raised are all known.

4. Using a diagram of a gear train furnished by the examiner, find the speed and direction of rotation of the output shaft when the speed and direction of the input shaft are known.

5. Convert a list of Celsius temperatures into Fahrenheit temperatures.

6. Convert a list of Fahrenheit temperatures into Celsius temperatures.

7. Using a battery hydrometer, measure the specific gravity of the electrolyte in a lead-acid battery.

8. Give examples of heat transfer by conduction, convection and radiation.

Maintenance Publications

Study Materials

Aviation Mechanic Series: General textbook .... ASA .... Chapter 11
Advisory Circular Checklist AC 00-2 .... FAA
Status of the Federal Aviation Regulations AC 00-44 .... FAA

Typical Oral Questions

1. What is an FAA Advisory Circular?

   A publication put out by the FAA for information, rather than for regulation.

2. What is a Federal Aviation Regulation?

   The actual law regarding the conduct of aviation activities.

3. Where can a mechanic find specific instructions for the maintenance of a particular aircraft?

   In the FAA-approved maintenance manual produced by the manufacturer of the aircraft.

4. What is the purpose of an Airworthiness Directive?

   An Airworthiness Directive is issued by the FAA to warn the owner or operator of an aircraft of a condition that has been discovered that renders the aircraft, engine or component unairworthy.

5. How does a mechanic record the compliance with an Airworthiness Directive?

   An entry must be made in the aircraft maintenance records stating that the AD has been complied with. This entry must include the AD number and revision date, the date of compliance, the aircraft total time in service, the method of compliance and whether or not this is a recurring AD. If it is a recurring AD, the time of next compliance must be noted.

6. Where can a mechanic find a list of major alterations that have been made and approved for FAA certificated aircraft?

   In the Summary of Supplemental Type Certificates.

7. In what part of the regulations can a mechanic find the airworthiness standards for normal, utility and acrobatic category aircraft?

   14 CFR Part 23.

8. In what part of the regulations can a mechanic find the airworthiness standards for transport category aircraft?

   14 CFR Part 25.

9. In what part of the regulations can a mechanic find the airworthiness standards for normal category rotorcraft?

   14 CFR Part 27.

10. In what part of the regulations can a mechanic find a list of items that must be inspected on an annual or 100-hour inspection?

    14 CFR Part 43, Appendix D.

11. In what information provided by the FAA can a mechanic find a list of the engines that are approved for a specific FAA certificated airplane?

    In the Type Certificate Data Sheets for the aircraft.

12. In what part of the regulations can a mechanic find the specifications for the identification numbers that must be displayed on an aircraft?

    14 CFR Part 45.

13. What type of information is issued by the manufacturer of an aircraft or engine that allows the mechanic to properly maintain the aircraft or engine?

    FAA-approved service manuals.

14. How does the manufacturer of an aircraft or engine keep the mechanics in the field aware of changes that affect the safety and performance of the aircraft or engines?

    By the issuance of service bulletins.

15. In what government publication can a mechanic find the category in which a particular aircraft is certificated?

    In the Type Certificate Data Sheets for the aircraft.

Aviation Mechanic Privileges and Limitations

Study Materials

Aviation Mechanic Series: General textbook .... ASA .... Chapter 12
Aviation Maintenance Technician Handbook—General FAA-H-8083-30A .... FAA .... Chapter 13
Title 14 of the Code of Federal Regulations, Part 65 .... FAA

Typical Oral Questions

1. What part of the Federal Aviation Regulations gives the requirements for the issuance of a mechanic certificate?

   14 CFR Part 65.

2. What are the two ratings that can be issued to a mechanic certificate?

   Airframe and Powerplant.

3. For how long is a mechanic certificate valid?

   It is effective until it is surrendered or revoked.

4. What is the recency of experience requirement for keeping a mechanic certificate valid?

   The holder of the certificate must have used it technically or in a supervisory capacity for at least six months of the preceding 24 months.

5. For how long is a temporary mechanic certificate valid?

   For 120 days.

6. Is it legal for a certificated aircraft mechanic to make a minor repair to an aircraft instrument?

   No, not unless they are operating under the authority of a Certificated Repair Station approved for this operation.

7. Who is authorized to approve an aircraft for return to service after a major repair has been made to its basic structure?

   An A&P mechanic holding an Inspection Authorization.

8. Is it legal for a certificated powerplant mechanic to make a major repair to a propeller?

   No, not unless they are operating under the authority of a Certificated Repair Station approved for this operation.

9. In what part of the Federal Aviation Regulations can a mechanic find a list of operations that are considered to be major airframe repairs?

   14 CFR Part 43, Appendix A.

10. In what part of the Federal Aviation Regulations can a mechanic find a list of items that should be inspected on a 100-hour inspection?

    14 CFR Part 43, Appendix D.

11. Is it legal for a certificated mechanic to supervise an uncertificated person while the uncertificated person performs a 100-hour inspection on an FAA-certificated aircraft?

    No, only a certificated mechanic can perform a 100-hour inspection.

12. Who is authorized to conduct an annual inspection on an FAA certificated aircraft?

    An A&P mechanic who holds an Inspection Authorization.

13. Under what conditions can a mechanic with only a powerplant rating perform maintenance on the airframe of a FAA-certificated aircraft?

    They can perform maintenance (not the required inspections) under the supervision of a mechanic who holds an airframe rating.

14. Who is responsible for ensuring that all of the aircraft maintenance records are kept up to date?

    The registered owner or operator of the aircraft.

15. Who is authorized to perform the inspection on an altimeter that is required under 14 CFR §91.411?

    An FAA-certificated repair station approved for this particular function.

16. How soon must the holder of an FAA mechanic certificate notify the FAA of a permanent change in their address?

    Within 30 days of any permanent change in their address.

Typical Practical Projects

1. Given a list of maintenance functions, identify which of them are major airframe repairs, minor airframe repairs, major powerplant repairs, minor powerplant repairs, major airframe alterations, minor airframe alterations, major powerplant alterations, minor powerplant alterations, and which are preventive maintenance.

2. Given a list of maintenance functions, identify the ones that a mechanic with only a powerplant rating can perform.

3. Given a list of maintenance functions, identify the ones that a mechanic with only an airframe rating can perform.

4. Given a list of maintenance functions, identify the ones that an A&P mechanic cannot perform.

5. Prepare the correct type of notification that is necessary to advise the FAA of a permanent change of address.

6. Explain to the examiner the difference in the privileges of a certificated mechanic and those of a certificated repairman.

7. Explain to the examiner the differences between a 100-hour inspection and an annual inspection.

8. Explain to the examiner the portion of the altimeter and static system inspection required by 14 CFR §91.411 that may be performed by a mechanic with an airframe rating.

Aviation Mechanic
Oral & Practical
Exam Guide
The comprehensive guide to prepare you for the FAA Aviation Mechanic General, Airframe, and Powerplant Oral & Practical Exams
Fourth Edition
Based on original text by
Dale Crane
GENERAL
AIRFRAME
POWERPLANT
FAA-S-ACS-1
FAA-G-ACS-1
Airman
Certification
Standards
Aviation
Mechanic
General, Airframe,
and Powerplant
GENERAL
AIRFRAME
POWERPLANT
Also available as eBooks